Buddhist Ethics

BUDDHIST ETHICS

Hammalawa Saddhatissa

Introduction by Charles Hallisey

Wisdom Publications · Boston

WISDOM PUBLICATIONS
361 NEWBURY STREET
BOSTON, MASSACHUSETTS 02115

First published in 1970 by George Allen & Unwin Ltd under the title *Buddhist Ethics: Essence of Buddhism.*
Second edition published in 1987 by Wisdom Publications under the title *Buddhist Ethics: the Path to Nirvana.*
This revised edition published in 1997.

© Hammalawa Saddhatissa 1970, 1997

Library of Congress Cataloging-in-Publication Data

Saddhatissa, H.
    Buddhist ethics / Hammalawa Saddhatissa; introduction by Charles Hallisey.
        p.   cm.
    Includes bibliographical references and index.
    ISBN 0-86171-124-6 (alk. paper)
    1. Buddhist ethics.   2. Buddhism—Doctrines. I. Title.
BJ1289.B223   1997
294.3'5—dc21   97–5412
                                                                         CIP

ISBN 0-86171-124-6

02 01 00 99 98
 6   5   4   3   2

Designed by: L·J·Sawlit

Wisdom Publications' books are printed on acid-free paper and meet the guidelines for the
permanence and durability of the Committee on Production Guidelines for
Book Longevity of the Council on Library Resources.

Printed in the United States of America

CONTENTS

PREFACE TO THE
THIRD EDITION

THE PASSING OF ALL THINGS is one of Buddhism's central tenets. But with correct understanding and insight, the passing of people and things no longer produces anguish or suffering. Instead, through meditation on the impermanence of all mental and physical phenomena, one learns to cultivate a state of dispassion and equanimity with regard to such worldly fluctuations as birth and death, gain and loss. From this state of dispassion one sees with increased clarity how the world, through its ignorance, continues to grasp at that which is impermanent and attempts to construct a fortress of immutability against the relentless tides of change. For one who has recognized the inevitability of impermanence, the suffering that the world encounters in its futile attempts to outwit change evokes a deep sense of compassion and universal responsibility. While still maintaining a personal sense of equilibrium, such a person will speak forcefully, convincingly, and lovingly of the need to reexamine our basic assumptions about the nature of reality. And such a person will act as a guide, teaching us not only how to overcome the poisons of attachment, anger, and ignorance, but showing us as well how to live life in the most beneficial, peaceful, and noble manner possible.

The Venerable Hammalawa Saddhatissa was such a person. His passing in 1990, therefore, should in no way be taken as an occasion for lamentation and grief, but rather as a fresh opportunity to review his message for humanity. Among the many invaluable contributions that Saddhatissa made to the elucidation of the Buddhist path, *Buddhist Ethics* stands out for its depth, its clarity, and its obvious compassionate intent. Seeing the world around him suffer as a result of its ignorance, attachment, and hatred, Saddhatissa here shares his vision of reality as a highly educated, socially engaged, and concerned Buddhist practitioner and monk. The result is this classic volume of ethical teachings that seeks to explain traditional Buddhist ethical theory through terms comprehensible to the Westerners to whom it was addressed.

Although he was born and raised in Sri Lanka, Saddhatissa spent much of his adult life in foreign lands—true to the ideals of renunciation and homelessness espoused by the Buddha in ancient India. His sojourn in India, where the Buddhist path had long since elapsed, brought him into contact with the prominent social reformer Dr. B.R. Ambedkar, whose conversion to Buddhism in 1956 led to a whole new community of ex-untouchable Indian Buddhists. There, too, he mastered Pali, Sanskrit, and other Indian languages, enabling him to increase his understanding of the full range of Buddhist philosophical and ethical materials, as well as to serve as the religious advisor for the new Indian Buddhist community. In 1957, he moved to London, where he became the Head of the London Buddhist Vihāra of the British Mahābodhi Society. In Europe, he furthered his pioneering work for the transmission of Buddhism outside Sri Lanka through the foundation of a number of Buddhist centers for the study and cultivation of the Buddhist path.

Saddhatissa's scholarly achievements are also remarkable. His concern for the lay practitioner of Buddhism is evinced by his critical edition and study of the *Upāsakajanālankāra*, a 12th century Pali manual on the Buddha's teachings for the laity. As the former Vice President of the Pali Text Society, he has contributed to the field of Buddhist studies through his work on the Pali Tripitika Concordance and his various translations and editions of Pali texts. Among his numerous articles and books, works such as *The Buddha's Way* (London: Allen & Unwin, 1971) have had widespread influence and are now considered as classics of his time. The present volume, *Buddhist Ethics*, is now in its third edition. It stands as a tribute to a life well lived and as an impetus to our own self-examination and growth. As one of the first works by a Buddhist author to specifically present Buddhism in terms that Europeans and Americans could understand, it is a seminal work in the transmission of Buddhism to the West. It is, therefore, with great happiness and high admiration that we commemorate the life of Venerable Hammalawa Saddhatissa through this new edition of *Buddhist Ethics*. May it bring benefit to all suffering sentient beings.

WISDOM PUBLICATIONS
Boston, 1997

PREFACE TO THE
SECOND EDITION

THE LAST HALF CENTURY has seen a steady decline in the teaching, understanding, and observance of religious, ethical, and moral principles and ideas. The greed for money and material possessions, the overriding desire for personal advancement in day-to-day life, the wish to control other human beings, living things, and the environment, both politically and economically, have been the characteristics of the path along which modern civilization has developed in recent years.

This development is contrary to the ordinary, just, and reasonable nature of man. As a result, mankind is today confronted with enormous destructive forces. These forces are so powerful and compelling that the minds of most people, especially the young and the mentally weak, cannot grapple with them nor cope with them. Instead, they succumb to these forces. They take refuge in apathy, anarchy, drugs, alcohol, and other forms of conduct which lead to superficial feelings of well-being, but do not contribute to any long-lasting or substantial happiness. This decline in the religious, ethical, and moral standards has caused a breakdown in the social fabric of mankind.

The only way one can retrieve the situation, the only sensible way forward, is to live according to the religious, ethical, and moral standards accepted by one's own traditions and in understanding and compatibility with those of others.

This book analyses, examines, and explains the ethical concepts from a Buddhist point of view. The emphasis is on the ethical concepts accepted by all the schools of Buddhism and, indeed, there is no difference between these concepts among the different schools, either Theravāda or Mahāyāna. Furthermore, today there is a tendency to study not just one religion, but different religions side by side, sometimes separately and sometimes on a comparative basis. This method of study brings about an appreciation and understanding of the similarities in the tenets and ideas of all the different religions. This is not a surprising factor, as these concepts have been formulated for the well-being of mankind, to enable men to live a life of peace, harmony, and happiness.

In this context the second edition of *Buddhist Ethics* being published at this juncture is an event of prime importance. I have the honor to be able to offer the world the fruits of a lifetime of study of Buddhism and other religions, and of teaching Buddhism and comparative religions as a contribution to the further elevation of humanity.

Whilst writing this book (in 1969), I was deeply appreciative of the help provided by my friends and colleagues, amongst whom I would like especially to thank Miss I. B. Horner (President of the Pali Text Society), and Mr. M. O'C. Walshe. And for the republication of this work, my grateful thanks are due to Dr. Nicholas Ribush, Director, Wisdom Communications.

H. SADDHATISSA
London, 1987

INTRODUCTION

THIS IS THE THIRD EDITION of Venerable Hammalawa Saddhatissa's *Buddhist Ethics*. For more than a quarter of a century, those in search of an introduction to Buddhist moral thought have turned and returned to this little volume, but, like other examples of the genre of introductions, it also presents particular challenges for its readers.

These challenges stem, in part, from the very reason that we take up any introductory book: we want to explore a subject about which we know little. Our lack of knowledge also means that we are relatively unprepared to understand what we encounter because we lack familiarity with the requisite vocabulary, concepts, and contexts of thought. Ven. Saddhatissa anticipated such expectations and difficulties in his book by including in it a remarkable range of information on Buddhist history, thought, and practice as background for understanding the fundamental issues of Buddhist ethics. He also collected and quoted extensively from the Pali canon, the scriptures of the Theravāda tradition, which allow readers their own access to the sources that inform his presentation. He presented all of this as commonly Buddhist, saying that his emphasis was "on the ethical concepts accepted by all the schools of Buddhism" (p. ix). Since the original appearance of Ven. Saddhatissa's book, advances in knowledge about the historical diversity of the Buddhist traditions across Asia—and now Europe and the Americas—may make this claim to representativeness seem exaggerated, but this does not take away from the book's inherent value as an introduction.

Adequate and comprehensive acknowledgment of the diversity of Buddhist thought and practice would not only be impossible in an introduction, but inappropriate. Indeed, for someone new to a subject, the lack of familiarity with Buddhist terms and the concepts they express, with the texts and traditions of understanding that they are drawn from, can make understanding of even the most basic material about a single school of thought elusive. In using any introductory book, we inevitably encounter a cycle of expectation and frustration. We want to know more, but we find that we can't learn all that we sense is before us because we don't already know enough. Readers and authors naturally have opposing reactions to this cycle, given their respective vantage points of purpose and understanding. A reader wants ready access to information and insight. An author, in contrast, may find it counterproductive to try to minimize the challenges of the material, preferring to trust that the rewards of an introductory work can be in inverse proportion to its rigors. The author must be responsible to the integrity of the material he or she wishes to introduce, even while acknowledging the valid expectations of readers. There is probably no happy medium in this regard, no standard that will satisfy the desires of all, but readers can negotiate the inevitable challenges of the unfamiliar by keeping in mind the contexts of thought in which the choices and responsibilities of a particular introduction gain cogency.

Authors usually try to identify such contexts of thought for their readers with words of preparation and purpose in a preface. This third edition of *Buddhist Ethics*, however, is a posthumous work, Ven. Saddhatissa having passed away in 1990. We cannot know whether Ven. Saddhatissa would have said something different from what he wrote in his preface to the second edition. That preface is included in this third edition and readers who turn to it will quickly see that Ven. Saddhatissa offered this book to us with some urgency, seeing in the world around him a profound need for social reform and moral regeneration.

This perception of urgency gives cogency to *Buddhist Ethics* and helps us, for example, to appreciate Ven. Saddhatissa's inclusion of a chapter about the layman's relation to the state as opposed to a more meta-ethical discussion about, say, the foundations of moral knowledge that the more philosophically inclined might have preferred. A sense of urgency about the moral state of the world in fact animated much of Ven. Saddhatissa's lifework, which was devoted to the career of a *dhammadūta*, "a messenger of Truth" or "messenger of Dhamma." He was born in Sri Lanka in 1914 and took novice ordination as a Buddhist monk in 1926. After his education at monastic and secular colleges in Sri Lanka, he went to India in the forties to engage in missionary work sponsored by the Mahbodhi Society. From the start of his mature career, however, he combined his labors as a dhammadūta with more academic interests, and his first book was a grammar of the Pali language written in Hindi.[1] While in India, Ven. Saddhatissa was associated with and advised Dr. B. R. Ambedkar's movement for social justice for the Dalit (former "untouchable") communities, a movement which culminated in the mass conversions of a half million people to Buddhism in 1956.

In 1957, he was invited by the Mahābodhi Society to go to the London Buddhist Vihāra, which had been founded earlier in the century by Anāgarika Dharmapāla but which had declined in public activity during the Second World War. Ven. Saddhatissa was to spend the rest of his life in Europe, again combining the life of a Buddhist monk with the life of an academic in a modern university. In addition to his duties as incumbent of the London Buddhist Vihāra, he taught regularly at the School of Oriental and African Studies and he was a diligent and regular laborer in its library. He received a doctorate in 1963 from the University of Edinburgh for his critical edition of a medieval Pali handbook for Buddhist laypeople, the *Upāsakajanālaṅkāra,* which was subsequently published by the Pali Text Society in 1965.

Buddhist Ethics clearly reflects Ven. Saddhatissa's academic interests and abilities, but it also reflects his identity as a dhammadūta. I think we can see something of Ven. Saddhatissa's understanding of himself as a dhammadūta in the book itself, and it is worth pausing to consider what he has to say. One example of his self-presentation is characteristically indirect. Ven. Saddhatissa closed an account of a dialogue between the Buddha and an ascetic named Kassapa by noting that, for the Buddha, any "discussion which would lead to useful results would be better begun with points of agreement of the debaters than with their differences" and "that these hopeful beginnings would deal with things accepted by all shades of reputable opinion as definitely 'good' or definitely 'evil'; in other words, the starting points should be moral values" (p. 92).

This exemplary sense that productive beginnings are best sought on common ground was apparently adopted by Ven. Saddhatissa in his role as a dhammadūta. This may be surprising to some, since an orientation towards common ground is not usually associated with a "missionary," the ordinary translation of the word *dhammadūta* into English. Throughout his life, Ven. Saddhatissa upturned such unreflective stereotypes. For example, in the course of a lecture introducing meditation, Ven. Saddhatissa commented:

[W]e sometimes pay excessive attention to such labels as Christianity, Buddhism, Hinduism but none or very little to the teachings which they impart. Therein lies the root of the trouble. We should not pay excessive attention to labels. We should accept that those teachings are for all humanity. The great teachers came into the world to improve it. . . . I stress that the basic desire of the great teachers was to make a better world and that they had no interest at all in labels. Anyone can avail themselves of their teachings and so, for example, meditation on universal love, on higher thoughts and on breathing, all can be used by all human beings and not solely by Buddhists. These meditation practices make possible control over the mind and the overcoming of aggression, confusion, selfishness and evil desires. All these enemies can be overcome and one can cultivate, on the other hand, compassion and universal love, friendliness, generosity and positive qualities in general.[2]

A similar orientation towards an initial and productive common ground is evident in *Buddhist Ethics*, as can be seen in Ven. Saddhatissa's own words in the preface to the second edition. They make it clear that the reader's sensitive alertness to a global ethic which is conducive to "the elevation of humanity" provides the most important context of thought against which *Buddhist Ethics* should be read. It goes without saying that an orientation to common ground is not blindness to difference. Common ground instead provides the very rationale for careful attention to different viewpoints because they are about issues that we *already* care about. Beginning on common ground encourages us to endure the momentary awkwardness of speaking with new terms, to explore in a searching way unfamiliar categories of thought, and to appreciate, in imagination and in action, relatively novel practices for the improvement of character.

When I keep this orientation to common ground in view, I am mindful that Ven. Saddhatissa would have been disappointed if readers of *Buddhist Ethics* finished his book with only a sense of knowing more about Buddhist thought, and not also an awareness of knowing more about themselves and their moral embeddedness in the world.

Such general observations, when specified further, can aid readers thinking about how to get the most out of this book. For example, in the first chapter, "Definitions and Historical Background," Ven. Saddhatissa reviews a number of discussions of ethics from the history of Western philosophy, ending with allusions to an entry in the *Encyclopaedia Britannica* by Abraham Wolf. Conventional habits of reading may incline one to hurry past Ven. Saddhatissa's use of this entry, somewhat incongruously mentioned alongside Plato and Aristotle, but to do so would be to miss one of the keys that Ven. Saddhatissa gives to the structure of his book, and thus to miss a broader context of thought that he asks us to keep in mind as we read.

Ven. Saddhatissa takes from Abraham Wolf a ready-at-hand list of "the main problems of ethics." These are: 1) questions about what is the highest good of human conduct; 2) the origin or source of moral knowledge; 3) sanctions of moral conduct; and 4) the motives that prompt right behavior (p. 3). Just as rapidly as he introduces this list, Ven. Saddhatissa rearranges its order, and in the process subtly and with little comment adjusts the contents of some of the list's members: "The present consideration will be made under four main headings: 1) origin and source of knowledge of the highest; 2) the sanctions of moral conduct: the Three Refuges; the Precepts; 3) moral principles as possessing value in view of a standard or ideal; 4) the ultimate aim which may serve as the ultimate standard. . ." (p.4).

Keeping these headings in view helps us keep the many details of each chapter in perspective. The expectations of an introductory text require Ven. Saddhatissa to present various kinds of relevant information, all essential as background for understanding, but they unfortunately can also sometimes obscure the economy of presentation. It is incumbent on us, his readers who are in need of this background information, to remind ourselves repeatedly of the bigger picture that gives his presentation force. One way we can do this is by keeping these four headings in mind, but it will be easier to do this if these four headings are correlated with the seven chapters that form the bulk of the book:

(1) The origin and source of knowledge of the highest is discussed in chapter 2. It is a crucial account of the nature and career of the Buddha, which can be usefully enhanced by the historical material introduced at the end of chapter 1.

(2) The sanctions of moral conduct are covered in chapters 3 and 4, which treat the Three Refuges and the precepts. The inclusion of the Three Refuges as a moral sanction, something that makes particular courses of action like the five precepts valid, is very distinctive and one of the most compelling aspects of Ven. Saddhatissa's presentation. It is worth emphasizing that Ven. Saddhatissa presents the Refuges in connection to a consideration about what dictates ethical choice, and not as a reaction to the Buddha as a source of knowledge of the highest. I am sure that I am not alone among Ven. Saddhatissa's readers to have found it fruitful to reflect on what is entailed in discerning a moral sanction in one's relationship to the Three

Gems rather than in an abstract principle comparable to Kant's categorical imperative, in which only actions that can be willed as universal should be sanctioned as moral. I have also found it productive to consider the similarity in Saddhatissa's appreciation of human freedom, which he sees represented in the Three Refuges, and the appreciation of freedom as the sine qua non of moral thought in the modern West.

(3) The heading of "moral principles as possessing value in view of a standard or ideal" organizes well the material in chapters 5, 6, and 7. A striking statement made by Ven. Saddhatissa in chapter 5 shows his integrative concerns in these chapters: "Whatever the position assigned to the laity, whether in the Buddha's day or whether visualized to cover the centuries, the statement of the Four Noble Truths must, in the last instance, determine the role which the layman should assume and play in the Buddhist life" (p. 89). Ven. Saddhatissa's long interest in the normative character of the Buddhist lay life is everywhere in evidence in these chapters, and his focus on issues of family life is especially noteworthy. Of course, this reflects Ven. Saddhatissa's general orientation to common ground, but, as we shall see in a moment, his interest in lay life reflects his total understanding of the Buddhist life on its own terms.

(4) Finally, "the ultimate aim which may serve as the ultimate standard" is taken up in the last chapter about Nirvāṇa, the realization of enlightenment itself. In addition to an account about the nature of Nirvāṇa, one will also find discussions of material appropriate to Abraham Wolf's fourth heading. Chapter 8 surveys Buddhist teachings on some crucial aspects of Buddhist moral psychology connected with motivation, both as that which prompts right conduct and that which inhibits right conduct.

Ven. Saddhatissa gave two reasons for the changes he made to Abraham Wolf's list of the main problems in ethics (these reasons call attention to two changes made by Ven. Saddhatissa, but careful attention to the list will reveal a number of other significant changes as well). The first has to do with the conception of "the highest" as a state "which lies beyond good and evil."[3] The second change is more crucial for our understanding of the book as a whole, for it represents a key organizing principle in the book: Buddhist practice is crucially integrated into one whole, and a failure to appreciate this integration is inevitably a source of misunderstanding and distortion. Indeed, the last sentence of *Buddhist Ethics* is a ringing affirmation of this practical integration seen as an intent of the Buddha himself: The Buddha's teaching "began with the most elementary of the moralities, and proceeded *without a break* to the realization of the ultimate goal: the realization of Nibbāna with the realization of the Four Noble Truths" (p. 149; emphasis added). In this respect, Ven. Saddhatissa is quite at odds with many other modern interpreters of Buddhist practice, who tend to see a sharp divide between the practices of virtuoso monks and everyone else.

Without trying to adjudicate between these two accounts of practice in the Buddhist community, let me simply say that Ven. Saddhatissa's perspective has abundant support in Buddhist literature. One of the most famous verses in the *Dhammapada* goes:

> Refraining from what is detrimental,
> The attainment of what is wholesome,
> The purification of one's mind:
> This is the instruction of Awakened Ones.[4]

What is clear from this verse is that the moral life is intimately connected with the mental cultivation associated with Buddhist meditation. This association is twofold. First, the moral life is a preliminary to the proper practice of mental discipline and progress in meditation is not possible without the stability that morality lends to human life. Secondly, and conversely, meditation enhances the practice of morality, extending and perfecting it. One of the most interesting passages in *Buddhist Ethics*, and a point where Ven. Saddhatissa is deeply in tune with the religious heritage of the Theravāda Buddhist tradition, is the long account in chapter 4 about how meditations on *mettā*, loving kindness, are integral to the keeping of the first precept not to do harm to others.

The location of the moral life in a larger Buddhist life—a life which includes meditation and aspires to the attainment of wisdom—is an insight that allows Ven. Saddhatissa to affirm that "Buddhism can be said to provide the complete ethical study" (p. 4) and leads to the creative tension at the heart of this book. That Ven. Saddhatissa was probably aware of this tension is indicated by the different subtitles which were given to the two previous editions. The first edition appeared in 1970 with the full title *Buddhist Ethics: The Essence of Buddhism*, while the second edition appeared in 1987 entitled *Buddhist Ethics: The Path to Nirvana*. The latter title suggests the crucial role that the moral life plays in the larger program of character development and realization taught by the Buddha and summarized in the schema of the Noble Eightfold Path. Some might, erroneously, take this to mean that morality is a mere preliminary stage in the higher life, which those who advance on the Path somehow leave behind. It must be admitted, of course, that in some respects this is true, as with the eradication of the anger inherent in human life, so crucial to perfection of morality through meditation and the attainment of wisdom and compassion. But in other respects, such an impression is profoundly wrong, and Ven. Saddhatissa communicated the constancy of morality in the total Buddhist life with his original subtitle that ethics is the essence of Buddhism: the moral life is not transcended in enlightenment, only perfected.

To respect this creative tension, to keep both poles in play as key to the cogency of Ven. Saddhatissa's presentation, this new edition appears without a subtitle.

CHARLES HALLISEY
Cambridge, Massachusetts
December, 1996

1

DEFINITIONS AND HISTORICAL BACKGROUND
SCOPE OF THE STUDY OF ETHICS

THE TERM ETHICS derives from the Greek *ethikos*, that which pertains to *ethos*, or character. It is also called "moral philosophy" from the Latin custom. Popularly, ethics is described as "the science treating of morals"[5] but since precise definition of the term is lacking it is necessary to state the ground that a consideration of ethics is intended to cover. G. E. Moore, in his *Principia Ethica*, refusing to take as adequate a definition of ethics as dealing with "the question of what is good or bad in human conduct," declares: "I may say that I intend to use 'ethics' to cover more than this—a usage for which there is, I think, quite sufficient authority. I am using it to cover the general inquiry into what is good."[6]

A more detailed description is given by Rev. H. H. Williams: "In its widest sense, the term 'ethics' would imply an examination into the general character and habits of mankind, and would even involve a description or history of the habits of men in particular societies living at different periods of time." Observing the exceptionally wide field that would be so covered, the author concludes: "Ethics then is usually confined to the particular field of human character and conduct so far as they depend upon or exhibit certain general principles commonly known as moral principles. Men in general characterize their own conduct and character and that of other men by such general adjectives as good, bad, right, and wrong, and it is the meaning and scope of these adjectives, primarily in their relation to human conduct, and ultimately in their final and absolute sense, that ethics investigates."[7]

We are therefore concerned with certain terms as they are used in a particular connection and also with their meaning in the absolute sense. In conjunction with these aspects the opinion of Professor Muirhead may also be borne in mind: "We have two kinds of sciences . . . those concerning themselves with the description of things as they are, and those which concern themselves with our judgments upon them. The former class have sometimes been called 'natural,' the latter 'normative,' or, as is better, 'critical' sciences. Ethics is critical in the sense explained. Its subject-matter is human conduct and character, not as natural facts with a history and causal connections with other facts, but as possessing value in view of a standard or idea."[8]

The various ethical systems are therefore more likely to show divergence when one comes to consider the standard or ideal that furnishes the value of human conduct rather than the prescriptions for the conduct itself. For example, killing, thieving, and lying are in general considered to be evils, though whether they are at any time justifiable will depend on the terms of the ideal; on the other hand, happiness is invariably associated with good.

The study of ethics as a particular discipline contributing to philosophical inquiry as a whole was due originally to Aristotle, since he distinguished between "first principles," or the investigation of the ultimate nature of existence as such, and the subsidiary disciplines which, though having the same purpose, themselves dealt with only a particular approach to it. Ethics constituted one such approach and, of the many hundreds of Aristotelian writings, three major works on ethics have come down to us. Aristotle maintained throughout the fundamental doctrine of Socrates and Plato that "virtue is happiness," a doctrine with which Buddhist thought would, in general, be in agreement,[9] and on two occasions was inspired to poetry concerning this tenet. In the *Elegy* to Eudemus of Cyprus he praised the man who first showed clearly that a good man and a happy man are the same, and in the *Hymn* in memory of Hermias he begins: "Virtue, difficult to the human race, noblest pursuit in life."[10] Two of Plato's successors at the Academy showed the same belief in the necessity of virtue, division of opinion occurring only with the view as to what good is.

Some two centuries earlier, a learned and eminent brahman expounded his teaching that morality and wisdom are essential to the character of a true brahman—the "true brahman" here representing the ideal. The Buddha then asked the man what morality and wisdom are. The brahman answered: "That is the farthest we have advanced, Gotama. It would indeed be well if the esteemed Gotama would clarify with regard to these words."[11] The lengthy exposition with which the Buddha replied[12] constituted a standard basis for the development of his teaching and will be referred to in detail in the course of the present text.

Returning to Aristotle, the theory that happiness is activity is contained in two of his most authoritative works, the *Metaphysica* and the *De Anima*, as well as in the three ethical treatises, the *Nicomachean Ethics*, the *Eudemian Ethics*, and the *Magna Moralia*, these three proceeding on similar lines up to this point. The *Nicomachean* then continues to the theory "that the highest happiness is the speculative life of the intellect . . . but that happiness as a human also includes the practical life of combining prudence and moral virtue; and that, while both lives need external goods as necessaries, the practical life also requires them as instruments of moral action." The treatise concludes with the means of making men virtuous; contending that virtue requires habituation, habituation law, law legislative art, and legislative art politics. Ethics thus passes into politics.[13] The *Eudemian Ethics* and *Magna Moralia* continue to considerations of good fortune and gentlemanliness, the latter being regarded as perfect virtue, containing all particular virtues.

Herein lie no indications of an ultimate or transcendental state, and for these one must look to later developments of the science of ethics, whether they arise in logical continuity or exist merely as arbitrary attachments introduced for the sake of convenience. Only the former condition would provide justification for considering ethics as a genuine contribution to the science of philosophy proper. In his article on ethics in *Encyclopaedia Britannica*, Professor Wolf has this to say of the study: "Ethics is not a positive science but a *normative* science—it is not primarily occupied with the actual character of human conduct but with the ideal. Many moral philosophers, indeed, have stated explicitly that the business of ethics merely consists in clearing up current moral conceptions and unfolding the ultimate presuppositions involved in them, and that it is not its function to discover any new moral ideas. It may be remarked that even the ethics of Aristotle attempted no more, although he was not bound by anything like this authority, and the traditions of the Christian Church."[14] Professor Wolf then states that the main problems of ethics "turn chiefly on the following conceptions: (i) The highest good of human conduct, or its ultimate ideal aim, which may serve as the ultimate standard of right conduct; (ii) the origin or source of our knowledge of the highest good or of right or wrong; (iii) the sanctions of moral conduct; (iv) the motives which prompt right conduct. Another problem discussed by moral philosophers is that of Freedom of the Will."

In a consideration of Buddhist ethics these problems may be rearranged with advantage for two reasons. In the first place, according to Buddhist and other Indian thought, the highest state is one that lies beyond good and evil. In the second place, according to Buddhism there is no break between the moral teaching and that which pertains directly to the ideal state. Humanity, sufficiently advanced in the practice of the moralities, rises and continues to rise above the common limitations of time and space, whether these terms are interpreted from the point of view of the physical sciences or with reference to historical and geographical location. The first of the main problems set forth by Professor Wolf, namely, the ultimate ideal aim which may serve as the ultimate standard of right conduct, relates, according to Buddhist thought, to the supramundane or *lokuttara* state. The connection between the moralities of everyday life and this *lokuttara* state is entirely covered by the Buddha's teaching. This connection is, in fact, known to Buddhists as *mārga* or *magga*, the Path or the Road, along which each person must travel for himself, beginning with the practice of the common moralities up to the supramundane state beyond good and evil. From this point of view Buddhism can be said to provide the complete ethical study.

After certain introductory remarks to clarify the position taken up by Buddhist thought, the present consideration will be made under four main headings: (1) origin and source of knowledge of the highest; (2) the sanctions of moral conduct: the Three Refuges; the Precepts; (3) moral principles as possessing value in view of a standard or ideal; and (4) the ultimate ideal aim which may serve as the ultimate standard, namely: the realization of the Four Noble Truths.

INDIAN THOUGHT IN THE SIXTH CENTURY B.C.E.

It must be emphasized at the outset that recognition of a state beyond good and evil in no way implies that a person who has performed a number of "good" deeds may then relax morally and do anything he pleases; it merely hints at a state described by the Buddha when he was asked: "Where do the four primary elements, earth, water, fire and air, entirely cease?"[15] He replied that the question should not have been put in that way. It should have been thus:

> Where do water, earth, fire, air, find no place?
> Where do "long and short," "fine and coarse,"
> "pleasant and unpleasant," not occur?
> Where are mind and body, mental and physical
>   states, entirely stopped?[16]

And the answer to this is:

Where the consciousness that makes endless
comparisons is entirely abandoned,
Here "long and short," "pleasant and unpleasant"
do not occur.

Here are stopped name and form, mental and physical states.
Here with the dying away of consciousness these
things have no place.[17]

In this description the terms "long and short," "fine and coarse," "pleasant and unpleasant" carry their customary meaning; the significance of "name and form, mental and physical states" is less obvious since the expression *nāmañ ca rūpañ ca* has a variety of associations. In the early *Upaniṣads*, *Brahman* was the Absolute Reality, while the term *nāma-rūpa* stood for the things of common experience. According to the ideal of Brahman as *niṣprapañca*, the things of common experience represent phenomena with Absolute Brahman as the noumenon; Brahman is here the mere ground of subject and object.[18] According to the *saprapañca* ideal, the things of common experience emerge from Brahman and are later reabsorbed into it.[19] So far Brahman was not personified, but in early Buddhist literature it is the personification that comes under discussion, sometimes as *Brahmā*, though also on occasion as *Brahman*, while *Brahmā* appears also in the early portions of the epic *Mahābhārata*. In the latter case, however, Brahmā is frequently identified with *Prajāpati*, a much older concept than Brahmā that at one time represented the creative power of nature.[20] Confusion arose since both Prajāpati and Brahmā were considered, at different times, to be the ultimate sources of all. But in whatever form Absolute Brahman is presented, it is distinguished from the things of common experience, which are *nāma-rūpa*. *Rūpa* is the specific form and nature of a phenomenon, while *nāma* is the word or name serving as its sign; taking the terms together, *nāma-rūpa* should be understood as the particularity or determinate character of individual things. A further connection between *nāma* and *rūpa* is indicated in the *Bṛhadāraṇyaka Upaniṣad* which mentions a triad consisting of *nāma*, *rūpa* and *karma* (action), the implications of which are very considerable;

consideration of them is therefore deferred.[21]

Excluding karma for the moment, in Buddhist teaching *nāma* is also a metaphysical term used to embrace the four mental groups, or *khandhas,* of feeling, perception, mental formations, and consciousness.[22] These, together with the material principle *rūpa*,[23] make up the individual person as distinguished from other individuals. *Nāma-rūpa* thus becomes "individual being" or "individuality." In the above quotation from the *Kevaḍḍha Sutta* we understand for *nāma-rūpa* "mental and physical states,"[24] so that when these cease without remainder the consciousness that makes endless comparisons will also cease and the supramundane state will be attained.

Still one point remains which may have been present in the first linking up of *nāma* and *rūpa* and which is again prominent in present-day thought: this concerns the singling out of any one phenomenon from the whole mass of phenomena, an act that in general is called a "discovery." With *nāma* closely associated with *rūpa*, the singling out is not entirely disconnected from those parts of the discoverer's mentality that could hardly be classified as "perception"; therefore he may look to recognize a closer union between *nāma* and *rūpa* than has so far been possible to demonstrate.

If, however, Indian thought looked toward an ultimate state in which pairs of opposites did not figure, considerable distinction has always been drawn between the conventional "right" and "wrong" of the present existence. The idea of a fixed physical law, like the uniformity of nature or the ordered course of things such as the alternation of day and night, was formed at a very early date, probably well before the separation of the Aryan migrants into Indian and Iranian contingents. In the *Ṛgveda* it was known as *ṛta*, but the word occurs in Persian proper names as early as 1600 B.C.E. in the form *arta*, and in the *Avesta* as *asha*. By the time of the Mantras *ṛta* had also taken on the significance of a moral order, and expressions such as *gopārtasya* (guardians of *ṛta*), and *ṛtayu* (practicers of *ṛta*), are frequently encountered.[25] The Vedic gods were therefore both maintainers of cosmic order as well as upholders of moral law. In course of time other views appeared, but the main line of development of Indian thought did not lie in a unity of godhead, in the reduction of many gods to one who would be assumed to make and guide the world; but in a monism that traces the whole of existence to a single source. Although the performance of sacrifices was often dominant, since they were taken to be essential to the satisfying of man's desires, the idea of morality was never superseded. There existed a triad of obligations *(rna-traya)* for the fulfillment of which sacrifice was only the first; the second was indebtedness to the culture inherited, and was discharged by handing on the traditions to the rising generation. The third lay in continuing the race. The ideal includes the practice of adherence to the truth, of self-restraint and kindness. Benevolence was particularly praised and meanness deplored. "He who eats by himself will keep his sin to himself," says the *Rgveda.*[26]

The earlier gods were upholders of the moral order to the extent of rewarding virtue with happiness in heaven in their company. There is no explicit reference to "hell" in the *Rgveda*, though in the *Atharvaveda* and in the *Brāhmaṇas* it is a place of eternal darkness from which there is no escape. The idea of *iṣṭāpūrta*, however, occurs in the *Rgveda, iṣṭa* standing for the sacrifice to the gods and *pūrta* the gifts made to the priests, the merit accruing from these acts preceding a person into the next world where it secured him happiness. This merit is not entirely ethical but may become so if the reference to sacrifice is excluded and if the results of both good and bad deeds are assumed to pass on to determine the circumstances and conditions of the next existence. In that case we have an elementary idea of karma. Moreover, in the scale of rewards and punishments corresponding to the good and evil deeds of the present life, the *Brāhmaṇas* include among their serious punishments *punar-mrtyu*, repeated dying, which takes place in some other world. There is no mention of repeated births, though obviously these must occur if there are repeated deaths. In the early *Upaniṣads* the whole conception was clarified by recognition of a series of births and deaths taking place either in this world or in a realm of better or worse conditions, according to one's record here. Concern was then principally with the natural fruits of good and evil deeds maturing either in the present life or in some future life, irrespective of deities. What, then, was the position of a "god"?

The Sanskrit word *deva*, from *div*, to shine, means god; it is cognate with the Latin *deus*. It points to an era preceding the Aryan settlement in India, in which the conception of god was associated with the luminous powers of nature. The spirit of veneration with which the early Aryans regarded such powers is also indicated by *yaj*, "worship," a root found in many European languages. We have the association with the Vedic *yaj*, "to sacrifice," as in the title *Yajurveda*. But with the development of the idea of karma and consequent lack of authority of the deities over man, the value of *deva* was modified.

In Buddhism the rendering of *deva* as "god" is acceptable only in the sense that the being indicated is of a type superior to the average human. Whereas the gods of mythology resemble largely the creations of poetic fancy, taking their status more or less in accordance with the importance of the natural phenomena with which they are associated, the *devas* exist in definite grades according to their condition of mental development. In the *kāmaloka*, or world of desire, there exist six grades of *devas*; in the *rūpaloka* or world of form there are four; and in the *arūpaloka* or immaterial world there are also four grades. Beings attain to these spheres in accordance with the doctrine of karma, the spheres corresponding to the degrees of mental concentration and one-pointedness of mind (*cittass' ekaggatā*) which, from time to time, have been experienced temporarily in the present existence. In the Indian religions these mental states are known as the *jhānas*, or *jhānic* states. They are described frequently in the Buddhist texts, notably in the *Poṭṭhapāda Sutta*, the ninth of the *Long Discourses of the Buddha*, otherwise known as the *Dīgha Nikāya*, where the sequence is complete, the theme being that with study and discipline states of consciousness arise and with study and discipline they pass away. The substance of the account is as follows.

Being well practiced in the moralities, having attained a state of mindfulness and awareness, and being accustomed to simplicity of life, the meditator retires to a solitary place. He must overcome, at least temporarily, sensual desire (*kāmacchanda*), ill will and anger (*vyāpāda*), sloth and torpor (*thīnamiddha*), restlessness and worry (*uddhacca-kukkucca*), and doubt (*vicikicchā*). These are the five hindrances (*pañcanīvaraṇa*) to mental development and vision and, having subdued them, he feels extremely happy. So is born joy, a calming of the body, ease, and the ability to achieve much concentration of mind. He separates himself from sensuous enjoyment but, continuing to apply and sustain his thoughts with regard to external and ideational objects, attains and remains in the joy and ease resulting from his detachment. This is the first jhānic state. The second is attained by withdrawing his thought from the object, thereby attaining serenity of mind and singleness of purpose. Withdrawing his thought from joy, he observes his mental states with equanimity (*upekkhā*), but always remains alert; this is the third jhānic state. For the fourth he withdraws from all ease and dis-ease, retaining only his equanimity and one-pointedness of mind. These four jhānic states concern the consciousness of the world or sphere of form, *rūpaloka* or *rūpāvacara*.

The meditator may now proceed to the consciousness of the formless, *arūpāvacara citta,* of which there are four states. In this case there is no gradual suppression of the factors of consciousness, which have already been reduced to the two mentioned. There is, however, progressive change of the plane of thought, and the meditator is always directing his own mind. The first stage is the jhāna-consciousness dwelling on the infinity of space (*ākāsānañcāyatana*) or noncollision of objects, the second on the infinity of consciousness (*viññāṇañcāyatana*) or noncollision of ideas, the third on nothingness (*ākiñcaññāyatana*), and the fourth, in which cognition is so extremely subtle that it cannot be said whether it exists or not (*nevasaññānāsaññāyatana*).

Of the whole succession of jhānic states, the first two may be wrongly assumed from causes producing a temporary joy and ease that has no moral foundation whatever. If from such a state of mind it is not possible to proceed to the equanimity and alertness of the third jhānic state then the assumption that the joy and ease had any connection with jhāna is entirely wrong and harmful in the extreme. With regard to the *arūpāvacara jhāna,* the third consciousness, "nothingness" has been reached (if one may judge by the descriptions of practiced meditators of a variety of theological beliefs, Christian mystics included), so that the progress through the jhānas is genuinely one of increasing mental concentration and is independent of creed. But whatever values are attached to the jhānic states, to the Indian mind they are connected with the general structure of their cosmology. The deva realms, for example, represent states or types of existence into which are born beings who in the present existence have attained various jhānic states. The five physical senses do not necessarily persist through all the grades of devas since presumably they are replaced by finer perceptions. The *Ābhassara* devas, for example, who correspond to beings with experience of the second jhāna, retain only sight and hearing. However, all devas are subject to birth and death. Therefore, for Buddhism the highest state, which constitutes complete emancipation, is beyond any of the devas; it is that of the Buddhas who are forever tranquil and stable and who see all things *yathābhūtam,* according to absolute truth. This view has been expressed in the following verse: "There is no track in the sky, externally there is no recluse. Conditioned things are not eternal; there is no instability in the Buddhas."[27]

At the other extreme, below the level of mankind, are the denizens of the demon world (*asuranikāya*), of the ghost realm (*petaloka*), the animal creation (*tiracchānayoni*), and hell (*niraya*). The whole range represents, therefore, a structure of grades of intelligence on either side of the human state as we know it at present, the higher grades being dependent on putting away the five hindrances to mental development and vision, which is to say, dependent on the moralities. The devas have no control over this mental development and vision of man; they merely represent states to which man may aspire with increasing morality and developing intelligence. But they can be no more than incidental, and to a person intent on the final goal they are of little interest.

The doctrine of karma was not known to the Vedas, but was accepted in principle and had been so for some time before the Buddha's day.[28] This is clear from the *Bṛhadāraṇyaka* and *Chāndogya Upaniṣads*, and since, according to much modern scholarship, these are the only two pre-Buddhistic *Upaniṣads*, further development of the karma concept may be due to either Brahman or Buddhist influence. Common to both, however, is the clear distinction between karma and karmic effects, for *karma* literally means *action* in the abstract, while karmic effects are effects of particular actions. In fact, the doctrine of karma was elaborated and developed by non-Vedic traditions such as Jainism and Buddhism. Buddhism briefly defines meritorious and demeritorious volition (*cetanā*) as karma. The Buddha said: "It is mental volition, O monks, that I call karma. Having willed, one acts through body, speech or mind!"[29] The expressions "good karma" and "bad karma," used frequently in the West, have therefore no logical significance, though obviously karmic effects may be either good or bad. Nor has karma anything whatever to do with "fate." The outstanding karmic effect for all Indian thought lay in the round of rebirths, and with the postulated means of breaking these rounds were associated the various developments of religious and philosophic thought. For the Brahmans the ideal came to be realization of the union of Ātman, the inner self of man, with Brahman, Absolute Reality or its personification, and this represented the impossibility of further rebirths. Stress was laid on theories that involved a transmigrating essence of the "soul" (*jīva*), which continued as long as the ideal remained unrealized. Buddhism recognized the karmic effect of the round of rebirths, but developed the doctrine of karma in conjunction with the *anatta* doctrine, or absence of a permanent indwelling self, and so presented life and the series of lives as a stream of consciousness. The form of this presentation may be seen in the following *gāthās* (verses) taken from the anthology of the earliest Buddhist literature or teaching, the *Dhammapada*.

The most elementary Buddhist exposition of karma reads as follows: "He who speaks or acts from a mind defiled, that one suffering follows as a wheel the foot that leads it," and "He who speaks or acts from a pure mind, that one happiness follows as his shadow that never leaves him."[30]

Many passages exist in the Buddhist texts to the effect that for an evil-doer "when his body is destroyed the fool arises in hell,"[31] but the statement is merely a generalization about worlds inferior to the present one and indicates the nature of the relationship between action and the results of actions. More precise indication is given in the *Dhammapada* chapter on "Pleasant Things":[32] "Just as a traveler who has been long absent and comes back safe and sound is greeted on his return by his kinsfolk, friends and comrades, in the same way when a man passes from this world to another after a life of merit, so his good deeds welcome him as dear kinsmen on his return."[33] Further: "Therefore amass good deeds for the other world; for men, everything in the other world rests on merits."[34] Correspondingly we have: "If in committing evil acts the fool does not awake to understanding, he is burnt by his own actions as by fire."[35] These quotations represent the more specific attitude of Buddhism towards action and the results of actions, the indication being more a running on of the deeds themselves than a distinct break, as might be inferred from specifying an act and its results to the performer. The idea is expressed, in particular reference to hatred, in the early verses of the *Dhammapada*: "Surely in this world enmities at no time cease through hatred; they cease through lack of hatred. This is the primeval law. Not having formerly perceived 'In this matter we touch the realm of death,' those who perceive this connection thereupon cease from strife."[36] The Sanskrit *Dharmapada* and Rockhill's translation from the Tibetan *Udānavarga* contain the first sentence of this; the second is peculiar to the Pali. Here we have the suggestion of the running on of the action, the effect being continuity of that particular action.

These quotations represent, however, only the latter part of the chain of events relating to an act, and for its whole history the origin of the act must also be taken into account. Regarding this origin we have the first lines of the two *Dhammapada* verses just quoted in part. They are identical in both cases: "Mind precedes all things; all things have mind foremost, are mind-made."[37] Here we have the key to Buddhist ethics and, in fact, to the whole Buddhist teaching, for Buddhism is essentially a mind-culture. Any improvement or retrograde step must occur initially in the mind of the person concerned, whether it proceeds to external manifestation immediately or at a later date, so that the importance of being aware of and of controlling one's thoughts is continually stressed. Each of the *Dhammapadas* has its chapter on mind, and each deals at length with the difficulty of achieving control. We have, for example: "Just as the arrow maker straightens his arrow, so does a wise man make straight his mind, which is agitated, fickle, difficult to keep guard on, difficult to hold back."[38] The simile is a very old one in Indian literature and furnishes the subject of a bas-relief at Bharhut.[39] It shows an arrow-maker seated at the door of his house; he has heated an arrow in a pan of coals and has made it wet with sour rice-gruel; closing one eye, he is looking down the length of the arrow and is making it straight. Standing by are a mendicant, formerly the king Janaka of Banaras, and his former queen, Sīvalī, who has followed him against his will. The ex-king asks the arrow-maker why he closes one eye, and is told that with both eyes open the vision is distracted whereas with one eye open the vision is true. The moral is that one's mind should be made pliable, subject to control, with the vision kept clear, and concentrated on the main aim.[40]

The Bharhut inscription and its theme of the king turned mendicant draws attention to another basic difference between Indian thought and Greek ethics from Aristotle onwards. Where the *Nicomachean Ethics* allows external goods to be necessary in the practical life of combining prudence and moral virtue as instruments of moral action, and in the highest life of the intellect as a means of physical subsistence, Indian thought offered nothing so accommodating. Though the value of the present life is emphasized as providing essential opportunities for realization of the ultimate truth—it is, in fact, a stage of development through which one is obliged to pass— Indian thought held that this truth lies beyond the present state and is not to be considered as merely an improvement on present conditions with those conditions persisting in principle. The renunciation of one's social status, as in the case of King Janaka of Banaras, was a natural preliminary step to the renunciation of the whole round of rebirths. From early days, even when the *Brāhmaṇas* were in process of compilation, certain people had left their homes to live in the forests; vivid pictures of this life are given in the *Rāmāyana*, and other facts concerning the hermits are found in the *Dharma Sūtras*. By the time of the early *Upaniṣads* there were several classes of people who had adopted the homeless life, some because they objected to the authority of the *Vedas*, some because they wished to conduct their inquiries into the truth with as little disturbance from the outside world as possible, and others who were said to have already attained the truth. Originally the hermits were known as *vaikhānasas*, from *Vikhanas,* the traditional originator of the Rule, but later the term *vānaprastha*, forest dweller, came into use. In course of time the leaders of the homeless life were wanderers (*parivrājakas*), wearers of matted hair (*jaṭilas*) or finders of subsistence (*ājīvikas*). Extreme forms of asceticism were often resorted to, but the Buddha, from his own experience of them, considered them to be useless or even harmful unless they were accompanied by, or came as the result of, a very high degree of mental development. Still, detachment from the things of the present life formed an essential part of his teaching.

Returning to the question of breaking the round of rebirth, if for Buddhism there was to be no Brahman, no god, no inherent self, did the whole spell complete annihilation? This the Buddha repudiated entirely, classing a doctrine of annihilationism along with other speculations concerning the future, happy or otherwise. The goal is completely unconditioned, and to attempt to describe it in terms of the conditioned state that we know at present is as futile as to attempt to describe a "happy" state. The point is illustrated in a conversation held by the Buddha with the well-known wandering mendicant of the day, Poṭṭhapāda:[41]

There are, Poṭṭhapāda, some samaṇas and brahmans who hold and expound the view: Certainly the self is completely happy and healthy after death. I went to them and said: "Venerable Sirs, I have heard that you teach the certainty of a happy and healthy self after death. Is this so?" They acknowledged that it was so. I asked: "Is the world, as you know it and see it, completely happy?" "No," they said. I asked them: "Have you produced for yourselves complete happiness for one night or one day, or even for half a night or half a day?" They replied, "No." Then I asked: "Do you, Venerable Sirs, know a path or a method by which a realm of complete happiness may be reached?" They replied that they did not. "Have you heard of gods, who have arisen in a completely happy world, saying: 'There is a path, O Sirs, which, entered on and followed thoroughly and exactly, will lead to this world of complete happiness?' We, Sirs, by following this path, have been reborn in a completely happy world." They replied: "No."

The Buddha compared this state of affairs to that of a man who declared himself in love with a beautiful woman whom he had never seen and whose appearance and lineage he knew nothing whatever about; alternatively he likened it to that of a man building a flight of steps to a palace whose location and details of construction he did not know.

If then we have no details of the state of happiness, other than that it is happy, it remains only to consider what things give rise to unhappiness and to avoid them. Hence the Buddha's teaching of the Four Noble Truths: "Suffering, the Origin of Suffering, the Cessation of Suffering, and the Way to the Cessation of Suffering."[42] Beginning with the seemingly simple practice of the ordinary moralities of everyday life, the teaching continues unbroken to the transcendental state known generally as *nirvāṇa*. There is no modification for any particular person or class of persons, lay or otherwise, and, if the progress is sufficient, nirvāṇa is obtainable in the present life. "Cut out the love of self as you would an autumn water-lily with the hand; develop the way to peace, to nirvāṇa, taught by the Happy One (the Buddha)."[43] There is no other training for the attainment of the highest state.

2

ORIGIN AND SOURCE OF
▨ KNOWLEDGE OF THE ▨
HIGHEST STATE

THE ENLIGHTENMENT OF THE BUDDHA

To THE BUDDHIST, the origin of the knowledge of the highest state lies in the enlightenment of the Buddha, and the Buddhist's knowledge of this is derived from the teaching of Gotama Buddha. That these should be sufficient, if followed sincerely, is evident from the declaration made by Gotama Buddha to his devoted attendant Ānanda shortly before his passing away (*parinibbāna*): "I have expounded my doctrine throughout, in its entirety, Ānanda; the Tathāgata[44] has not the closed fist of a teacher who holds back something of his Doctrine."[45]

Enlightenment consists essentially in knowing things in accordance with reality (*yathābhūtam*). In seeing thus there are no misconceptions or mental projections about the appearance of a thing or a course of events; the seeing is entirely clear and according to absolute reality. Gotama Buddha describes the climax of the Buddhist's training thus: "He comes to know what, in absolute truth, are the influxes (*āsavas*) (see p. 158, n.150), their origin, their cessation, and the way to their cessation. From knowing thus and seeing thus, his mind is freed from the influxes and he knows 'I am free.' He knows: 'Exhausted is birth; the Higher Life has come to perfection; that which should be done has been done; there will be no more of the present state.'" [46]

LIFE OF GOTAMA BUDDHA

The historic personage known to Buddhists as "the Buddha" is Gotama Śākyamuni. He was born around the middle of the sixth century B.C.E., probably in the year 566, in Lumbini Park in the neighborhood of Kapilavastu in the north of the Gorakpur district. A pillar, erected in 239 B.C.E. by the emperor Asoka, marks the place of his birth. Both his parents belonged to the Śākya clan, his father being a chief. Astrologers had foretold that Gotama would become either a world monarch or a great spiritual leader, and since it was taken for granted that in the latter case he would adopt the homeless life, his parents took every precaution to prevent his coming into contact with any form of unhappiness, surrounding him always with those things which, to them, seemed the best that life could offer. However, at the age of fourteen, one day in his father's garden, he experienced a state of mind in which he became aloof from his surroundings, though still maintaining his faculties of observation and application of them.[47] Many years elapsed before further developments occurred; Gotama married, had a son, and to all appearances led an existence suitable to a man of his rank. Then, in spite of all the precautions, he encountered an aged man, a sick man, a corpse, and a man wearing the yellow robe of the wandering mendicant. Appreciating that old age, sickness, and death are the lot of mankind, and that there existed persons who aspired to an existence in which these did not figure, he resolved that he too would devote himself to finding the truth about life and the cause of all the suffering it entailed.

According to tradition, Gotama was twenty-nine years old when he left his palace, his parents, his wife, and his child. One night he rode out with a single attendant beyond the city, dismounted, sent his horse back, and himself took to the homeless life of the forest. For some time he studied under famous teachers of the day but always found their doctrines deficient; the best of them could offer only a temporary, self-induced state of cessation of consciousness, and many relied merely on theorizing.[48] Practicing strenuous asceticisms, he became so weak that he was hardly able to stand; then, finding that these served only to dull his thought, he abandoned them. With returning health he came to remember his early experience in his father's garden and to see that the only means of arriving at a solution of man's sufferings lay in his own meditation. One night he took up his position under the Bodhi tree (*Ficus religiosa*), determined to remain there until he had reached complete understanding.

THE CHAIN OF DEPENDENT ORIGINATION OR PAṬICCASAMUPPĀDA

Canonical texts vary as to the hour at which Gotama reached this understanding and so became "enlightened"; the *Udāna* gives in each of its first suttas of the *Bodhivagga* accounts of the process of reasoning connected with the enlightenment, identical in every respect except that the first, second, and third watches of the night, respectively, are stated as the time of attainment.[49] However, the main importance lies in the facts that the process of reasoning immediately preceded the enlightenment, and that all the Buddhas attained their respective enlightenments by this process. It is known as the *paṭiccasamuppāda*,[50] or more popularly as the *nidāna chain* or *chain of dependent origination*.[51]

The *Mahānidāna Suttanta*[52] contains an account of the paṭiccasamuppāda as delivered by the Buddha, and in that text he reflects upon it as in the *Mahāpadāna Suttanta*.[53] As recorded in the latter, Venerable Ānanda remarked that the paṭiccasamuppāda was easy to understand, the Buddha replying: "Do not say so, Ānanda; do not speak like that. Deep, indeed, Ānanda, is this paṭiccasamuppāda, and it appears deep too. It is through not understanding this doctrine, through not penetrating it, these beings have become entangled like a matted ball of thread, like a matted bird's nest, like *mūñja* grass and rushes, subject to the round of rebirths (*saṃsāra*) in a state of suffering."[54]

Nāgārjuna opens the *Madhyamakakārikā*, the textbook of the Mādhyamika school, with the following dedication:

The Perfect Buddha,
The foremost of all Teachers I salute;
He has proclaimed
The Principle of Universal Relativity.[55]

Indeed, so revered is this doctrine, that the well-known Indian Mahāyānist scholar Śāntarakṣita offers his adoration to the Buddha in one of his treatises, the *Tattvasaṃgraha*, as the "Great Sage who taught the doctrine of paṭiccasamuppāda."[56]

It must be remembered that unlike the majority of other religious philosophies, Buddhism has never given importance to the idea of the first cause, nor indeed to any form of cosmology. Theology did not develop in Buddhism, since practical realization is expected of the *bhikkhu* (monk, recluse) and not abstruse disputation. In any case, Buddhism does not recognize a conflict between religion and science as religion is, properly speaking, a practical spiritual application of the principles of science.

As the universe comprises the sum total of sentient life, there are, as one would expect, a multiplicity of causes that brought this entity into being. And in this connection, the doctrine of paṭiccasamuppāda recognizes twelve distinct phases, links, chains, or divisions (*nidānas*) in the cycle of causation. These phases are interdependent, and so the whole doctrine can be termed that of "dependent origination."

The abstract formula of the doctrine's whole sequence has been schematized as follows, showing its logic without its contents:

> *Imasmiṃ sati idaṃ hoti;*
> *imass' uppādā idaṃ uppajjati;*
> *imasmiṃ asati, idaṃ na hoti;*
> *imassa nirodhā imaṃ nirujjhati*[57]

> That being thus this comes to be;
> from the coming to be of that, this arises;
> that being absent, this does not happen;
> from the cessation of that, this ceases.

There is a law in this process of causal sequence that makes it impossible to point out a first cause, simply because it forms a circle—the "wheel of life" (*bhavacakka*). Most people regard time as a line stretching from a finite past to a finite future. Buddhism, however, views life as a circle and life, reflected as such, is repeated over and over again, an endless continuum. Moreover, the whole series of phases must be taken in their entirety, the conception of the wheel of life being in relation to space and time.

As recorded in the scriptures, it is customary to begin the exposition of paṭiccasamuppāda with the factor of (1) ignorance (*avijjā*). This ensures the continuation of death and remains a crystallization of the acts one performed during life. Ignorance, therefore, as an antonym of knowledge (*vijjā* or *ñāna*), leads inevitably to (2) volitional activities or forces (*saṅkhāra*) good and bad, or rather wholesome and unwholesome (*kusala akusala*), the effect of which leads to the motive for, or will to, life. These two factors were regarded as the causes of the past.

In the present life, the first stage is (3) consciousness (*viññāna*) of mind or will towards life. When this takes upon itself (4) material form or mind and body (*nāma-rūpa*), this action constitutes the second step. The third phase soon manifests itself as (5) the six sense organs (*saḷāyatana*), of which (6) the sense of touch (*phassa*) predominates. The consciousness of the living being rears itself, followed quickly by (7) feelings (*vedanā*) that are pleasurable (*sukha*), painful (*dukkha*), or neutral (*adukkham asukha*) associated with seeing, hearing, smelling, tasting, and bodily and mental impressions.

In these stages, the individual is formed, but he is not entirely responsible for his present condition, owing to complex past causes. The first of three causes that will ensure a future life for each individual is (8) desire (*taṇhā*) which can be neutralized; but if joy, sorrow and the like are experienced, then (9) attachment (*upādāna*) is produced, which in turn leads one to cling to the object of desire. The formation of another, (10) becoming (*bhava*), is ensured (the latter term is preferable to that of *existence*, as this phase falls midway between this life and the next).

While the individual is enjoying the effects of his past, he is unaware that he is creating the conditions for a future life. The whole process may be likened to that of the growth of an ordinary plum tree: its very existence depends upon fertile soil, a suitable environment, and favorable weather. After the lapse of a considerable period of time, when at last the tree has reached maturity and is blossoming, the fruit is finally born; but then, in no time at all, the fruit perishes and dies and the stones drop and are scattered, only to become seeds and produce trees in their turn. In the matter under discussion, therefore, (11) birth (*jāti*), (12) decay (*jarā*), and death (*maraṇa*) in themselves constitute the causes for renewed life.

In Buddhism, every stage is a cause (*hetu*) when viewed from its effect (*phala*), and there is nothing rigid or unalterable in this theory. The ignorance that remains after death is regarded as *kamma*—a dynamic manifestation of physical and mental energy. This latent energy is potential action, the motivating force behind the cycle of life. A living being determines his own action and, as this cycle has been trodden over innumerable years, no beginning to this process can be seen.

Saṃsāra, or constant flow, is the sum total of conditioned existence, and as such has been likened to an ocean upon which the ripples of the waves denote each life, each one influencing the next. It follows from this analogy that just as each life can be influenced only by the one preceding, so no outside power, such as a divine being, can possibly trespass and claim property rights!

Before closing the subject, it is noteworthy to recall that there are four kinds of karma, or *kamma* in Pali, with regard to begetting future life: that having immediate effect in this life itself (*diṭṭhadhammavedanīya*), that having effect in the next succeeding life (*upapajjavedanīya*), that having effect in some afterlife (*aparāpariyavedanīya*), and that whose effect has completely lost its potential force (*ahosi*).

Finally, to sum up: there is only conditioned existence (*sahetudhamma*) with the necessary causes, the factors of which belong to every individual. A fundamental doctrine of Buddhism is to regard everything in the universe as dynamic becoming, but it is through this becoming that delusion increases and ignorance is prolonged. This fact, as Candrakīrti says, is in existence everywhere in the universe:

> Nothing at all could we perceive
> In a universe devoid of causes,
> It would be like the color and the scent
> Of a lotus growing in the sky.[58]

As associated directly with the enlightenment of the Buddha, the declaration of the paṭiccasamuppāda would end with the actual enumeration of the links of the nidāna chain. This and the realization of other noble doctrines (*dhammas*) would constitute the aspect of the enlightenment of the Buddha known as his *mahāprajñā*, or great wisdom. However, before considering the bearings of these on the Buddhist's knowledge of the origin and source of knowledge of the highest state, there remains, according to the *Mahānidāna Suttanta*, one more corollary declared by Gotama the Buddha in his instruction of Ānanda. This concerns the nature of the self.

THE SELF AND THE ANATTA DOCTRINE

The Buddha gives the current opinions concerning the self as: (1) my self is small and has material qualities; (2) my self is limitless and with material qualities; (3) my self is small[59] and without material qualities; and (4) my self is limitless and without material qualities. Again there were persons who would make no declaration concerning the self.[60]

The Buddha asks in what respects the self is perceived. It can be seen as follows: (1) feeling is my self; (2) feeling is not my self, my self does not experience feeling; (3) feeling is not my self, my self does not lack experience of feeling; (4) by my self are things felt, the thing that feels is my self. To those who hold these views that feeling is my self, it should be said that feelings may be happy, unhappy, or neutral; any one of these three feelings, while it endures, excludes the other two. All of them are impermanent, conditioned, arising from other relations, things of decay, age, destruction, annihilation.

If to a person experiencing any one of them it should seem "This is my self," then with the passing of that feeling it should also seem to him "Gone is my self." A person declaring "Feeling is my self" is taking for the self impermanence, a mixture of happiness and suffering, a thing coming into existence and dying away, here among the things of this world. Therefore the statement "Feeling is my self" is not acceptable.[61]

On the other hand, to a person who declares "My self does not consist in feeling, my self does not experience feeling," it should be said: "Where there is entirely no feeling, can it be said 'I am'?"

Again, whether it is claimed that "my self does not consist in feeling, my self does not lack experience of feeling," or the converse, it may also be replied that if feeling should cease utterly, in every respect, could it be said there that "I, this person, am"?

None of these statements concerning feeling and the self is therefore acceptable.[62] The Buddha concludes: "From the time, Ānanda, that the bhikkhu ceases to regard the self as consisting in feeling, experiencing feeling, and does not maintain 'my self experiences feeling, the thing that feels is my self,' he grasps at nothing in the world; and not gripping for support, he does not long for anything. Not longing for anything, he attains to his final release for himself.[63] He comes to know: 'Exhausted is birth; the higher life has come to perfection; that which should be done has been done; there will be no more of the present state.'"

Concerning the existence of the Tathāgata after death, the Buddha said that any statements that he did or did not exist, or both, or neither, were "foolish theories." Why? "As far as the contact of mind and mental objects and the range thereof, as far as language and the range thereof, as far as concepts and the range thereof, as far as intelligence and the roaming of intelligence, so far does there reach the cycle of rebirth and its turnings. Having thoroughly understood that, the bhikkhu is freed, and, being so freed, does not know and does not see in the same way. To him the theories are not intelligent."[64]

From the direct statements of the nidāna chain, it is clear that "life," in the usual interpretation of the term, moves as a vicious circle continuously kept in motion by a drive of anxiety that it should do so. It is necessary to bear in mind that the term *consciousness*, as used in the chain, refers to the general sense, as one might say that a person is conscious if he knows what is going on around him, unconscious if he does not. Having established contact with an object or event, one registers judgment on it; one may find it pleasant, unpleasant, or one may be indifferent to it. In the first two cases one wishes either to perpetuate the liaison or to destroy it; in the third one is merely not interested. Yet though in the main there are no fixed standards of pleasantness or unpleasantness, there are certain states that man, irrespective of time or place, dislikes, and certain others that he ardently desires. The outstanding example of the first is death, and of the second, life. Only the worst agonies to which man has been subjected have made him desire death, while dissertations on happy afterlives, Elysian fields, or whatever their appellation, have never superseded his desire to prolong the present existence. But the present existence has never shown any security of tenure, and to make it continue, or appear to continue indefinitely, it has always been necessary to provide a support.

Yet in existence as we know it at present, life as followed by death, or a series of lives punctuated by deaths, how much of man has ever "lived"? What is it of him that "dies," and what is it of him that is "reborn"? The sūtra and suttas quoted above supply the answer to these questions, and in the Buddhist teaching, far from living one single isolated life, man lives a long series of lives connected with each other by a potential constituted by his previous actions. As one life draws to a close, the characteristics that would previously have been taken to constitute "unconsciousness"—using the word in the general sense—disappear. There remains a consciousness, sometimes referred to as the subconsciousness, but which more accurately is the infraconsciousness, which is the potential mentioned above. This potential leads to a blind activity, the energy or effect of which is the will to live. At the moment of conception the first stage of the individual existence is that of the infraconscious mind, or the blind will towards life. Its next stage of development lies in that of mental and physical states, the stage of prenatal growth with the mind and body evolving in combination. From here onwards we have the development of the sense organs, the making of contact with the outside world, and so on. But throughout these events, and throughout the existence just started, is the undercurrent of potential, the result of past actions, which determines the personality of the individual in question and which constantly makes itself felt.

How much the individual can improve on this undercurrent will decide his circumstances and disposition in future lives, but there is no question of any organ representative of the individual, such as a *jīva* (soul), experiencing one existence only and fading out into some realm of happiness or misery, or with its potential lost in the general mass of the world's activity. Modern biologists tell us that there is no permanent part of the physical organism that sustains, or could possibly sustain, the whole process of life, but on the contrary, that life consists in the processes of growth, nourishment, and renewal, that were once assumed to be the accompaniments to life. In the same way there is no "self" that stands at the center of the mentality to which characteristics and events accrue and from which they fall away, leaving it intact at death. The stream of consciousness, flowing through many lives, is as changing as a stream of water. This is the *anatta* doctrine of Buddhism as concerns the individual being. Extended to all the phenomena of the universe, we have a parallel in the steady-state theory, or theory of continuous creation advanced by present-day astronomers. This is in contrast to the former periodical creations as developing from Brahma or a primeval atom, or with the creation once-and-for-all as put forward by the Zoroastrians and taken over by the Christians and other monotheistic religions.

THE THREE CHARACTERISTICS OF EXISTENCE

The *anatta* doctrine is counted among the three characteristics of existence as put forward in the Buddha's teaching, the other two being impermanence, or *anicca*, and suffering, or *dukkha*. They are essentially present in all teachings claiming to be Buddhist. The *Dhammapada* discusses them in a passage not presented identically, though often approximately, elsewhere in the Buddhist scriptures as we know them at present. According to the *Dhammapada:*

> 'All mental and physical phenomena are impermanent.' Whenever through wisdom one perceives this, then one becomes dispassionate towards suffering. This is the road to purity. 'All mental and physical phenomena are painful.' Whenever through wisdom one perceives this, then one becomes dispassionate towards suffering. This is the road to purity. 'All things are without self.' Whenever through wisdom one perceives this, then one becomes dispassionate towards suffering. This is the road to purity.[65]

Two points are of particular note in the translation of these verses. The first, "dispassionate towards suffering," is explained, both here and in the corresponding Sanskrit text, as "a sense of indifference to suffering arising out of a true knowledge of the real character of existence." The meaning is given thus by Buddhaghosa and is also born out in the Tibetan version. R. C. Childers, in an early translation of the Pali *Dhammapada*, gave the sense correctly as "only does he conceive disgust for (existence which is nothing but) pain."

The second point consists in the employment in the third verse of the word *things* as contrasted with the "mental and physical phenomena" of the first and second verses. The corresponding Pali terms are *saṅkhāra* and *dhamma*. The meaning of *saṅkhāra* is more comprehensive here than in the previous case mentioned and now extends to all mental and physical phenomena which are *saṅkhata* (i.e., put together, compounded, conditioned). *dhamma*, of which the corresponding Sanskrit form is *dharma*, carries a yet more extensive meaning. *Dharma* derives from *dhṛ*, to hold or bear, so that the noun *dharma* would be "that which is held to," therefore, figuratively, the "ideal." This to the Buddhas would be their enlightenment, the supreme wisdom, *sambodhi*. To their followers it would be "that to be realized," the seeing of things as they really are (*yathābhūtam*); expressed in words, *dharma* would be the Buddhas' teaching, the moralities, precepts, and general discipline of *magga*, the Path. But these meanings of *dharma* are not here applicable and are not intended, and *dharmas* in the everyday world as "that which is held to" are the things, material or otherwise, of everyday life. Used in this connection it is better not to translate *dharma*, but if translation is imperative, "thing" is the only possibility since it has no pretensions to being a scientific term. The rendering made by Stcherbatsky, "elements of existence," is merely an aggrandizement which does nothing to clarify the meaning, for, as will be seen by the forthcoming classifications of dharmas, the word *element* as used in the strict sense is not here applicable, while that which qualifies for "existence" from one point of view is "nonexistent" from another. The term does not seem to have met with Stcherbatsky's entire satisfaction for he states shortly after: "A Buddhist element is always a separate entity, it is neither 'compound' nor 'phenomenon,' but is an element (*dharma*)."[66]

The confusion becomes even greater when one finds *entity* to mean "a thing complete in itself, its actual existence as opposed to qualities and attributes; something with a real existence of its own."[67] Rhys Davids was nearer the mark when he translated *diṭṭhe va dhamme* as "in this very world," the context being to the following effect.[68] An inquirer, having observed that craftsmen such as mahouts, horsemen, high-ranking military officers, cooks, bath attendants, confectioners, garland-makers, accountants—many others were mentioned—were able, from the proceeds of their occupation, to support their families and enjoy themselves generally, *diṭṭhe va dhamme*, asked if there accrues to a person who becomes a recluse any comparable result *diṭṭhe va dhamme*. Taking *diṭṭhe* as "seen, perceived, understood," and *va* for *iva*, "like, as," with *dhamme* "that which is held to," we have for the whole expression "that which is held to in everyday life." Again, Rhys Davids and William Stede in their dictionary give for *diṭṭhe va dhamme* "in the phenomenal world," as contrasted with *samparāyika dhamme*, "the world beyond."[69] A. C. Banerjee, in his *Sarvāstivāda Literature*, gives for *dhamma* "existent things," and for *dhammas* "things."[70]

Taking the classifications of dharmas according to the Buddhist philosophical systems, the Sarvāstivāda and Vijñaptimātravāda schools enumerate seventy-five and a hundred dharmas respectively.[71] These divide into five groups entitled mind, mental concomitants, forms, things not associated with mind, and things which are not put together. The first four groups are *saṃskṛta* dharmas (*saṃskṛta* corresponding to the Pali term *saṅkhata)*, that is, dharmas that are formed, prepared, put together, etc., while the fifth group contains the *asaṃskṛta* dharmas, things which are not formed, prepared, etc. The *saṃskṛta* dharmas, which include the body and the four sense organs of eye, ear, nose, and tongue, include also the corresponding touch, sound, smell, and taste, as well as the eye-consciousness, ear-consciousness, and so on. Among the mental concomitants that all systems treat with great respect are feeling (*vedanā*), will (*cetanā*), and vigilance (*appamāda*), while the class "things not associated with mind" contains such various dharmas as birth (*jāti*), number (*saṅkyā*), region (*deśa*), and time (*kāla*). The *asaṃskṛta* dharmas comprise space, modes of exhausting the life process, and, in the Vijñaptimātravāda, that which transcends all specific character and conditions, namely, *tathatā* (thusness, i.e., truth, reality). The Pali Abhidhamma literature condenses the dharmas to four categories: mind, mental concomitants, form and the *lokuttara* (supramundane).

According to the *Dhammapada* verses 277–79 quoted above, one turns away from, or becomes dispassionate toward, an existence that, by reason of the transitoriness of the phenomena, brings only sufferings. This reminds us of the lack of stability of all things.

Dukkha, here translated as "suffering," may also represent misery, unsatisfactoriness, or evil. *Dukkha* is the first of the Four Noble Truths, and figures in feelings to the extent that these may be painful or unpleasant as regards the physical and mental senses. "Birth is painful, old age is painful, disease is painful, death is painful, grief, lamentation, suffering, misery and despair are painful, not to get what one wishes for is painful; in short, the clinging to the five khandhas is painful."[72] Yet these five sensorial aggregates condition the appearance of life in any form, and in an existence that is essentially conditioned, even to the extent that it itself "exists," we cannot know from our present standpoint anything that is unconditioned. Therefore we follow the Path pointed out by the Buddha, the Way to the cessation of suffering, and come to a position from which we may gauge that which is greater than happiness.

THE *MAHĀKARUṆĀ* OF THE BUDDHA

From this account of the Buddha's enlightenment it is clear that the enlightening consisted primarily in perceiving the real nature of life as experienced in the present existence and the beings living it. There was also the expectation of future existences, all more or less similar, and the means of bringing about cessation of the conditioning of all of them. But if the Buddha's teaching had been confined to these matters regardless of their application, though no doubt he would have drawn a considerable following of learned people throughout the ages, he would have come down in history as a great thinker and philosopher but as a theorist only. This was not his intention, and he took into consideration the ordinary person's estimate of the Buddha himself. This is clear from his exposition in the Pali *Brahmajāla Sutta* where, at the outset of this very comprehensive and profound discourse, he remarks: "An average worldling appraising the Tathāgata would speak of relatively small things, the things of this world, the moralities. What would he say?"[73] The text continues to the effect that the average worldling would say that the Samaṇa Gotama does not take life, does not take that which is not given, and so on, enumerating the moralities. Therefore, though he would not appreciate in detail the high attainments of the Buddha with regard to perfect wisdom and understanding, he could not fail to see the reflection of this in the Buddha's daily life of the present existence. Could the average person establish any connection between the supreme understanding and the ordinary moralities?

Many recent Western writers have adopted the stand that original Buddhism consisted entirely in a reformatory movement amongst recluses, and that the laity were considered only in so far as they were necessary to the physical maintenance of the bhikkhus. "Buddha's Church is a Church of monks and nuns. . . . He who cannot or will not gain this freedom (*i.e. leaving home*) is not a member of the Church," says Oldenberg, and continues: "But while there was framed from the beginning for the monastic Church an organization, clothed with strict forms of spiritual procedure, there was no attempt made at creations of a similar kind for the quasi-Church of lay-brothers and lay-sisters."[74] Quotations adduced in support of these statements and other similar ones are drawn almost exclusively from Vinaya texts which, of course, deal essentially with the rules of the order. But making due allowance for the facts that Oldenberg published his work over eighty years ago, that the Western nations had many centuries of strict Christian tradition behind them from which they were hardly beginning to get themselves free, and that such a term as *Church* pertained strictly to their own terminology, the idea that Buddhism was entirely the property of monks and nuns, or *bhikkhus* and *bhikkhunīs,* still persists. That the Saṅgha (community of monks) should form the nucleus wherefrom the Buddha's teachings should be perpetuated is reasonable enough; for if with the vicissitudes of time the laity became estranged from Buddhist teachings, provided the Saṅgha remained true to its trust the populace could reform around it. History has shown that such vicissitudes did occur on more than one occasion and that the laity did so reform. If it is contended that the laity might have been more rigorously controlled so as to have been more independent of the Saṅgha, then it must be recalled that the strict control, religious or political, which has been such a feature of Western religions, was entirely contrary to the whole spirit of the Buddha's teaching. It cannot be argued that the laity was not adequately provided for at the outset of the teaching of the Buddha Dhamma, or that Buddhism represented merely a new doctrine for the consideration of recluses. That these and kindred notions are grossly incorrect is evident from a study of the events immediately following the enlightenment itself.

It is a matter of extreme importance that the account of the enlightenment of Vipassi Buddha (the first of six Buddhas of previous ages) as given by Gotama Buddha ends, not with an exposition of the paṭiccasamuppāda, but with the conversation with the Great Brahmā. If the enlightenment of the Buddha constituted his *mahāprajñā* (great wisdom), the first result of this was his *mahākaruṇā*, or great compassion. The *Mahāpadāna Suttanta* gives: "Then there occurred to Vipassi, the Exalted One, Arahat, and All-

Knowing One: 'What if I should now teach the Doctrine, the Truth?' But there also occurred to him: 'I attained to this Truth, profound, difficult to discern, difficult to understand, of peaceful and excellent import, not of the order of logical deduction, subtle, which only the wise can appreciate. Yet this generation is attached to pleasure and delights in the attachment, and because of this it is difficult for it to understand the matters, namely, this causation and the Law of "This arises depending on That." These, too, are matters difficult to understand, namely: the calming of all mental concomitants, the forsaking of all substrata of rebirth, the destruction of craving, dispassion, quietude of heart, nibbāna. If I should teach the Dhamma and others did not understand it from me, that would be wearisome to me; that would be a vexation to me.'"[75]

At that point, the Great Brahmā appeared to him, asking him to preach the Dhamma, for the reason that there existed beings with few defilements who, without knowledge of the Dhamma, would dwindle away. Vipassi replied that he had considered preaching the Dhamma and gave his reasons for deciding against doing so. The Great Brahmā asked him a second time and received a similar reply. On the request being made a third time, "Vipassi felt compassion for all beings, and with his Buddha's vision, saw beings of various degrees of defilement, of sharpness and faculties, of various dispositions, of different capacities for learning, living in evil and fear, with small appreciation of a world beyond."[76]

Two *gāthās* follow this description, the first, spoken by the Great Brahmā, enlarges on this reason as to why the Buddha should preach the Dhamma.

> As a man who has climbed to the hill-top
> Looks down on the people below,
> So the Sage having reached to All-Vision
> Sees men as afflicted with woe.
> He considers their birth and decaying,
> And attaining to victory himself,
> A leader, a man free from grasping
> Who has broken the rounds of rebirth,
> Sees others possessed of ability—
> May he teach them the Dhamma himself!

To this Vipassi replied:

The doors of the deathless state are open wide.
Let those who have ears abandon blind beliefs!
Brahmā! Perceiving vexation in teaching,
I did not declare my Dhamma to mankind.[77]

Vipassi immediately set about his task of teaching the Dhamma, and, under similar circumstances, Gotama Buddha did likewise.

Though the incident may seem familiar to Buddhist readers, it contains one point that is often passed over, namely, that as long as the prospect lay in teaching a few people in comparatively advanced states, the Buddha refused to teach; but when he considered the whole heterogeneous mass of mankind and its sufferings he decided without hesitation that he would teach his Dhamma. Therefore, any statement to the effect that the Buddha Dhamma was intended for a select few only, of whatever nature that few might be assumed to be, is not in accord with the statement made by Gotama. Remembering the *mahāprajñā* of the Buddhas, it is incumbent on one to remember their *mahākaruṇā*. One may consider, in passing, the import of the presence of the Great Brahmā. Should it be taken that this superbeing did present himself to the ocular vision of the Buddha? Or did the Buddha become conscious of that which the Great Brahmā was popularly assumed to represent, namely, the creator of the world and the living creatures in it? Great Brahmā or Mahā Brahmā was not Absolute Reality; technically he was a *rūpāvacara* deva, or a god of the world of form. However exalted he may have been in his own particular realm, he still created in terms of form and was still subject to birth and death. The question "Where do earth, water, fire and air entirely cease?" was put to the Buddha (see p. 4); immediately before that, it had been put to the Great Brahmā who admitted that he did not know the answer and referred the question to the Buddha. From the Buddha's reply that the question should have been stated as: "Where do earth, water, fire and air not occur?" it is clear that the raising of the world from its present condition must be a matter for someone or something greater than its creator. Hence the Great Brahmā's request to the Buddha to preach his Dhamma here.

Therefore, in our consideration of the origin and source of knowledge of the highest state, we have to bear in mind that the great compassion of the Buddha is inseparable from it. If after enlightenment the doors of the deathless state were open wide, the Buddha, with the profound knowledge of mankind and its needs which his compassion brought him, was ready to show the way in.

3

THE SIGNIFICANCE
OF THE REFUGES

THE THREEFOLD REFUGE

IN BUDDHISM THERE IS NO formal code of prohibitions. A follower of the Buddha lives according to the Buddha's teaching and declares his intention to do so using the following formula, called *Tisaraṇa,* or Three Refuges.

Since the full implication cannot be conveyed in short English phrases, it is necessary to consider the Pali words. They are: *Buddhaṃ saraṇaṃ gacchāmi. Dhammaṃ saraṇaṃ gacchāmi. Saṅghaṃ saraṇaṃ gacchāmi.* They may be translated, word for word, as: "To the Buddha as a refuge I go; to the Dhamma as a refuge I go; to the Saṅgha as a refuge I go."

Saraṇaṃ, however, does not denote exclusively "refuge," and in the comprehensive sense in which it should be taken lies the relationship of the Buddhist to the Buddha, which will eventually determine his whole attitude towards life. *Saraṇa* is common to both the Sanskrit and Pali languages, and for the Sanskrit Monier Williams gives: "*Śaraṇa*: protecting preserving. (Vedic. *say rakkhake, Ṛgveda* VI. 47. 8); one who protects or preserves; a protector, preserver, defender. (a) n. help, defense; a refuge, place of refuge, sanctuary, asylum (sometimes applied to a person); a private apartment, closet; a house, habitation, abode, lair, resting-place (of an animal)."[78] Regarding the Pali we have from Rhys Davids and Stede: "*Saraṇa*: (Cp. Vedic.) . . . shelter, house, refuge, protection, etc."[79] Buddhadatta Mahāthera gives: "Protection, help, refuge, a shelter."[80]

"Refuge" is therefore the most acceptable short translation of *saraṇaṃ,* but in no sense can the declaration of taking the Three Refuges be interpreted as undertaking to comply with blind, unreasoning obedience to a series of orders or commandments. In contrast to the monotheistic religions which depend entirely on faith, and to the systems that have developed *bhakti,* devotion, as an end in itself, the Buddha denounced blind faith, pointing out that it is merely a form of ignorance that retards one's purification and therefore one's development. When consulted by the Kālāmas of Kesaputta as to how they should choose between the various pronouncements of their many visiting teachers, each of whom claimed that his dogma or method was the only one leading to the desired perfection, the Buddha replied: "Whenever you find out for yourself . . . 'these things are bad, reprehensible, condemned by the wise, are not rightly taken upon oneself, lead to harm and suffering,' you should abandon them . . . . Whenever you find out for yourself 'these things are good, blameless, extolled by the wise, are rightly taken on oneself, lead to welfare and happiness,' you, having attained to this, should there remain." Frequently throughout this address he observed: "Do not accept anything because of report, tradition, hearsay, the handing on in the sacred texts, or as a result of logic or inference, through indulgent tolerance of views, appearance of likelihood, or as paying respect to a teacher."[81] Of his own teaching the Buddha said: "As a wise man uses gold as a touchstone, heating and cutting, so you, bhikkhus, should take my words after investigation and not because of reverence for me."[82] So is achieved *śraddhā*, confidence, an attitude directly opposed to that of blind faith. Of it the Buddha said: "Confidence is the greatest wealth of man in the world."[83]

Concerning *saraṇa* as "protection," the Buddha never made any declaration to the effect: "Abandoning all duties (*dharmāṃ*), come to me as the only shelter. Do not be grieved; I will liberate thee from all evils."[84] But he does make clear that one will achieve liberation as a result of one's own efforts made in accordance with the refuge described in the following passage: "Many persons, indeed, driven by fear, move quickly to mountains, forests, the parks and trees of shrines, as a refuge. That is not a safe refuge; it is not the best refuge. Having come to this refuge one is not freed from all suffering. But he who goes for refuge to the Buddha, Dhamma and Saṅgha, by right wisdom and insight perceives the Four Noble Truths: Suffering, the Origin of Suffering, the Passing-Beyond Suffering, and the Way to the Calming of Suffering. This is the safe Refuge, this is the best Refuge. Having come to this Refuge one is freed from all suffering."[85]

It should be noted that the protection sought is not only from worldly ills but from the whole mass of suffering to which mankind is subject. The true nature of the Refuges was to be understood as follows:

> The disciple of the Noble Ones is possessed of this clear confidence in the Buddha: that the Exalted One is rightly named the Fully-Enlightened One, perfect in knowledge and conduct, wise as

to the words, an incomparable guide to man's self-mastery, happy, a teacher of devas and men, a Buddha, an Exalted One. The disciple of the Noble Ones is possessed of this clear confidence in the Dhamma: the Dhamma is well-preached by the Exalted One, is evident in this life, is not subject to time, invites every man to come and see for himself, and brings near that which should be known to the wise each for himself. He has this clear confidence in the Saṅgha: that the Saṅgha of the followers of the Exalted One is entered on the direct right path, is walking in the right path, the proper path, namely the four pairs of persons, the eight classes of individuals;[86] that the Saṅgha is worthy of offerings, of hospitality, of gifts, or being honored; that the Saṅgha is the incomparable source of merit for the world, that it is possessed of the precepts believed in by the wise, in entirety, without defects, continuously, which bring freedom to men, are extolled by the wise, which are uncorrupted, and which lead to *samādhi*.[87]

It is now quite clear that the taking of refuge means resolving to follow the guidance or shining example of the Buddha, Dhamma, and Saṅgha.

THE FIRST REFUGE: THE BUDDHA

Taking refuge in the Buddha implies no personal guarantee that the Buddha himself will effect one's arrival at the goal. To the contrary, he says: "Surely by oneself is evil done, by oneself one becomes pure. Purity and impurity are of the individual. No one purifies another."[88] When referring to progress toward the goal he frequently used the expression *sayaṃ abhiññā sacchikatvā*, "having thoroughly understood and experienced for oneself."

According to the doctrine of karma, future happiness is a direct result or continuation of maintaining a satisfactory standard of conduct in the present. But there were wrong actions in the past which must produce their effects in the present and in the future. If inevitably one reaps the results of one's actions, good or bad, and there is no means of avoiding the results on the strength of the moral excellence of another person, the best that can be done to gain secure and lasting well-being is to decrease the evil actions and increase the good ones. There is freedom of will in making a choice, but clearly there must be cultivation of vision and discernment to detect when a choice should be made. Buddhist teaching stresses the cultivation of discernment more than the cultivation of will-power; since blind obedience is not encouraged, unless a person is convinced that he is pursuing a wrong course he is unlikely to abandon it if it seems to be attractive. The *Dhammapada* says: "If by renouncing a relatively small happiness one sees a happiness great by comparison, the wise man abandons the small happiness in consideration of the great happiness."[89] It is therefore necessary that one should be willing to discern a possible comparison and be able to draw it.

Such matters are not always evident in the devotion and pageantry associated with Buddhism in the Buddhist countries, and the mental attitude of persons participating in these must be made clear. Nowadays the central tangible object of a ceremonial display consists, almost invariably, in a Buddha-*pratima*, or image of the Buddha, but such figures were unknown until the first century B.C.E. When before that date it was desired to reproduce a scene including the Buddha, his presence was indicated by a symbol such as a Bodhi tree, wheel, lotus, or feet, these being also employed to represent certain ideas of Buddhism. It is generally considered that non-Indian influences, notably perhaps the Greek, brought about the representation of the Buddha as a human figure. But a Buddhist goes before an image and offers flowers or incense not to the model but to the Buddha as the perfection; he goes as a mark of gratitude and reflects on the perfection of the Buddha, meditating on the transiency of the fading flowers. As he offers the flowers the Buddhist recites: "With diverse flowers to the Buddha I do homage (*pūja*), and through this merit may there be release. Even as these flowers must fade, so does my body progress to a stage of dissolution."[90] This is not a canonical text but a very old traditional verse.

Though an image or some such symbol is useful to the ordinary person in helping him to concentrate his attention, an intellectual could dispense with it since he would direct his thoughts, probably concentrating on a passage such as the following: "Such indeed is the Exalted One, Worthy One, Fully Enlightened One, Perfect One in wisdom and virtue, the Happy One, the Knower of the world, an Incomparable Guide to man's self-mastery, a Teacher of gods and men, the Blessed One."[91]

But genuine reverence for the Buddha is measured only by the extent to which one follows his teaching. "He who, having entered on the course, lives in conformity with the Dhamma, having engaged in practices in conformity with the Dhamma, pays reverence to the Tathāgata."[92]

How does this attitude affect the moral outlook of the Buddhist? In contrast to the theistic religions where man is a subservient creature, forever below God or the gods until such being or beings should feel inclined to raise his status, the Buddhist has it in his own power to rise as high as he likes provided he is willing to make the effort. The Buddhist's mentality is never enslaved; he does not sacrifice freedom of thought or freedom of will. Here is the advantage of *śraddhā* or *saddhā*, "confidence born of understanding," over blind faith. The Buddhist pilgrim starts out on a worthwhile journey in happy expectancy, with plenty of equipment and good chance of success; he is never a "miserable sinner."

THE SECOND REFUGE: THE DHAMMA

"He who sees the Dhamma, Vakkali, sees me; he who sees me sees the Dhamma," said the Buddha to one of his disciples who was anxious to get a glimpse of him.[93]

We have already considered the term *Dhamma* as "things in general" and from its derivation can attribute to it a meaning as of duty or duties; we now take *dhamma* in the sense of teaching or doctrine, and here distinguish between the teaching itself and the sacred texts recording that teaching.

Regarding notable pre-Buddhistic doctrines, the Brahman-Ātman ideal and the derivatives of the personification of Brahman as Brahmā have been mentioned, but in order to appreciate fully the innovations of the Buddha's teaching we will consider in some detail the current opinions with which he had to deal. Many of them have figured in philosophic and religious thought throughout the centuries, and still form subjects of considerable debate.

In one of the oldest records that have come down to us, namely, the *Brahmajāla Sutta*, also known as the "Discourse on the Net of Brahmā," from the *Dīgha Nikāya*, dating from the sixth to fifth century B.C.E., the Buddha described various classes of beliefs. He dealt first with persons who attempted to reconstruct the ultimate beginnings of things and who deduced the eternality of the world and the self. In this case, by reason of extreme ardor, striving, and right attention, a *samaṇa* (homeless wanderer) or Brahman is able to call to mind his earlier existences. He recollects: "In such-and-such a place my name, ancestry, food, and happy and sorrowful experiences were thus and thus, coming to an end at such-and-such an age. Then my consciousness died down, arising again in such-and-such a place. There my name, ancestry, appearance, food, and happy and sorrowful experiences were thus and thus, coming to an end at such-and-such an age. Then my consciousness died down, arising again in such-and-such a place. There my name, ancestry, appearance, food, and happy and sorrowful experiences were thus and thus, coming to an end at such-and-such an age; my consciousness died down and arose again here." In such fashion he calls to mind, point by point, the activities and circumstances of the existences in which he was previously engaged. He says: "The self is eternal; and the world, producing nothing new, stands out immovable as a strong pillar. Living beings moving continuously through existences, pass away and rise up again; yet it is eternally the same."[94] With greater application the ascetic or Brahman remembers existences more remote, while a similar conclusion may also be reached by the sophist-logician who is practiced in specious argument and is possessed of a ready wit.

The second class comprises the belief that some things are eternal and others are not. Here it is suggested that the sometime inhabitants of the present world have been reborn as devas, in this case in the realm of the radiance (Ābhassara). After a lengthy period one of these beings, either because his merit is exhausted or because his duration of life is spent, re-arises in a lower sphere equivalent to that of Brahma. This is still a fine-material sphere,[95] and birth and death still occur. The fallen one is lonely and wishes for companions. These appear, also from the Ābhassara, and for similar reasons. To the first arrival in the Brahma-world they seem to have come in accordance with his wish; to them, from his being there first, he is the ruler of the realm. He is therefore the Great Brahmā, Overlord, the Unvanquished, to be perceived by others as Be-It-So (i.e., self-existent), wielding power, the Master, the Maker by Creation, the Most Excellent to be produced having power, the Father of all produced in the states of existence. Subsequently one of the Brahma-world re-arises in the present world. Disgusted with the prevailing conditions, he becomes a samaṇa, or homeless wanderer. He recalls his former existence in the Brahma-world, though not elsewhere, and thinks of Brahmā in the terms described above. But to him it seems also: "We were created by Brahmā because he is permanent, constant, eternal, a changeless thing; he stands eternally the same, the Truth. Moreover, we who were created by Brahmā have come to the present state as being impermanent, subject to change, of short life, as things that fall away and die."[96] Hence, said the Buddha, arises the opinion that some things are eternal and some are not, that the self and the world are partly eternal and partly not eternal.

Other instances of this belief arise from the falling from the state of gods blemished by pleasure (*khiḍḍāpadosikā*), or blemished in mind (*manopadosikā*). These re-arise in the *kāmaloka* (this world), become recluses and, realizing their former existence, come to the conclusion reached by the beings fallen from the Brahma-world. A fourth case cited is that of the sophist-logician accustomed to specious argument and to use of his own ready wit. Such a person holds: "That which is called eye, ear, nose, tongue, body, that 'self' is impermanent, subject to change, noneternal, a changing thing. That which is called thought, or mind, or consciousness, that 'self' is eternal, a changeless thing, standing eternally the same and thus the Truth."[97]

Other classes of beliefs that confronted the Buddha and on which he also pronounced a verdict, consisted in the following: the belief in limitation or infinite extension of the world in one or more directions, the existence of the world as occurring by chance, the conscious or unconscious existence of the self after death (with variations as to form, duration, modes of perception, states of happiness or misery), the belief in total annihilation, and the highest bliss obtainable in this world. A short dissertation concerning persons who, through lack of understanding, avoid expressing definite opinions is also included. The supporters of the theories of limitation, the fortuitous origin of the world, and the conscious or unconscious existence of the self after death rely for their evidence largely on experience of an exalted state of mind which is here not clearly defined. The annihilationists and the supporters of the particular states of bliss in this world adduce evidence from their experiences of the jhānic states.

We come now to the verdict passed by the Buddha. Of the ascetics and Brahmans who reconstruct the past and arrange the future, or both, he says: "These view-points, thus taken up, thus adhered to, will have for result future rebirth. That the Tathāgata knows, and he knows immeasurably beyond. But he is not attached to the knowledge, and from this lack of attachment has found out for himself the final bliss. Having come to know, as they really are according to the Truth, the origin of feelings, their passing away, their satisfaction and disadvantages, and the way of departure from them, the Tathāgata, from not grasping at the world, is freed."[98]

Of the speculations he says: "They derive from the lack of knowledge and understanding of the ascetics and brahmans, and from the resulting feeling and cravings with their attendant worry and struggle. They are due to contact (with the senses). They all experience feelings from constant touching in the six fields of contact. To them, with feeling as cause and conditioning factor comes craving; with craving as cause and conditioning factor comes the grasping for support; from grasping for support, the process of life; from the process of life, birth; and from birth as cause and conditioning factor come decay and death, with the arising of grief, lamentation, ill, suffering, and all trouble. From the time the bhikkhu comes to know, as they really are according to the Truth, the origin and passing away, the satisfaction and disadvantages of, and the way of departure from the six fields of contact, he comes to know that which lies beyond them all."[99]

To the Buddha, then, the individual theories concerning the ultimate beginnings and ends of things were merely unintelligent, and since they were all founded on one basic error the only worthwhile course to pursue lay in exposing that error. Summing up his own experience he said: "Repeated birth is suffering. Housebuilder, you are seen! You will not again build the house. The ribs of the hall are broken, the peak of the house is thrown apart. Having come to a condition divested of all phenomena, mind has obtained destruction of craving."[100] But there remains also for consideration the effect of teachings regarding the ultimate beginnings and ends of things, and, in view of the deficiencies of these teachings, the estimate of the Buddha's reasons for declaring his own teachings was made by him on many occasions. These were enunciated very clearly on the occasion of his visit to the debating hall in Queen Mallika's[101] park where Poṭṭhapāda, the wandering mendicant, was staying at the time.[102]

Having been welcomed, the Buddha inquired after the subject of the debate in progress, but Poṭṭhapāda introduced instead that of cessation of consciousness, a matter on which discussion was frequently held. After exchange of opinions the Buddha remarked: "It is difficult for you, Poṭṭhapāda, through your other views, other beliefs, inclinations, connections, procedures, to understand either 'Consciousness is a man's self' or 'Consciousness is one thing and the self another.'" Poṭṭhapāda then put forth the question: "(i) Is the world eternal, or (ii) is it not eternal, (iii) is the universe finite or (iv) is it infinite, (v) is soul the same as body or (vi) is soul one thing and body another thing, (vii) does the Tathāgata exist after death or (viii) does he not exist after death or (ix) does he both (at the same time) exist and not exist, and (x) does he both (at the same time) not exist and not not exist?" The Buddha replied: "I have made no declaration with regard to these ten problems."[103] Then Poṭṭhapāda asked:

"Why has the Exalted One made no declaration concerning these matters?"[104]

"I have made no declaration concerning these matters because they do not lead to that which is connected with welfare, truth, or the leading of the Higher Life, to disenchantment (with the world), to the absence of desire, to calm, to thorough understanding, to the Highest Wisdom, or the Final Bliss (*Nibbāna*)."

"What, then, *does* the Exalted One teach?"

"'Suffering' is my teaching. 'The Origin of Suffering' is my teaching. 'The Cessation of Suffering' is my teaching. 'The Way to the Cessation of Suffering' is my teaching."[105]

"Why does the Exalted One teach these things?"

"I teach them because they lead to that which is with welfare, with truth, with the leading of the Higher Life, to disenchantment (with the world), to the absence of desire, to calm, to thorough understanding, to the Higher Wisdom, and to the Final Bliss (*Nibbāna*). That is why I teach concerning them."[106]

In the same manner the Buddha dismissed those ten questions posed by Māluṅkyaputta, a young monk.[107]

Buddhism, therefore, does not provide an explanation of all the metaphysical problems that interest mankind. The Buddha explained whatever he thought was necessary in order to get rid of *dukkha* (suffering) and not in order to satisfy curiosity. It is a means of deliverance and a doctrine of reality that gives every encouragement to investigate the riddle of life. It is not necessary to indulge in idle speculation or theorizing; neither is faith demanded with regard to a first cause. This knowledge does not bring us any nearer to the goal; it only gratifies childish curiosity. Whatever other religions may teach, Buddhism does not speak about a first cause of life. Nevertheless it stresses the cause and effect with regard to the life continuum according to the doctrine of dependent origination (*paṭiccasamuppāda*). It clearly shows how the cause becomes the effect and the effect becomes the cause. The continuous recurring of birth and death, *saṃsāra,* has been aptly compared to a circling. It is inconceivable to ascertain a beginning in such a circle of cause and effect; therefore, with regard to the ultimate origin of life, the Buddha declares: "Without cognizable end is this recurrent wandering (*saṃsāra*), a first beginning of beings who, obstructed by ignorance and fettered by craving, wander to and fro, is not to be perceived."[108]

One should not worry in vain seeking for a beginning in a beginningless past. Life is a process of becoming, a force, a flux, and as such necessitates a beginningless past whether one is ape or man. One should seek the cause of this faring on and live in the present and not in the past. One should utilize one's valuable energy to transform the life stream into the sorrowless, dukkha-less state which is Nibbāna. As the life span is short, one should try to learn only the important things. There is no time to waste: one may live a hundred years or more but this is not sufficient time to study more than a few subjects. A library contains books on many interesting subjects but we must select the most useful subjects and specialize in them. There is no time to devote to metaphysical speculation. Those who pose questions for the mere sake of argument defeat their own ends. One might argue that life had a beginning and a finite past and that the first cause was a creator-god. In that case there is no reason why one should not question who had created the creator. In other words, no first cause is to be found. Science does not care to investigate into the first cause simply because such an attempt is directly inimical to the advancement of knowledge. The law of paṭiccasamuppāda does not investigate either, because the very conception of a first cause itself is a complete check in the progress of knowledge.

Sīla, Samādhi, Paññā

The teachings of the Buddha are authoritatively grouped under three headings; sīla (morality), samādhi (concentration), and paññā (wisdom). A later addition appears to be vimutti, deliverance,[109] but the three originals were undoubtedly as stated. To appreciate the authority for the grouping as well as its nature, it is necessary to consider the discourse in the sutta known as "The Fruits of the Life of a Recluse" (Sāmaññaphala Sutta)[110] which, though stated in the text to have been delivered to King Ajātasattu of Magadha, son of Bimbisāra, must have been made originally at a much earlier date. According to modern chronology, Ajātasattu succeeded his father only about seven years before the parinibbāna of the Buddha, whereas the address contained in the Fruits sutta was quoted on many occasions, some of which date from the very early days of the Buddha's teaching career. It was clearly a standard address that the Buddha quoted at length, then referred to in order to emphasize or clarify the particular points under review. Moreover, if anything is to be argued from the order of the arrangement of the suttas in the *Dīgha Nikāya*, and at least the first thirteen of these, perhaps the first sixteen, are amongst the earliest of the Discourses that have come down to us, it appears that they were arranged by the compilers in an order that would produce a cumulative account of the Buddha's teachings. For the first of the sixteen we have the *Brahmajāla*, or "Net of Brahmā," which contains the lengthy exposition of contemporary views, then the *Sāmaññaphala* which contains the exposition of the Buddha's views. Other developments like, for example, the stages of the path, the enunciation of the goal, the paṭiccasamuppāda, together with dissertations on the nature of true sacrifice, asceticism, and so on, follow in the course of the next sixteen suttas, the sixteenth being the *Mahāparinibbāna Suttanta*. In the meantime, *Sāmaññaphala* traces the development of the prospective Buddhist recluse from the time he decides to adopt the homeless life until he finally attains realization of the Four Noble Truths. Rhys Davids points out in the introduction to his translation of the sutta that though the "fruits" mentioned contain only one that is "exclusively Buddhist," yet "the things omitted, the union of the whole of these included into one system, the order in which the ideas are arranged, the way in which they are treated as so many steps of a ladder whose chief value depends on the fact that it leads up to the culminating point of Nirvāna in Arahantship—all this is exclusively Buddhist."[111] In point of fact, the fruits, other than the realization of the Four Noble Truths, already existed in Brahman thought in stages varying from the most rudimentary to that of developed growth, so that the enumeration of the whole series formed the ideal basis from which to expound. In the course of the sixteen suttas are introduced the four *Brahmavihāra*,[112] also previously known to Brahmanic thought, and, far more importantly, almost the whole of the *Paññā* section is recast.[113] For the present, however, we consider the *Sāmaññaphala* discourse as it stands in the sutta bearing that name.

We first have the recognition of the arising of an arahat in the present world, the hearing by an ordinary person of his teachings, and that person's decision to adopt the homeless life. We then have the section on the *sīlas*, or moralities, of which the main ones are described in terms of the ordinary man's estimate of the Buddha. The text states that such a person would say:

> Having abandoned the taking of life and continued to abstain therefrom, the Samaṇa Gotama, who has laid the stick and sword aside, feeling shame now shows kindness to all beings; he lives their

friend. Having abandoned the taking of that which is not given, and continued to abstain therefrom, the Samaṇa Gotama, taking only what is given, waits for the gift. Committing no theft, he lives as one whose being is pure. Having abandoned the world and become a follower of the religious life, the Samaṇa Gotama lives away from the world and abstains from sexual intercourse. Having abandoned the speaking of falsehood and continued to abstain therefrom, the Samaṇa Gotama is a speaker of truth. Linked to truth he is reliable and trustworthy, never breaking his word to the world. Having abandoned slander and continued to abstain therefrom, the Samaṇa Gotama, having heard a thing in one place does not declare it in another to cause dissension to the people there. Or, having heard a thing elsewhere, he does not repeat it here to cause dissension with the people here. Thus to the disunited he is a conciliator; to the united he is one who strengthens the existing union. He takes delight in peace and his words make for peace. Having abandoned harsh speaking and continued to abstain therefrom, such is the Samaṇa Gotama; whatever words are pure, comforting to the ear, kind, reaching to the heart, gentle, gracious to the people, such is the quality of his words. Having abandoned trivial conversation and continued to abstain therefrom, the Samaṇa Gotama's words are timely, in accordance with the truth, and of things bearing advantage—of the Dhamma and the Discipline of the Order. His speech is as a hidden treasure. It is in accordance with the occasion, cumulative and endowed with gain.[114]

Other and minor moralities are recounted, these referring almost entirely to recluses, after which, with the bhikkhu complete in the moralities, the discourse proceeds to the samādhi section.[115] Here are described the guarding of the doors of the senses, whereby the bhikkhu is restrained in his faculties; he no longer experiences covetousness, grief and evil things, but experiences "within himself" an unimpaired ease. Samādhi includes also: mindfulness and awareness, contentment with simplicity, and the destruction of the five hindrances to mental development and vision.[116] He now enters on the jhānic states but the present sutta mentions only the *rūpāvacara* jhānas.

The third section, *paññā*, is entered upon with the following realization: "This is my body, possessing material qualities, formed of the four great elements, produced by mother and father, on accumulation of rice and fluid, a thing by its nature impermanent, fragile, perishable, and subject to total destruction; and this is my consciousness, bound up with and dependent on it."[117] The meditator then concentrates on producing a mind-made body, on acquiring psychic powers such as passing through rocks and walking on water, on attaining supernormal hearing, on the knowledge of other people's thoughts, on recollection of his own previous births, and on the knowledge of other people's previous births. The last concerns the acquiring of the purity of the celestial eye. From this point he proceeds to the realization of the destruction of the *āsavas* (influxes) and so to the realization of the Four Noble Truths.[118]

Such were the terms in which the Buddha so frequently outlined his teaching. With regard to the amendments mentioned—the possible substitution of the *Brahmavihāras* for the jhānic states, a much wider use of the term *samādhi* than is indicated here, and a reconstruction of the paññā section—these will be considered in connection with the ultimate ideal aim. Returning to the authority on which the grouping into the sections of sīla, samādhi and paññā is based, we have the incident recounted in another of the early *Dīgha* suttas, namely, *Subha Sutta*, no. 10.

Shortly after the parinibbāna of the Buddha, Venerable Ānanda was approached by Subha, a young man from Tudi, a village near Savatthi and now in the territory of Nepal. Subha said to him: "You, Ānanda, were for a long time the attendant of the Venerable Gotama, intimate with him, keeping near him. You would know what were the doctrines he extolled, the doctrines with which he aroused people and in which he established them. What are those doctrines?" Venerable Ānanda replied: "There were three groups of that which the Exalted One extolled: the noble group relating to *sīla* (morality), the noble group relating to *samādhi* (concentration), and the noble group relating to *paññā* (wisdom)." Venerable Ānanda then quoted the moralities, concluding the section with the remark: "And after that there is certainly more to be done." He then described samādhi, concluding with the same remark, but after describing the paññā sections he stated: "And now there is indeed nothing further to be done."[119]

The placing of the moralities as the first section of the Buddha's teaching is not incidental, but essential if the student is to proceed with the mind-culture that is the core of Buddhism. The Buddhist scriptures give frequent warnings regarding the extreme danger of attempting to experience states of mental concentration without thorough grounding in the practice of the moralities. Any teachings that are issued or that have become extant—and many have done so in recent years—that do not insist on practice of the moralities before embarking on exercises in mental concentration are fraught with disaster and are to be utterly condemned. At the same time, if the moralities are to be kept to increasing degrees, then cultivation of samādhi and paññā are essential; the dictum of Soṇadaṇḍa,[120] endorsed by the Buddha, to the effect that morality is washed round with wisdom and wisdom with morality,[121] that these two together constitute the heights of the world, is incontrovertible. What cannot be maintained is that either morality or wisdom should exist independently of the other.

However, of the above address in *Sāmaññaphala Sutta*, there is much that might be held to be too advanced for the ordinary layman. The *Dhammapada* tells us: "The extent to which one is well versed in the Dhamma is not measured by the amount one talks, but if one has heard even only a little and really discerns the Dhamma through the mental body (intelligence), one is, indeed, well versed in the Dhamma who does not neglect it."[122] The great point is, therefore, that one should understand what one hears or reads of it, and that one should put that into practice. Moreover, the qualities that the Dhamma texts particularly stress should be cultivated are energy and vigilance. "Guard your own thoughts. Take delight in a vigilance. From a place difficult of access, pull yourself up as an elephant does out of the mud."[123] One may quote: "Vigilance is the way leading to the deathless state; negligence is the road to death. Those who are vigilant do not die; those who are negligent are as if dead already."[124]

The Noble Eightfold Path

In a very practical sermon known as the "Discourse of Setting in Motion the Wheel of the Doctrine" (*Dhammacakkappavattana Sutta*)—in fact, it was the first sermon given by the Buddha, at Isipatana near Banaras—he declared that those who wish to lead a pure life should avoid the two extremes of self-indulgence (*kāmasukhallikānuyoga*) and self-torture (*attakilamathānuyoga*). He said: "Self-indulgence is low, vulgar, ignoble and harmful, and self-mortification is painful, ignoble and harmful—both are profitless."[125] In fact, the former surely retards one's spiritual progress and the latter weakens one's intellect.

Both of these erroneous doctrines of extremes were actually propound-ed by two religious groups at the time: one, materialist (*cārvāka*), supported hedonism; and the other believed in a transcendental self or soul bound to a material body which should be annihilated by severe ascetic practices in order to release the true self.

The Buddha himself put into practice both these doctrines before his enlightenment: the first, when he was a prince in his father's palace before he renounced the world; the second, as an ascetic in the Uruvelā forest prior to his enlightenment. Hence, he realized their futility and discovered that only self-conquest in moderation leads to the ultimate goal—Nibbāna.

Avoiding the two extremes, the Buddha therefore asked his followers to take the Middle Way (*majjhimāpaṭipadā*) which opens the eyes and bestows understanding, which leads to peace of mind, to the higher wisdom, to full enlightenment.[126] In fact, according to the Four Noble Truths, (1) life is sub-ject to sorrow (*dukkha*); (2) this sorrow is caused by ignorance which results in desire-attachment (*samudaya*); (3) this sorrow can be eliminated by the elimination of desire-attachment (*nirodha*); and (4) the path to eliminate desire-attachment (*magga*). One can, therefore, put an end to sorrow by adopting and following the path—the Middle Way—which to the Buddhist is the philosophy of life itself. This Middle Way of self-conquest, which leads to the ultimate goal, is eightfold, namely: (1) right understanding (*sammā-diṭṭhi*); (2) right thought (*sammā-saṅkappa*); (3) right speech (*sammā-vācā*); (4) right action (*sammā-kammanta*); (5) right livelihood (*sammā-ājīva*); (6) right effort (*sammā-vāyāma*); (7) right mindfulness (*sammā-sati*); and (8) right concentration (*sammā-samādhi*).

1) Right understanding: To begin treading the Path, we must see life as it is, in accord with its three characteristics of impermanence (*anicca*), suffering (*dukkha*), and no-soul (*anattā*); we must possess a clear understanding of the nature of existence, of moral law, of the factors and component elements (*dhammas*) that go to make up this *saṃsāra* or conditioned realm of life. In short, we must have the clear understanding of twelve nidānas or the depen-dent origination (*paṭiccasamuppāda*) and the Four Noble Truths. We should, therefore, make these the bases of our acceptance of the vicissitudes of life.

2) Right thought: This means that our mind should be pure, free from lust (*rāga*), ill will (*vyāpāda*), cruelty (*vihiṃsā*), and the like. At the same time,

we should be willing to relinquish anything that obstructs our onward march and unselfishly transfer merit we obtain to all sentient beings. Three other steps conjoin with and accompany right thought, namely: right understanding, right effort, and right mindfulness.

3) Right speech: By refraining from lying (*musāvāadā*), backbiting (*pisunāvācā*), harsh talk (*pharusāvācā*), and idle gossip (*samphappalāpā*), we create a connecting link between thought and action, one, moreover, which is characterized by wisdom and kindness. Correct speech should not be unduly loud or excitable, not prompted by infatuation, ill will or selfish interests; it should be free from dogmatic assertions and discrimination; finally, it should not be such as to inflame passions. Three steps are accompanied by right speech as in right thought.

4) Right action: This generally consists in observing the five precepts, which can be shown in both their negative and positive aspects: i) not to kill but to practice love and harmlessness to all; ii) not to take that which is not given, but to practice charity and generosity; iii) not to commit sexual misconduct, but to practice purity and self-control; iv) not to indulge in false speech, but to practice sincerity and honesty; and v) not to partake of intoxicating drinks or drugs that cause heedlessness, but to practice restraint and mindfulness.

It is important to notice that *sexual misconduct (kāmesumicchācāra)* has wrongly been translated as "adultery" on many occasions, whereas the original Pali usage *kāmesu,* being in the plural, denotes that *all* abnormal or illegal practices should be avoided, in addition to any other practice or pursuit that tends to overstimulate any of the senses. For the ordinary disciple, moreover, it is essential to practice all these injunctions if he wishes to aspire to the higher life.

Particularly abstaining from taking life, from taking that which is not given, and from sexual misconduct is right action. This is also conjoined with the first, sixth, and seventh steps.

5) Right livelihood or vocation: The layman should only pursue an occupation that does not cause harm or injustice to other beings.

To practice deceit, treachery, soothsaying, trickery, and usury is regarded as wrong living. The traditional trades from which the layman is barred are: dealing in arms, in living beings, in flesh, in intoxicating drinks, and in poison.

He should be free from acquisitiveness or any connections with money-making (legalized or otherwise) or prostitution of any kind, and should have a sense of service and duty in life. As the homeless life is the ideal state at which to aim, he should, although encumbered with family and business responsibilities, simplify his needs and devote more time to meditation.

The first, sixth, and seventh steps are conjoined with right livelihood in practice.

6) Right effort: Self-perfection can be achieved by avoiding and rejecting ignoble qualities while acquiring and fostering noble qualities. This stage is, therefore, subdivided into four parts: the effort to prevent the arising of evil that has not yet arisen; the effort to expel that evil that is already present; the effort to induce good that has not yet arisen; and the effort to cultivate that good that is already present.[127]

By conscientiously practicing the above, the layman will more easily cultivate the higher spiritual ideals, the best-known formulation of this being termed the ten perfections (*dasapāramitās*): generosity (*dāna*), morality (*sīla*), renunciation (*nekkhamma*), wisdom (*paññā*), energy (*viriya*), patience (*khanti*), honesty and truthfulness (*sacca*), determination (*adhiṭṭhāna*), loving kindness (*mettā*) and equanimity (*upekkhā*).

7) Right mindfulness: This implies a state of constant awareness with regard to the body, feelings, mind, and ideas engendered therein and is, in effect, an additional sense. The development of this type of mindfulness is necessary to prevent the practitioner from being led astray by erroneous views. Thus, it is the culmination of the intellectual process which links up with the intuitive process, namely vipassanā, or direct insight into things as they truly are. This step marks a further advance from the stage when things were known only by the differing features each displayed, since here all such discrimination is discarded. Although things seem corporeal, good or bad, right or wrong, such attitudes only go to prove how the mind views things on an incomplete basis. The process of thoughts is only food for the intellect to enable the mind to diagnose the truth more clearly as such discriminating things first make themselves aware. Hence, we should transcend the intellectual mind if we are to progress further and realize the true significance and relationship of all compounded things.

The above four fundamentals of mindfulness, practiced and developed, bring the seven factors of enlightenment (*bojjhaṅga*) to full perfection; they are: mindfulness (*sati*), investigation of the Law (*dhammavicaya*), energy (*viriya*), rapture (*pīti*), tranquillity (*passaddhi*), concentration (*samādhi*), and equanimity (*upekkhā*).

8) Right concentration: At the final stage, we should aim at one-pointedness (*ekaggatā*) of mind directed towards a wholesome object. Through desire and craving, the root of all evil kamma is accumulated, making rebirth necessary. To overcome this process, we must understand that everything is impermanent, unsatisfactory, and substanceless. True knowledge of this nature is acquired through the practice of meditation, which has two aspects: the active aspect of practice, and the passive aspect of realization of truths.

Of these eight components of the Middle Way, the first two constitute paññā, the next three sīla, and the last three samādhi. Clearly the components are not to be accounted as consecutive steps, but even though one takes the right speech, right action, and right livelihood components of the sīla group first, in accordance with the order of the three sections sīla, samādhi, and paññā, one remarks immediately that neither right speech nor right action, much less right livelihood, is possible without right understanding. The interrelation of the components is inevitable, and recognizing this one comes again to the strength of the Buddhist teaching, namely, that the moralities are never an end in themselves; they are inextricably bound up with all the other components which form the Path to final release from suffering. To what extent, then, is it necessary to study and develop them?

This is the Middle Way, the Buddhist's philosophy of life, by which one lives and progresses in accord with the principles of moderation and detachment. Once deliverance is thus obtained from suffering, and the freedom appreciated, it cannot be lost by those who have once won it. The first principle of all reality is that whatever has a beginning must have an end. The Buddha said: "Whatever is subject to arising must also be subject to ceasing" (*Yaṃ kiñci samudayadhammaṃ sabbaṃ taṃ nirodhadhammaṃ*).[128] Suffering is no exception to this law.

The Texts of the Dhamma

The Buddhist scriptures are divided traditionally into three main groups known as "baskets" (*piṭakas*), the Pali terms being *Vinaya, Sutta, Abhidhamma*, and the Sanskrit *Vinaya, Sūtra, Abhidharma*. Until the early part of the twentieth century it was assumed that the Pali texts represented the only complete canon, for though the discovery of the Hodgson manuscripts in Nepal in the 1830s and 1840s did bring to light some Sanskrit texts, it was not until the explorations of the very late nineteenth and early twentieth centuries that the one-time existence of a Sanskrit canon became evident. Even so, the Nanjio Catalogue listed 781 sūtras, including the *Āgamas*, in addition to 299 other sūtras originating between 960 and 1280 C.E., 85 *Vinaya* texts, and 131 *Abhidharma* texts; another 342 titles classified as "Miscellaneous" were also in it.[129] These figures do not include Pali works since Nanjio was dealing largely with Chinese translations. Though some of the Pali texts correspond sufficiently to some of the Sanskrit originals of the translations to make it obvious that the works in question derived from a common source,[130] there is also evidence that some of the Sanskrit texts evolved independently of the Pali, though the titles might seem to suggest a parallel.[131] A large quantity of Sanskrit texts has for long been known only in Chinese and Tibetan translations, but more recent archaeological research and expert examination have made available the contents of such texts, as for example the *Sarvāstivāda Vinaya*[132] and the *Upatissa* commentary relating to *vimutti*, or deliverance (*Vimokṣamārgaśāstra*).[133] However, since all too little information is available concerning the Sanskrit works of dates comparable to those of the Pali, we examine in detail the Pali canon, of which we have a lengthy record, only touching on the texts of Buddhist schools other than the Pali Theravāda or Sthaviravāda.

The Vinaya Piṭaka

The *Vinaya Piṭaka* is concerned with the rules of discipline governing the order of bhikkhus and bhikkhunīs. It is divided into three sections, *Suttavibhaṅga, Khandhakas*, and *Parivāra*.

Suttavibhaṅga deals with the rules for bhikkhus and bhikkhunīs. The *Bhikkhu-suttavibhaṅga* enumerates 227 rules concerning eight classes of offenses, the first four of which involve expulsion from the order. They are: incontinence in sexual intercourse, theft, taking life or inciting to suicide, and false boasting of supernormal attainments. For the other four classes suitable penances are required. The *Bhikkhunī-vibhaṅga*, providing similar guidance for bhikkunīs, is somewhat longer.

The *Khandhakas* are subdivided into the *Mahāvagga* and *Cullavagga*. The *Mahāvagga* covers the rules of admission to the order, the *Uposatha* meeting with the recital of the code of rules (*pātimokkha*),[134] residence during the retreat in the rainy season (*vassa*), the ceremony concluding the retreat (*pavārana*), the rules for articles of dress and furniture, medicine and food, the annual distribution of robes (*kathina*), the rules for sick bhikkhus, sleeping, and the material of robes, the mode of executing proceedings by the order, and the proceedings in cases of schism. The *Cullavagga* covers the rules for dealing with offenses that come before the order,[135] the re-instatement of bhikkhus, rules for dealing with questions that arise, miscellaneous rules for bathing and dress, etc., dwellings, furniture, and lodgings, etc., schisms, classes of bhikkhus and duties of teachers and novices (*sāmaneras*), exclusion from the recital of the *Pātimokkha*, the ordination and instruction of bhikkhunīs, the account of the First Council at Rājagaha, and the account of the Second Council at Vesāli.[136]

The *Parivāra* summarizes and classifies the rules of the Vinaya, arranged as a kind of catechism for instruction and examination purposes.

The Sutta Piṭaka

The Pali *Nikāyas* and Sanskrit *Āgamas* are among the Buddhist texts that resemble each other sufficiently to point to a common origin. Wherever they may have been separately compiled, the important incidents in the Buddha's teaching career occurring in Magadha are reported in the *Āgamas* no less than in the *Nikāyas*. Only a few discourses are individual to either the *Āgamas* or *Nikāyas*, the main differences between the compilations lying in the order in which the component discourses are arranged.[137] From an editorial point of view, it seems clear that the natural development of the line of thought as evident in the Sanskrit compilation must lead to a presentation of Buddhism commonly referred to as Mahāyāna rather than to one with Theravādin characteristics, but such an opinion arises solely from the impression given by the order of the sūtras and suttas and in no way concerns variation in the matter contained.

Of the remaining *Nikāyas*, *Majjhima*, the Medium-Length Discourses, *Aṅguttara*, the Gradual Discourses, and *Samyutta*, the Kindred Discourses, are comparable, respectively, to the *Madhyamāgama*, *Ekottarāgama* and *Samyuktāgama*. The *Khuddaka Nikāya* is not present, as a collection, in the *Āgamas*. Of the *Khuddaka* texts, the *Dhammapada* contains the "Flower" chapter in which is put the question: "Who shall conquer this world and the realm of Yama together with that of the gods (*devas*)? Who shall assemble the verses of the Law (*Dhammapada*) well-preached as a skillful person selects a good flower?" The reply to the question is that a disciple in training (*sekho*) will so conquer. Since this text bears the title of *Dhammapada*, or equivalent, and since these are the only verses contained which mention the term *dhammapada*, it is evident that the simile of selecting flowers is intended to provide evidence that the *Dhammapada* is a genuine anthology which contains the ethical teachings of the Buddha. The value of the Dhammapada texts[138] is therefore inestimable. Other components of the *Khuddaka Nikāya*, though in many cases very old and of great interest, can only be of lesser value.[139]

The Abhidhamma Piṭaka

The *Abhidhamma* literature contains the philosophy of Buddhism in analytical form. It is based on the Discourses of the Buddha, many of which were philosophical treatises (as for example the *Poṭṭapāda Sutta*, the *Mahā-Nidāna Sutta*, or the *Saṅgīti Sutta*[140] and many other suttas), but which were not necessarily worked out into complete philosophical systems. Some details of the systems have already been given in connection with the classification of recognizable states (*dharmas*), but a rough indication of the fundamental differences consists in the Sarvāstivāda assumption that all things exist, the Vijñānavāda that nothing exists apart from mind, and the Pali *Abhidhamma* that some things exist and others do not. The exact sense of *exists* is not the same in all three cases, but whatever the differences between the systems they all come under the cover of the three characteristics of Buddhism: *anicca* (impermanence), *dukkha* (suffering), and *anatta* (no self). The sets of philosophical literature were compiled entirely independently of each other, so that it is evident that they belong to a period subsequent to sectarian divisions, the date of the *Vijñānavāda* being already well established.

The Pali *Abhidhamma* contains seven books, generally known as the seven *Pakaraṇas*, namely: *Dhammasaṅgaṇī*, the enumeration of the dhammas; the *Vibhaṅga*, supplement to the *Dhammasaṅgaṇī*; *Dhātukathā*, the relationship of the dhammas; *Puggalapaññatti*, types of individuals; *Kathāvatthu*, refuting misinterpretations of the Pali *Abhidhamma* philosophy; *Yamaka*, a treatise of applied logic; and *Paṭṭāna*, which continues in six volumes from the foregoing *Pakaraṇas* to the Buddhist philosophy of relation. Of the seven *Pakaraṇas*,

Puggalapaññatti and *Kathāvatthu* do not contribute to the development of the main theme.

According to the *Nidānakathā* of the *Atthasālinī*, the commentary on the first of the seven *Pakaraṇas*, the Buddha ascended to the *Tāvatiṃsa* realm to teach the Abhidhamma, his mother being the chief witness, but there is no mention in the suttas of the visit, and the highly technical style of the *Abhidhamma* texts has no parallel in the simple, intimate style of the suttas. Moreover, Mahā-Kassapa, addressing the five hundred arahats composing the First Buddhist Council, said merely: "Now friends, let us recite the Dhamma and *Vinaya* before the anti-Dhamma (or non-Dhamma) comes to the forefront and the Dhamma is warded off; so with the *Vinaya*."[141] It is of further interest that the call was made to recite the *Dhamma,* as containing the material for teaching the ordinary person, before the *Vinaya* which pertained particularly to the Saṅgha.

THE THIRD REFUGE: THE SAṄGHA

The Third Refuge taken is in the Saṅgha. In the very early days after the Buddha's enlightenment, before the formation of the Saṅgha, only two Refuges could be taken; such a declaration was made by two tradesmen, Tapassu and Bhalluka. The circumstances were as follows. For seven weeks after his enlightenment, the Buddha remained in the neighborhood of the Bodhi tree experiencing the bliss of Nibbāna; at the close of the seventh week when he was at the foot of the Rājāyatana tree, two merchants passed on the road from Ukkala. A deva spoke to them, and, pointing out the tree where the Buddha sat, told them he had recently become enlightened and instructed them to offer him rice cake and honeycomb as a sign of reverence. The Buddha accepted the food, and when he had removed his hands from the bowl they said: "We take our Refuge, Sir, in the Blessed One and in his Dhamma; may he receive us as lay devotees (*upāsakas*) who from this day on, while our life lasts, have taken their refuge."[142] Tapassu and Bhalluka were the first lay disciples of the Buddha, and since they could take only the two Refuges, were known as the *dvevācika* ("one who teaches or recites the two-word formula") *upāsakas*.

The formation of the Saṅgha took place at Isipatana after the first declaration of the *Dhamma* to the five recluses[143] who had previously been companions of the Buddha, but the term *tevācika* ("three-word formula") is used in Pali literature for the first time in connection with the parents of Yasa

Thera of Banaras. During the Buddha's stay in that city, his expositions attracted many people by reason of their originality, and one night he was visited by Yasa, the son of a wealthy guild master. Yasa, tired of the luxury and constant entertainment in which he had been brought up, came to Isipatana, where the Buddha was staying, and was instructed by the Buddha, who discoursed to him on the evils and vanity attendant on worldly desires, pointing out the path of deliverance. Yasa's father, missing his son from his home, went in search of him; following his track, he came to the Buddha. The Buddha comforted him and discoursed to him also, whereupon he took the Three-fold Refuge (*Tisarana*), thereby becoming the first *tevācika upāsaka*, using the three-word formula. In the meantime Yasa, who had heard the instruction given to his father, attained arahatship. As he was free from all attachments and could not therefore return to the worldly life, he was ordained and became the seventh member of the saṅgha. The first women to become lay disciples (*upāsikās*) were Yasa's mother and wife, both of whom used the *tevācika* formula.[144]

The word *saṅgha* derives from *saṃ* plus *hṛ*, literally: "comprising." In practice it signifies multitude or assemblage, but in Buddhist terminology the saṅgha is one assembly and one only, namely, the order of bhikkhus and bhikkhunīs; this without distinction of race, nationality, caste, or age. Within the Saṅgha the only distinction is that of the *ariyasaṅgha* or *ariyapuggala*, the Noble Ones, and the *sammutisaṅgha*. The former are sometimes referred to as "saints," but correctly described they are those who have "entered the stream" (*sotāpatti*), or attained the supramundane plane.[145] The *ariyasaṅgha* is represented conventionally by the *sammutisaṅgha*, but it is in the *ariyasaṅgha* that the Buddhist takes his refuge since it consists of those who have realized the truth and are able to teach it from their own experience.

Here, however, we have something of an anomaly. Of the persons who have "entered the stream," and who therefore belong to the four pairs of persons and eight classes of individuals (see note 86), it is possible that laymen will be included. Such a layman would therefore be a member of the *ariyasaṅgha* but not of the *sammutisaṅgha*; the point is extremely important in estimating the position of the laity in early Buddhism. At the same time, it is not justifiable to assert without qualification, as Dr. Radhakrishnan has done, that "The Saṅgha contains both lay-members and monks. While the laymember assents to the doctrine, the monk is the missionary."[146]

The Saṅgha, in the sense of the *sammutisaṅgha*, consists exclusively of bhikkhus and bhikkhunīs; it does not include *upāsakas* and *upāsikās*. The term *parisā*, meaning company, assembly, association, is used correctly to cover all these four types of disciples, but the terms *parisā* and *saṅgha* are not interchangeable. The *Kaṅkhāvitaraṇī* categorically explains that an assembly of at least four bhikkhus is called a saṅgha.[147] In practice, both lay members and monks—the latter more correctly called bhikkhus—assent to the doctrine, and though the preaching of the Dhamma is an auxiliary activity for the bhikkhu he is not a missionary in the modern sense of the term since he does not engage in converting from one religion to another.

Various definitions have been offered for the word *bhikkhu*. The Sanskrit *bhikṣu* derives from *bhiks*, beggar, and long before the Buddha's day a *bhikṣu* represented one of many types of ascetics, as did the *parivrājakas*, *ājīvakas*, and others (see page no.13); now the terms *bhikkhu* and *bhikṣu* are exclusively Buddhist and the bhikkhus and bhikṣus are not "beggars." Though they may make spontaneous requests to their parents or close relatives, and may also state a need to professed supporters who have previously requested them to ask for anything they want, the rules of a bhikkhu do not permit him to ask anything from any other person, though he may accept gifts of the four "requisites" of robes, alms, shelter, and medicine if they are offered to him.

Nor is it correct to refer to the bhikkhu as a monk since he is not bound by any vows; he may, in fact, leave the order at any time he pleases. Most important in view of frequent mistranslations, he is not a priest. Since Buddhism recognizes no Deity, there is no being on whose behalf the bhikkhu could act as intermediary with man, either for the performance of ritual and ceremonies, for the asking of favors, or for any other reason. Moreover, no intervention such as asking pardon for misdeeds is possible since, automatically, one suffers or enjoys the results of one's actions. Possibly the nearest translation of the word *bhikkhu* is *mendicant,* though this term may be employed only in the sense of living on alms.

The Buddha was once asked by Mahāli the Liccavi if it was for the cultivation of samādhi that the bhikkhus led the religious life under him. He replied that it was not, but that there were "other things, higher and more excellent" for which they did so.[148] The form in which he proceeded to describe them, though considerably simpler than that adopted in many other places,[149] brings forward clearly the continuity between the moralities side of his teaching and the conditions necessary to attain to the *lokuttara* (supramundane) state from the destruction of fetters and is therefore quoted here.

There are 10 fetters (*dasa saṃyojanas*) by which beings are bound to the continuity of existence (*saṃsāra*): (1) belief in personality (*sakkāyadiṭṭi*); (2) doubt, uncertainty of judgment (*vicikicchā*); (3) belief in the efficacy of ceremonial observances (*sīlabbataparāmāsa*); (4) sensual lust (*kāmarāga*); (5) ill will (*paṭigha*); (6) greed for fine material existence (*rūparāga*); (7) greed for immaterial existence (*arūparāga*); (8) conceit (*māna*); (9) restlessness and worry (*uddhacca-kukkucca*); and (10) ignorance (*avijjā*).

First from the destruction of the [first] three fetters, the bhikkhu becomes a *sotāpanna,* one who is sure to have done with all suffering and is sure of liberation at the final end.

Further, the bhikkhu, from the destruction of the three fetters and from the reduction of the foolishness of sensuous craving and ill-will, becomes a *sakadāgāmī,* one who, having come once more to this world, makes an end of suffering.

Further, the bhikkhu, from the destruction of the five fetters belonging to the world of desire (i.e. the *aforementioned five*), becomes one who arises independently of the ordinary processes of birth (*opapātika*), in that condition obtaining final release, one who does not return to a succession of rebirths here.

Further, Mahāli, from the complete destruction of the influxes (*āsavas*),[150] the bhikkhu, having come to understand thoroughly and to experience for himself, freeing of mind and freeing of insight, here amongst things as seen in the present world, having so attained therein continues. This is the thing, higher and more excellent, for the experiencing of which the bhikkhus lead the religious life under me.[151]

To Mahāli's next question as to whether there is a "way of progress by which these things may be experienced," the Buddha replies: "There is a Way. It is the Noble Eightfold Path *(ariyo atthaṅgiko maggo)*."[152] He enumerates the components (see pp. 44-48).

Concerning the beings who have arrived at the supramundane plane, that is to say, *sotāpannas* and beings of still higher development, those who have reached the goal may be *Sammāsambuddhas, Pacceka* Buddhas, or

Arahats. A *Sammāsambuddha* is a fully enlightened one who comprehends the truth by his own intuition, without the help of any others, and who can preach and make others understand the truth. A *Pacceka* Buddha also comprehends the truth by his own intuition only, but he is unable to preach to others. An arahat realizes the truth after first hearing it from another; he is able to preach and so make others understand the Dhamma. The Buddhas, *Sammāsambuddha* and *Pacceka*, are not members of the sangha; the arahats and the persons on the three lower stages of the Path comprise the *ariyasangha*.

Bhikkhus of the *sammutisangha* lead the religious life intending to attain the *ariyasangha*, first "entering the stream," or becoming *sotāpannas*, then rising to the higher stages. They teach others, both by example and precept, without remuneration. Purity, voluntary poverty, selflessness and service are among their characteristics. There are no hard and fast rules regarding admission of candidates to the order. Race, color, caste, and social class are immaterial in this respect, the only rank recognized within the order being length of membership. Entry is barred to deformed persons, those suffering from such diseases as leprosy or tuberculosis, and to debtors, professional soldiers, or such persons having mundane allegiances. There is no age limit; a boy who is "old enough to scare away a crow" may join the order. Entrants below the age of twenty are known as *sāmaneras* and later may become bhikkhus. In the meantime they observe the ten precepts (see chapter 4) and prepare for the higher ordination known as *upasampadā*. If they possess the necessary qualifications, when they complete their twentieth year they are admitted to the order of bhikkhus.

Any senior qualified bhikkhu who has counted more than five years in the order is empowered to ordain a candidate as *sāmanera*; no self-ordination is permissible. To be initiated into the higher order there should be at least five Theras (elders) at the ceremony.

A newly ordained bhikkhu is obliged to remain under a competent teacher for a period of not less than five years, studying and practicing the Dhamma, until the teacher considers it advisable for him to live by himself. According to his temperament a bhikkhu may choose either the studious course (*ganthadhura*) or the meditative course (*vipassanādhura*). Those who adopt the former study and practice of the Dhamma may travel from place to place preaching the doctrine to others throughout the year except in the rainy season. Those who prefer the latter retire to a place of solitude and engage in meditation.

Having renounced everything worldly, the bhikkhu claims no property, does not regret his past, and does not worry about the future; he lives essentially in the present, free from the responsibilities and the trammels of the world. He clings to no abode and in all vicissitudes maintains a balanced mind. The energy at his command is directed to the activities that tend to universal happiness.

Clearly the bhikkhu's self-appointed mission is no easy one, for he has no centralized authority in the shape of a governing body on which to base any claim or to which he can look for any support. Though the tradition of the saṅgha, maintained over a period of some 2,500 years, must count for much in many countries, in the main it is by the example of his own life that he must achieve the good for others that he sets out to do.

4

SANCTIONS OF MORAL CONDUCT: THE PRECEPTS

THE FIVE PRECEPTS (*PAÑCA SĪLA*)

HAVING TAKEN THE Three Refuges, the Buddhist layman takes it upon himself to observe the precepts. In the first instance these number five, but in particular cases and on particular occasions they are extended to eight or even ten. The five precepts are:

1) *Pāṇātipātā veramaṇī sikkhāpadaṃ samādiyāmi* (I undertake the precept to abstain from the taking of life).
2) *Adinnādānā veramaṇī sikkhāpadaṃ samādiyāmi* (I undertake the precept not to take that which is not given).
3) *Kāmesu micchācārā veramaṇī sikkhāpadaṃ samādiyāmi* (I undertake the precept to abstain from misconduct in sensual actions).
4) *Musāvādā veramaṇī sikkhāpadaṃ samādiyāmi* (I undertake the precept to abstain from false speech).
5) *Surā-meraya-majja-pamādaṭṭhānā veramaṇī sikkhāpadaṃ samādiyāmi* (I undertake the precept to abstain from liquor that causes intoxication and indolence).

The First Precept

By the first precept the Buddhist undertakes to abstain from destroying, causing to be destroyed, or sanctioning the destruction of a living being. *Living being* implies anything that has life, from insects up to and including man. In taking this precept a Buddhist recognizes his relationship with all living things, a relationship so close that the harming of any living creature is inevitably the harming of himself. The Buddha taught the advisability of comparing one's own life with that of other beings: "Everyone fears violence, everyone likes life; comparing oneself with others one would never slay or cause to slay."[153] In the conventional sense, however, *pāṇa*, or in the Sanskrit, *prāṇa*, is a "sentient being"; but in the highest and ultimate sense it is only psychic life or vital force. Preventing the existence of a sentient being is taking away life or killing.

The precept applies to all creatures irrespective of size. It does not exclude the killing of animals for the Vedic sacrifices (*yajña*) or, as do the commandments of some religions, that of lower animals. A Buddhist does not sacrifice living beings for worship or food, but sacrifices instead his own selfish motives; in India the Buddha stopped cow killing and all blood sacrifices. On one occasion he was asked by a well-known brahman, Kūṭadanta, what was the procedure for an elaborate sacrifice, suitable for the expression of the gratitude he felt for gifts and possessions variously acquired.[154] The Buddha, remarking on the cruelty and suffering involved in the usual type of sacrifice, suggested better means to express gratitude: open largesse, perpetual alms to guarantee the upkeep of a number of bhikkhus and bhikkhunīs, and the building of dwelling places for them. But, he continued, a sacrifice bearing greater fruit and advantage is to take upon oneself, with devoted mind, the Precepts: abstinence from taking life, from taking that which is not given, etc., enumerating the five precepts mentioned above.[155]

The extent of moral guilt in killing depends on the physical and mental development of the being that is killed and the circumstances under which the deed is committed. The karmic results of killing a man and killing a child vary in proportion to the physical and mental development of the two. Patricide, matricide, the slaughter of innocent people and of people of considerable mental development are therefore particularly productive of evil results to the killer. The distinction is drawn between being culpable to a lesser degree (*appasāvajja*), and to a greater degree (*mahāsāvajja*). The injunction runs: "Do not kill a living being. You should not kill or condone killing by others. Having abandoned the use of violence you should not use force either against the strong or the feeble."[156]

There are five conditions that constitute the immoral act of killing: (1) the fact and presence of a living being, human or animal; (2) the knowledge that the being is a living being; (3) the intent or resolution to kill; (4) the act of killing by appropriate means; and (5) the resulting death.[157] In the absence of any one of these conditions, the act would not constitute killing even though death should follow; the event would be considered an accident and would not entail any evil effect for the performer of the act.

There are six means of killing: (1) killing with one's own hands (*sāhatthika*); (2) causing another to kill by giving an order (*āṇattika*); (3) killing by shooting, pelting with stones, sticks, etc. (*nissaggiya*); (4) killing by digging trenches, etc., and entrapping a being (*thavara*); (5) killing by the powers of *iddhi*, or occult means (*iddhimaya*); and (6) killing by mantras, or occult sciences (*vijjāmaya*).[158] Whatever device may be used, the individual who kills or destroys the psychic life of a sentient being commits the evil deed of *pāṇātipātā-kamma-patha*. This kamma may be caused through the door of speech since the act of killing could be performed on receiving an order from another person.

Among some of the kammic results that a man brings upon himself by committing injury to a life are suffering in an unpleasant state for a long period, and rebirth in some lower form of being. If born again as a man he may be infirm, ugly, unpopular, cowardly, divested of companions, subject to disease, dejected and mournful, separated from the company of loved ones, and unable to attain ripe age. So much is recorded in the suttas. The *Telakaṭāhagāthā* states: "He who destroys the life of any being may, in his next birth, meet death unexpectedly while in the prime of life, even though he is possessed of all the amenities of life, wealth and beauty, like an Adonis."[159]

Noninjury (*ahiṃsā*) has also its positive counterpart. It demands not only abstention from injury but also the practice of loving kindness, *mettā*, to all.

One who wishes to create this force within himself, that is, who wishes to meditate on mettā, should first sever the impediments inimical to his peaceful surroundings. Then he should choose a suitable time and a secluded place where he can, without interruption, devote himself to his meditation practice. He should then perceive the danger of anger arising and, at the same time, should realize the advantage of possessing patience, because anger has to be abandoned and patience has to be fostered in the development of this meditation. The dangers of anger should be understood in every possible way. The most effective method would be to understand it in accordance with the teaching of the Buddha.

After that, the aspirant should embark upon the development of mettā for the purpose of ridding the mind of hate, which is a danger, and for the acquisition of patience, which is an advantage. However, mettā should at first be directed only toward certain types of persons and not to others. It is absolutely unwise, as well as dangerous, at the commencement of the practice of mettā, to direct one's thoughts toward the following six kinds of persons: an antipathetic, a very dearly loved, a neutral, a hostile, or a deceased person, or a member of the opposite sex.

Why should mettā not, in the preliminary stages, be developed towards

these six kinds of persons? To direct thoughts of mettā towards an antipathetic person, a very dearly loved one, or a neutral one is mentally fatiguing,
and in the case of a very dear person there may be emotional involvement.
Anger springs up if a hostile person is recollected. If mettā is directed toward
a deceased person, neither absorption (*appanā*) nor access (*upacāra*) concentration is reached. Should mettā be developed towards the opposite sex, lust
may arise.

There is a story of a young monk who had started the practice of developing mettā but, on making no headway, went to a *mahāthera* and said:
"Venerable Sir, I am quite familiar with the attainment of absorption (*jhāna*)
through mettā, yet now I cannot attain it. What is the matter?"

The *mahāthera* replied: "Seek the sign, friend, the object of your meditation."

When the young monk did so, he discovered that his teacher, to whom
he had been directing his thoughts of mettā, had died. He then proceeded
to develop it towards another and attained full absorption (*appanā*). This,
therefore, is the reason why mettā should not be developed toward one who
is deceased.

For a successful meditation, one should be in a peaceful situation as free
from distraction as possible. To begin meditation, the practitioner should be
in a posture convenient to him. The proper postures include lying, walking,
and sitting. If it is convenient, the ideal position is sitting cross-legged, with
spine erect, head straight, eyes half-closed and hands in the lap.

The first step: For the beginner in this practice of meditation on mettā, it
should be developed first of all toward *oneself,* mentally repeating the following or any other formula similar in sense, either in Pali or in one's own tongue:

Ahaṃ avero homi (May I be free from enmity);
abbyāpajjho homi (may I be free from ill will);
anīgho homi (may I be free from distress);
sukhī attānaṃ pariharāmi (may I keep myself happy).

But does this not conflict with what is said in the texts? For there is no
mention of any development of mettā toward oneself to be found in the
Vibhaṅga, which says: "How does a monk dwell pervading one quarter with
his heart filled with loving-kindness?"[160] In the *Paṭisambhidā* it is said: "In
what five ways is mind-deliverance of loving-kindness practiced with

unspecified pervasion? 'May all beings be free from enmity, affliction, and anxiety and live happily. May all breathing things; all who are born; all individuals of whatever kind be free from enmity, affliction, and anxiety, may they live happily.'"[161]

In the *Metta Sutta* we find the following:

Whatever living beings there be—
Feeble or strong, tall, stout or medium,
Short, small or large, without exception—
Seen or unseen,
Those dwelling far or near,
Those who are born or who are to be born,
May all beings be happy[162]

The reason why this does not conflict with the texts is because the latter refer to absorption (*appanā*)[163] alone and not to the initial development of mettā in oneself which is only by way of example; for even if one developed it for a hundred or a thousand years in this way, mentally repeating, "May I be free from enmity" and so on, absorption would never arise. Taking oneself as the example, one then extends the wish to other beings' welfare and happiness arises in one.

So first, one should, by way of example, pervade oneself with mettā.

The second step: In order to proceed easily, one should recollect gifts received, kind words, etc. (*dānapiyavacanādīni*), that inspire loving kindness and endearment, such as virtue, learning, and so on (*sīlasutādīni*), which give rise to respect and reverence toward a religious teacher, preceptor or his equivalent, developing mettā toward him by thinking, "May this good person be free from ill will." With thoughts directed to such a person one may attain absorption.

The third step: If, however, one who meditates wishes to proceed further, in order to break down subtler, spiritual barriers (*sīmāsambheda*), one should follow up the development of mettā toward a dearly loved friend.

The fourth step: One should then develop it toward a neutral person just as one would to a very dearly loved friend.

The fifth step: Finally, one should develop it toward a hostile person, considering him as neutral. As one does this, one's mind becomes malleable in each case before passing on to the next. On the other hand, if one is the type of individual who perceives none as his enemy, even though one may suffer harm at their hands, this question will not arise.

Only one who believes he actually has any enemy should develop mettā toward a hostile person as a neutral.

Overcoming Resentment

The first method: Should resentment arise in one when the mind is directed toward a hostile person because of the memory of past wrong done by him, one should endeavor to overcome this feeling by entering repeatedly into the state of absorption brought about by the development of mettā and directed toward any of the aforementioned persons. Thus having emerged each time, one should direct one's feelings of goodwill toward the hostile person in question.

The second method: If, in spite of one's efforts, the feeling of resentment continues to exist, one should strive and strive repeatedly to leave resentment far behind. One should admonish oneself, reviewing the Dhamma in this way: "Why should I get angry? Has not the Buddha said this: 'Monks, even if bandits brutally severed [one] limb from limb with a two-handled saw, he who entertained hate in his heart on that account would not be one who carried out my teaching.'?"[164]

Further, one should admonish oneself by reviewing the teaching of the Buddha as contained in the following verses of the *Dhammapada*:

> In those who harbor such thoughts: "He abused me, he struck me, he overcame me, he robbed me"—hatred never ceases. (v. 3)

> In those who do not harbor such thoughts hatred will cease. (v. 4)

> Hatred never ceases by hatred in this world; through non-enmity it comes to an end. This is an ancient law. (v. 5)

> Some do not think that all of us here one day will die; if they did, their dissension would cease at once. (v. 6)

> One should give up anger, renounce pride. (v. 221)

> Let a man overcome anger by loving-kindness; let him overcome evil

by good; let him overcome the miser by liberality; let him overcome the liar by truth. (v. 223)

One should speak the truth, not give way to anger. (v. 224)

There is none in the world who is not blamed. (v. 227)

One should guard against misdeeds caused by speech. Let him practice
restraint of speech. Let him practice virtue with his mind. (v. 232)

The wise who control their body, speech and mind are indeed well-
controlled. (v. 234)

"Monks, there are these five ways of removing annoyance, by which
annoyance can be entirely removed by a monk when it arises in him. What
five? (i) Loving-kindness can be maintained towards a person with whom
you are annoyed: this is how annoyance with him can be removed. (ii)
Compassion can be maintained . . . (iii) Onlooking equanimity can . . . (iv)
The forgetting and ignoring of a person with whom you are annoyed can be
practiced: this is how . . . (v) Ownership of deeds in a person with whom
you are annoyed can be concentrated upon thus: 'This good person is owner
of his deeds, heir of his deeds, his deeds are the womb from which he is born,
his deeds are his kin for whom he is responsible, his deeds are his refuge, he
is heir to his deeds, be they good or bad': this too is how annoyance with
him can be removed."[165]

The third method: If, after striving according to the above method, one's
resentment subsides, it is good; if not, one should remove irritation by recollecting some controlled, pure, and pleasing qualities in that person which,
when recalled, help one's anger to subside.

Admonition to Oneself

The fourth method: If, however, in spite of one's efforts, irritation continues to arise, one should think thus:

Suppose an enemy has hurt you
In what is now his domain,
Why try yourself as well to hurt

Your mind? That is not his domain.

This anger that you entertain
Is gnawing at the very roots
Of all the virtues that you guard—
Where is there such a fool as you!

Another does ignoble deeds,
So you are angry—how is this?
Do you then want to copy, too,
The sort of acts that he commits?

Suppose another, to annoy,
Provokes you with some odious act,
Why suffer anger to spring up,
And do as he would have you do?

If you get angry, then may be
You make him suffer, may be not;
Though with the hurt that anger brings
You certainly are punished now.

If anger-blinded enemies
Set out to tread the path of woe,
Do you, by getting angry too,
Intend to follow heel to toe?

If hurt is done you by a foe
Because of anger on your part,
Then put your anger down, for why
Should you be harassed needlessly?

Since states last but a moment's time,
Those aggregates, by which was done
The odious act, have ceased, so now
What is it you are angry with?

Whom shall he hurt, who seeks to hurt
Another, in the other's absence?
Your presence is the cause of hurt;
Why are you angry, then, with him?[166]

Reviewing Ownership of Deeds

The fifth method: If, however, resentment fails to subside when one admonishes oneself thus, one should then call to mind the fact that oneself and others are owners of their deeds (*kamma*).

Thereupon one should reflect as follows: "What is the point of becoming angry with another? Will not this *kamma* that has anger as its source lead to my own harm? Since I am the owner of my deeds, heir of my deeds, having deeds as my origin, deeds as my kin, deeds as my refuge; I will become the heir of whatever deeds I commit."[167] It leads not to enlightenment or even to a favorable rebirth in the world, but is rather the kind of action that may lead to my downfall and to manifold suffering in states of woe.

"By allowing anger to arise I am like one who wants to hit another and picks up a burning ember or excrement and by so doing either burn or soil myself." Having reviewed one's own deeds in this way, one should proceed to review others' also. "What is the point of his becoming angry with me? Will it not lead to his own harm? For he is the owner of his deeds, heir of his deeds; he will become the heir of whatever deeds he commits. They are not the kind that can bring him to enlightenment or even to a high social position; rather they will lead to his downfall or to manifold sufferings in a miserable state."

By becoming angry one is like a man throwing dust against the wind— he only soils himself.

The sixth method: If after reviewing ownership of deeds, anger still persists, then one should recollect the special qualities of the Master's former conduct; for when the Master was but a bodhisattva, prior to attaining full enlightenment and while engaged in fulfilling the perfections, he allowed no hate to corrupt his mind even when his enemies on various occasions attempted to kill him. Many are the examples of self-control to be found in the "Birth Stories." It is, therefore, unworthy of one to allow thoughts of resentment to arise if one is attempting to emulate the Blessed One who reached omniscience and whose special quality of patience has no equal in this world.

Reviewing the Suttas

The seventh method: But if, as one reviews the special former qualities of the Master, resentment still remains, as one has long been a slave of the defilements, then one should read the suttas that deal with the endless round of birth and death.

In the *Saṃyutta Nikāya* we read: "Bhikkhus, it is not easy to find a being who has not formerly been your mother, or your father, your brother, your sister or your son or daughter."[168]

Reviewing the Advantages of Mettā

The eighth method: Should one still be unable to quench the feeling of anger in this way, one should then review the advantages of loving kindness as follows: "Has it not been said by the Blessed One: Bhikkhus, when the mind-deliverance of lovingkindness is cultivated, developed, much practiced, made the vehicle, made the foundation, established, consolidated, and properly undertaken, eleven blessings can be expected. What are the eleven?"

1. One sleeps in comfort.
2. One awakens in comfort.
3. One doesn't have bad dreams.
4. One is dear to human beings.
5. One is dear to non-human beings.
6. Devas guard one.
7. Fire, poison, and weapons do not affect one.
8. One's mind is easily concentrated.
9. One's mien is serene.
10. One dies unconfused.
11. If one penetrates no higher, one will be reborn in the world of Brahma.

If one fails to arrest the thought of anger, therefore, one will be deprived of these advantages.

The Resolution into Elements

The ninth method: But if one is *still* unable to prevent the arising of anger, one should try "resolution into elements." How is this accomplished?

One should ask oneself when angry with someone: "What is it I am angry with? Is it the hairs of the head, the earth element therein, etc., or the water element, or the fire element, or the air element that I am angry with? Or among the five aggregates or the twelve bases or the eighteen elements with respect to which this one is called by such-and-such a name—which material aggregate, then, am I angry with? Or the feeling aggregate, the formation aggregate, the consciousness aggregate, the perception aggregate that I am angry with? Is it the eye base that I am angry with or the visible-object base, the ear base or the audible-object base, the nose base or the olfactive-object base, the tongue base, or the gustative-object that I am angry with?

"Or is it the eye-element I am angry with or the visible-object element, or the eye-consciousness element, the ear, audible or ear-consciousness elements, the nose, olfactive or nose-consciousness elements, the tongue, gustative or tongue-consciousness elements, the body, tactile or body-consciousness elements that I am angry with?

"Or the mind, mental-object or mind-consciousness elements that I am angry with?

"For when one tries the resolution into elements, one's anger finds no foothold, like a mustard-seed on the point of an awl or a painting on the air."

Giving a Gift

The tenth method: If, however, one cannot effect the resolution into elements, one should try giving a gift. This can either be given by oneself to the other person or accepted by one from the other. For example, taking the case of a bhikkhu, if his requisites are incomplete, then the gift may be made by oneself and any annoyance with that person will entirely subside.

Breaking Down the Barriers

The sign: When one's resentment toward the hostile person has been allayed, then one can turn one's mind with loving kindness toward that person too, just as one can toward the one who is dear, the very dear friend, and the neutral person. One should then endeavor to break down the barriers that separate one from them by practicing loving kindness continuously, accomplishing mental impartiality towards the four persons, that is to say: oneself, the dear person, the neutral person, and the hostile person.

The special characteristics of this practice are as follows: suppose this person is sitting in a place with a dear, a neutral, and a hostile person, oneself being the fourth. Then suppose a party of bandits come to one who is meditating and say: "Venerable Sir, let us have any one of you!" On being asked why, they answer: "So that we may kill him and use the blood of his throat as an offering." If on hearing this the meditator thinks: "Let them take this one or that one," he has not broken down the barriers. Should he think: "Let them take me but not any of these three," again he has not broken down the barriers. Why? Because he seeks the welfare of the others only. However, when he does not see a single one among the four of them who should be given to the bandits while he directs his mind impartially towards himself and the other three, only then can it be said that he has broken down the barriers.

Thus this person simultaneously obtains the sign and access with the breaking down of the barriers. When this has been effected, he reaches absorption without difficulty by cultivating, developing, and repeatedly practicing the same sign.

At this point, one has attained the first jhāna which, among other things, is accompanied by loving kindness. When that has been obtained, one should continue to cultivate, develop, and repeatedly practice the same sign and successively reach the second and third jhānas. It is by means of these jhānas that one "dwells intent upon one direction with one's heart endued with loving-kindness, likewise the second direction, the third and fourth directions; also above, below and around; everywhere and equally one dwells, pervading the entire world with one's heart imbued with loving-kindness, abundant, exalted, measureless, free from enmity and free from affliction."[169]

The Second Precept

The second precept of good conduct, the *adinnādānā veramaṇī*, advises a Buddhist to abstain from taking things that are not given. According to the *Brahmajāla Sutta*, the Samaṇa Gotama "waits for the gift" (*dinnādayī*).[170] Bhikkhus and bhikkhunīs who live on charity should accept their requisites (*paccaya*) only when they are offered. Lay devotees should lead an honest life according to the right livelihood (*sammā-ājīva*). Any sort of thieving, even at the risk of one's life, was denounced by the Buddha.

Two modes of thieving are recognized, the direct and the indirect. The first consists in appropriating anything belonging to another person without first securing his consent.

The second comprises frauds and deceptions whereby a man may cheat another out of something that rightly belongs to him. Of these Buddhaghosa says: "One or other of these means may be carried out according to circumstances, in stealing by false means and weights, by force, by concealment, by design or by forgery. This is an outlined account of theft."[171] In short, any scheme, intrigue, or device, whether adopted in the sale of houses, horses, cattle, or any other commodity, constitutes a violation of the precepts of *adinnādānā veramaṇī*, of the injunction to abstain from taking anything without the consent of the owner, for in such cases the buyer is not aware that the purchase is worth less than he is paying for it. The second precept is therefore an injunction against any form of dishonest dealing.[172] "One should avoid that which is not given, whatever or wherever it is. The disciple, perceiving this, does not steal or condone stealing. Everything that is not given he should avoid."[173]

The second precept may be considered also as the reverse of *dāna*, or liberal giving, the first of the Ten Perfections (*dasapāramitā*). These are enumerated in *Buddhavaṃsa* and *Cariyāpiṭaka*. They are covered largely in the *Bhikkhuvagga* of the *Dhammapada*; the *Udānavarga* treats them in a *Sīlavarga* where the following two notable verses occur: "Firmly established in the moralities, the bhikṣu cultivates his mind and his wisdom; energetic and prudent he will attain to permanent destruction of suffering . . . .Those who are pure and moral, and who live by practicing vigilance, made free by right penetration, Māra does not know their road."[174] The first of these verses does not occur in the *Dhammapada* but resembles *Saṃyutta Nikāya* I.13; the second compares with *Dhammapada* 57. On the other hand the *Dhammapada* mentions the *sīlas* relating to all Five Precepts explicitly in verses 246 and 247: "He who in this world destroys life and speaks falsehood, takes what is not given or goes to someone else's wife, and he who takes intoxicating drinks, this person destroys his origin in this world." However, to complete the observance of *dāna* a strict observance of the precepts *adinnādānā veramaṇī* is necessary, for the practice of *dāna* and *adinnādānā* cultivates the state of mind that gives rise to freedom from cleaving to mortal and changeable things, and it is on the purification from lust and longing that the release from the cycles of *saṃsāra* depends.

Adinna, "that which is not given," and *ādāna*, "taking," the immoral volition to take others' belongings, is known as the immoral act of stealing (*adinnādāna-akusalakamma*). Five factors constitute the immoral act of stealing, namely: others' property; awareness of the fact that it is others' property that is being taken; the immoral volition of stealing; the employ-ment of a device to steal; and the act of removing the property.[175] Whatever device is employed, so long as others' belongings are taken without the con-sent of the owner, it is the path of retributive *kamma* (*adinnādāna-kamma-patha*) that is committed. This *kamma* may also be caused through the door of speech, since the act of stealing may be performed on receipt of instruc-tions from another person.

Amongst the kammic results that accrue to the thief are the following: great suffering in an unhappy state for a long period, or, if by virtue of other merits the thief should be reborn as a man he would lack possessions in this new state. He would be unable to acquire wealth, or if he did so he would be unable to keep it, and would be subject to danger from kings, murderers, floods, and fire. He would be unable to enjoy sensual pleasures and would be discontented and despised by the people. According to the *Telakaṭāhagāthā;* "If a man in order to benefit himself is guilty of stealing the property of others, in his next birth he becomes a contemptible beggar clad in dirty rags; with a broken begging-vessel in hand, he ever begs his daily bread at the doors of his enemies while suffering a hundred insults."[176]

The Third Precept

The third precept of good conduct, *kāmesu micchācārāmaṇī*, is tradi-tionally interpreted as though *kāmesu* were in the singular form and is there-fore taken to advise Buddhists to abstain merely from unlawful sexual inter-course. Since this limitation is generally accepted, we defer consideration of the wider significance and take, for the present, that which may be inferred if *kāma* had been expressed in the singular.

By *kāma* is meant "lustful attachment to male or female," and by *micchācāra* "wrong conduct." The immoral act of unchastity (*kāma-micchācāra-akusala-kamma*) is the volition or sense-desire of a male for a female or a female for a male. The Buddha said: "A wise man should avoid unchastity as if it were a pit of burning cinders. One who is not able to live in a state of celibacy should, at least, not break the purity of another man's wife."[177]

That the sexual is the strongest instinct of living beings is widely recog-nized. Man is more sensitive to sexual stimulation than are other living crea-tures, since in the animal world the incentive is periodic and seasonal while in man it is continual. That mental development should result in increase of control of sexual desire would appear to be the logical course of events, but it would also seem logical to suppose that the desire should lessen as the general view of life and its possibilities extends and appreciates in value. In the case of the person of chastity (*brahmacariya*) this is certainly true, whatever his religious views may be or whatever name he calls the religious life; but in the stages intermediary between the least and the most developed of human types the sexual is still the strongest instinct, desire for food and aspiration to religious thought ranking second and third. One may take the view that mental development is always challenged by the physical world, that what is popularly called nature makes for quantity and not quality, irrespective of the waste and possible suffering entailed. But if one is not inclined to assume that the physical world exists entirely independently of the mind of man, then one looks to the mind of man to find the ultimate cause of the sex or any other instinct. Here one may consider two factors: the fear of recognizing the impermanence (*anicca*) of things, and the assertion of power. Regarding the first, the urge to make the world seem permanent is reflected in the universal desire to see one's children and grandchildren growing up around one, whether or not these are expected to ingratiate some superbeing on behalf of one's welfare in a future state. Briefly stated, the family instinct tends to dispel loneliness for the immediate present and to foster companionship, as well as to furnish a vague suggestion that one will never be entirely alone. Somehow, somewhere, it is felt, there might exist something familiar to which one can in a sense return. Family life represents the aspiration of the bulk of mankind and is by no means to be condemned out of hand. On the contrary, one may agree that it constitutes a means whereby some of man's best qualities may be developed, for it obliges him to take an interest in a community, whether limited to that of family or extended to that of city or state. Since, however, the present precept refers to misconduct and misuse of a sexual relationship rather than to its conduct in general, we defer consideration of the latter until the following chapter when we may examine the position of the laity as a whole. We may, nevertheless, include certain remarks since they are pertinent to the whole matter of sex.

Though the highest conduct of life has so often been taken to be religious celibacy, still the bulk of the world's population has always been unwilling or unable to adopt it. In the general interest, therefore, marriage must be recognized as a respectable and honorable state if only for the avoidance of promiscuity. In the very early days of Christianity celibacy was the rule for all Christians, but enforcement of this was not possible for long in view of the thriving contemporary Mithraism; this religion held a creed almost identical with that of the Christians except that it did not enforce celibacy. The Christian objection to marriage for the laity was withdrawn and marriage was celebrated as a holy rite. Centuries before, Indian thought, the Buddha's included, had held that religious celibacy represented the highest form of conduct of one's life, but though the Buddha gave much advice to the laity there was at no time any attempt to bring the state or ceremony of marriage under religious jurisdiction. Rather the line was taken that the householder should achieve the best possible results in his present sphere so that he would become sufficiently advanced in his understanding to choose, of his own volition, the religious life in a future existence.

The second factor is probably not entirely disconnected from the idea of gods as possessing superhuman powers and, more particularly, with the idea of a creating god or God. If in his struggles to attain *brahmacariya* man has to contend with the impulse of the large bulk of his fellow creatures to reject celibacy, he also faces their determination to idealize and emulate a "creator." The rejection of celibacy implies a materialization of the creating instinct, but the desire to create makes also for a lust for power, which brings envy to competition and peoples and nations to war. The necessity to find room for surplus populations then figures as a secondary rather than as a primary cause of bitterness and strife.

This places consideration of the sexual conduct of man on the level of thought rather than on the level of sensation, and it is noticeable that in his efforts to raise himself above the sensation level he has engaged in forms of physical training whereby he acquires control over his physique and therefore a certain mental control also. In our own times we have seen rapid advances in the standard of physical health and improvement of mental outlook where populations have taken an interest in outdoor exercises. That these are often exploited for commercial and similar reasons is, of course, a matter for regret, but recognition that the first steps in mental control lie in the control of the physique is obvious and essential.

To destroy abnormal sexuality at the root, it is imperative that an individual turn his mind from such thoughts the instant they present themselves. "As rain gets into an ill-thatched house, so lust penetrates an undeveloped mind. As rain does not get into a well-thatched house, so lusts do not penetrate a well-developed mind."[178] The man who solemnly undertakes to observe the third precept of right conduct should therefore purify the source from which actions flow, namely, his thoughts, remembering: "The harm that an enemy will do to an enemy or a foe to a foe is not so great as that which a wrongly-directed mind will do to oneself."[179]

Still, as in the case of the person committing an act of theft at the instigation of another, the latter, giving the instruction or impulse to steal, being no less guilty than the person who actually takes the article in question, so persons inciting others to dissolute behavior are also guilty. The matter is less easy to counter than might at first be supposed, for a large number of even the major works of world literature have sex for their basic theme, while pictorial advertisements displayed in city streets force its lowest aspects on the attention of communities at large. Here the person inciting others to dwell on evil is entirely to be condemned, for by dwelling in thought on, and witnessing pictorial examples of, lustful behavior, sex becomes a demon that drives man to his utter ruin. To sum up the third precept, it may be said that indulgence in unlawful sexual conduct is productive of much evil to the person concerned and to the whole of society.

Those in whom sensual thoughts arise should learn to control them by the practice of mindfulness. In the *Satipaṭṭhāna Sutta* it is said: "Herein, monks, when sense-desire is present in him, the monk knows, 'There is sense-desire in me,' or when sense-desire is absent, he knows, 'There is no sense-desire in me.' He knows how the arising of non-arisen sense-desire comes to be; he knows how the rejection of arisen sense-desire comes to be; and he knows how the non-arising in the future of the rejected sense-desire comes to be."[180]

Among the evil consequences resulting from unlawful sexual intercourse are the following: suffering in an unhappy state for a long period; and when reborn as a man by virtue of merits acquired in a previous existence the birth would occur in a lower form of mankind. Such a person would have many enemies, would be disliked by the people, would be destitute, unable to procure comfortable lodgings, food, and clothes, and would be full of anger and rage.[181]

We now return to the interpretation of the precept as with *kāma* in the locative plural form *kāmesu*. In such form the precept signifies abstinence from all indulgences in the five sensuous objects, namely, visible object, sound or audible object, olfactory object, sap or gustative object, and body impression or tactile object. *Kāmesu micchācāra* is therefore "wrong or evil conduct with regard to the five sensual organs." In many places in Pali literature, the fifth factor of *kāma*, that is, body impression, has been interpreted as "unlawful sexual intercourse"; it seems that it would be the most blameworthy of the five *kāmas*. In representing *kāmesu micchācāra* as relating only to sexual intercourse, the grammatical form of *kāma* has been ignored; to achieve complete observance of the precept, one must therefore desist from the five forms of self-indulgence, both directly and indirectly.

The Fourth Precept

The fourth precept of good conduct, *musāvādā veramaṇī*, concerns abstention from falsehood. This covers the act of telling an untruth, the concealing of the truth in such a manner as to convince another person that an untruth is a truth, the use of exaggerated language—in short, everything that is in any sense a departure from a reliable sober statement of fact. Less obvious, but no less important, *musāvādā* implies accepting as truth that which one knows to be untrue, lack of diligence in searching out the truth of a statement, or any lack of precision in thought insofar as one is able with one's present understanding and intelligence to probe to the utmost truth.

Taking the obvious features first, "Lying is applied to the effort of the body and speech, on the part of one who is deceitful, to destroy the good of others; the volition setting up the bodily and vocal effort to deceive, with intent to cheat others."[182] From the habit of speaking truthfully confidence is acquired, since there is no need then to dissemble or conceal the truth. Moreover, the speaker of truth inspires confidence in others who come to know that they may rely implicitly on his words. "The speech released by a wise man is full of feeling, expressing his true thought. Clumsy people whose language consists only in opening their mouths are not wise people."[183] Again, "Truth is the immortal speech, this is the primeval law. In Truth, well-being and law the saints are established."[184] Conversely, it is disadvantageous to associate with habitual speakers of untruth, and the results of lying can bring considerable harm. There are four constituent factors in this offense: the untruth itself; the intent to deceive; the effort so involved; and the act of communicating the untruth.[185] This act becomes the path of retributive *kamma* (*kamma-patha*) when the false words spoken are taken by others to be the truth. If they are not believed by others, only a bad karmic effect is produced; *kamma-patha* gives rise to both rebirth and a resultant during the present existence. The immoral act may also be committed as an act of writing, or such communication by hand, and is then said to be performed "through the door of the body" (*kāyadvārena*).[186]

The habit of speaking the truth depends on the habit of thinking accurately, since in an attempt to give an accurate account of an event one must be clear in one's mind as to exactly what took place. In such an instance the *musāvāda* may represent misapprehension, and not a deliberate lie such as that told by a person who is caught in a wrong act and who denies it or tries to explain it away for fear of punishment. Here the narrator's sequence of thought as he casts about for formulation of a likely-sounding story does have an effect on his later mode of thinking as a whole. With a sustained effort to think precisely, and so to speak precisely, the constant devotee of truth gradually acquires a faculty of detecting falsehood whenever he encounters it, however much it may be disguised.

The penalty that falls on the habitual liar is that he loses all sense of truth, and much the same may be said concerning the casual or superficial thinker. In considering the first of the Three Refuges, the Buddha, attention was drawn to Buddhism's stress on the cultivation of discernment. But if truth and untruth are to be automatically confused there will be no possibility of discernment, and the person accustomed to falsehood will be far from an understanding of the teaching of the King of Truth (*Dharmarājā*), the Buddha. On the other hand, the follower of *Dharmarājā*, cleaving to truth in all his words and ways, will qualify himself to arrive at a right understanding. He will proceed steadily in the cultivation of discernment, which will make him ever less subject to doubt (*vicikicchā*), one of the five hindrances to mental development and vision, and also one of the fetters (*saṃyojana*) binding man to the rounds of rebirth (*saṃsāra*).

In assigning importance of the highest order to the precept relating to *musāvāda*, one may quote in support the *Dhammapada* verse: "Speak the truth. Do not be angry. When you are asked, give—if only a little. From these three conditions one may go into the vicinity of the *devas*."[187] If one is accustomed to speaking and thinking with precision, one has sufficient clarity of vision not to feel anger and not to pass over an occasion on which another person is in need of a gift. If, then, one wishes to be "near the devas," or in other words, to rise above the human state, then the cultivation of thinking and speaking truly is the means *par excellence*. It is, in fact, the foundation of Buddhism.

The Fifth Precept

The fifth precept concerns the Buddhist's abstention from taking distilled and fermented intoxicating liquors. "He should not take intoxicating drinks. The householder who likes this teaching does not urge others to drink and does not condone drinking, knowing that it ends in madness. Through drunkenness foolish people commit evils and cause them to be committed by other foolish people. Avoid that which is a realm of evils, maddening, deluding, and the delight of the foolish."[188]

Though it is recognized in the present day that certain drugs, including alcohol, are efficacious in the treatment of illness or disease, they are not necessary to a person in a normal condition. The basic objection to alcoholic drinks and such drugs lies in the fact that they distort the mental vision, if only temporarily; in such case it is not possible to preserve the vigilance and alertness that Buddhists should continuously practice. Possibly the best illustration of this distortion, even though very slight, may be taken from the experience of drivers of motor vehicles who are, as a rule, averse to taking any alcoholic drinks when driving or about to drive. If alcoholic drinks and drugs are taken frequently and in large quantities, the harm done to the addict is, of course, very grave. Whatever temporary pleasure he may think to derive from the indulgence, there can be no source of satisfaction, either to him or to his companions, in experiencing a waning control of his mind or in the subsequent recollection that he has behaved foolishly.

In view of certain current misapprehensions, it should be firmly stated that the use of hallucinogenic drugs for the purpose of attaining allegedly "higher" meditative states is highly dangerous and a contravention of the fifth precept. In this connection the words of a former supreme patriarch of Thailand, Prince Vajirañāṇavarorasa, may be quoted with reference to cannabis: "INDIAN HEMP. Another kind of narcotic drug is called hemp or Indian hemp (*Cannabis Sativa*). In small doses it may be used for medicinal purposes producing sleep and dullness of the senses. It is also habit-forming and has an intoxicating effect. The addicts prefer to smoke. It reacts mainly on the nervous system, producing both the visionary and auditory hallucination. Thus what a person addicted to it sees or hears is often distorted and exaggerated. Very often a rope is to him a snake and the sound of a drum becomes thunder or the roar of a cannon. This in turn gives rise to a morbid fear and an uncontrollable excitement leading eventually to delirium and insanity."[189]

The Buddhist texts allude only briefly to the matter of drinking, the causes being of far greater import. In general, these consist in an attempt to produce either a sort of exhilaration or a pacification. The former would connect with a temporary and false happiness, the latter with the lulling of a sense of grief. Rather than embark on wholesale denunciation of sufferers in either of these states, it would be more helpful to them to show how the states could be understood correctly and so remedied. Such understanding of mental states is an essential part of the Buddhist teachings.

THE EIGHT PRECEPTS (AṬṬHA SĪLA)

The foregoing Refuges and five precepts are declared by laymen who wish to account themselves followers of the Buddha, and to them the Refuges and precepts should be considered morally binding at all times. Three additional precepts, bringing the total to eight, form the *aṭṭha sīla*, or *Uposatha sīla*, since they are observed on *Uposatha* (weekly sacred) days.[190] The three additional precepts are:

(6) *Vikālabhojanā veramaṇī sikkhāpadaṃ samādiyāmi* (I undertake the precept to abstain from taking untimely meals).[191]

(7) *Nacca-gīta-vādita-visūkadassana-mālāgandha-vilepana-dhāraṇa-maṇḍana-vibhūsanaṭṭhānā veramaṇī sikkhāpadaṃ samādiyāmi* (I undertake the precept to abstain from dancing, singing, music, watching grotesque mime, from using garlands, perfumes, cosmetics and personal adornments).

(8) *Uccāsayana-mahāsayanā veramaṇī sikkhāpadaṃ samādiyāmi* (I undertake the precept to abstain from the use of high seats).

The sixth precept means that on days on which the aṭṭha sīla is observed the layman takes his main meal at midday and does not eat again during that day. The seventh precept is self-explanatory. The eighth precept has an ulterior meaning in that the occupying of high beds or high chairs may connect with the assumption of high rank or of personal importance. It need not mean that the bed or chair must be less than a certain height above the floor or ground. For a layman observing aṭṭha sīla at intervals, however, the suggestion of avoiding luxury is no doubt paramount.

Regarding the length of time during which the eight precepts should be observed, though the keeping may be periodical and therefore constitute "periodical virtue" (*kālapariyanta sīla*), Buddhaghosa says: "In the fifth dyad periodical virtue is that undertaken after deciding on a time limit. Lifelong Sīla (*āpāṇakoṭika sīla*) is that practiced in the same way but undertaken for as long as life lasts. *Aṭṭha sīla* is therefore of two kinds, periodical and life-long."[192]

A significant advance in the Uposatha sīla consists in the practice of celibacy. While the daily observance of the five precepts preserves the status of family life and only prevents the layman from indulging in unlawful sensual acts, the layman observing the eight precepts must practice complete celibacy. A layman strictly observing the Uposatha sīla is confined to meditation and other religious performances in Vihāras, woods, or separate apartments; for the period of observance he is dressed in the simplest of garments. But essentially, while observing aṭṭha sīla he must not live attached to his family, since the observation constitutes a form of temporary renunciation.

THE TEN PRECEPTS (*DASA SĪLA*)

The ten precepts, *dasa sīla*, were laid down by the Buddha for *sāmaṇeras* (members of the order below the age of twenty) and for the more pious of the laity who could remain unattached to their families. They could observe it for a certain period or for life. In the dasa sīla, the seventh precept of the Uposatha sīla is divided into two parts, so that we get for the seventh of the ten: "I undertake the precept to abstain from dancing, music, singing, and watching grotesque mime." The remainder, "I undertake the precept to abstain from the use of garlands, perfumes, and personal adornments," forms the eighth of the ten precepts. It is thought that the Buddha wished to stress the importance of a longer abstinence, possibly lifelong, from all sensual pleasures.

The ninth precept concerns the use of high seats, as in the aṭṭha sīla, while the tenth, which exists only in the dasa sīla, states: *Jāta-rūpa-rājāta-paṭiggahanā veramaṇī sikkhāpadaṃ samādiyāmi* (I undertake the precept to abstain from accepting gold and silver).

5

THE UNDERLYING IDEALS
OF THE MORALITIES

RELATING THE PRECEPTS TO THE REFUGES

HAVING CONSIDERED THE NATURE of the Three Refuges and the precepts separately, we now examine their import when taken together. Two aspects of the conjunction are presented: first the nature of the relationship of the precepts to the Refuges, second the effect of their being taken together on the whole view of life. Here we come to a study of the Buddha-Dhamma, rather than a study of the Buddha and the Dhamma as though they are separate entities.

Concerning the first aspect, if we try to consider the Buddha alone, we find ourselves postulating something of a transcendental state without the necessary knowledge and equipment for so doing. The result will be merely a "religion," and the precepts will represent merely an arbitrary code. But the Buddhist precepts had their natural root in the Buddha, and we may think of the Buddha both as a man who spent his youth and early manhood living in the world and also as one who experienced the passing from this stage to enlightenment. So will it be seen that the precepts were never ends in themselves, confined to the mundane life, but were the essential preliminaries, and the permanent accompaniments, to attaining the highest state.

The Buddha made the following statements regarding himself: "I am he who has overcome all things, who has found out all things; in all things I am free of taint. I have renounced all things; I am freed of the destruction of craving. From becoming possessed of the Higher Knowledge by myself, to whom should I point as teacher?"[193] The passage occurs frequently in the Buddhist scriptures but is in full context in the *Tathāgatavarga* of the *Udānavarga,* which includes the following stanza: "I shall go to Banaras; I shall beat the drum of the Deathless State; I shall make turn the wheel of the Law which in this world has not yet been turned."[194] Having set in motion the wheel of the Law, the Buddha said later: "Entered upon this course you will make an end of suffering. The road was declared by me when I had understood the removal of the darts."[195] The terms *salla* (or *śalya)*, for arrow, dart, or thorn, and *śokaśalya* for the arrows or thorns of grief, are common in Indian literature; *Lalitavistara* describes the Buddha as *mahāśalyahartā*, "the great remover of darts." The "darts" consisted in the following: lust (*rāga*), hatred (*dosa*), delusion (*moha*), pride (*māna*), false views (*diṭṭhi*), grief (*soka*), and indecision (*kathaṃkathā*).[196] They are the equivalents to the fetters binding one to the rounds of rebirth. Yet with such unparalleled attainments the Buddha is appraised by the average man only with regard to the moralities (see note 114).

The second aspect, that of the Refuges and precepts taken together, with the consequent overall view of life, brings up the question of how the Buddha-Dhamma was to be formulated and presented. It might be assumed that the laity would receive elementary instruction and the bhikkus more advanced instruction, but that was not always the case. There is no hard and fast line of demarcation between the practice of the moralities and the understanding of the paṭiccasamuppāda, nor is there any barrier between the intellectual capacity of the bhikkhus and that of the laymen. The point at issue was always the freeing of mind and freeing of insight, and though it was obviously likely that the bhikkhu would develop these more quickly than would the layman, still there was no holding back of the teaching for those who could absorb it, whatever their status.

We consider the days before the Saṅgha was formed, the days of the *dvevācika* (two-word formula). In the case of Vipassi Buddha, the first of the seven Buddhas mentioned in chapter 1, a following had formed around him from the time that he took to the homeless life. In order to retire to the solitude during which he became enlightened he was obliged to abandon his followers, but to form a nucleus of properly instructed people to help him after his enlightenment he went to two of his former friends in his native city of Bandhumatī, men whom he knew to be well informed and of a high moral standard. Gotama Buddha, after his enlightenment, went in search of five of his former companions, all of whom would have had considerable experience in philosophical study. Other than these five he had no following at the time. He went to Banaras, addressed gatherings, as did other teachers, and met with considerable success. The story of Yasa and his parents has already been recounted[197] and while the Saṅgha now counted seven members, three lay disciples (Yasa's father, mother, and wife) were there also. The class of followers known as *upāsakas* and *upāsikās* must therefore have come into being very shortly after the formation of the Saṅgha, whether *Sammuti* or the *Ariya* Saṅgha (see pp. 53-54). However, apart from Yasa and his family,

Gotama Buddha's teachings soon aroused sufficient interest to cause an out-cry in Magadha: "The Samaṇa Gotama has followed a method by which families are left without sons, women are widowed, and the line of succession of a clan is cut off."[198] At the same time the prospective recluses were saying: "The household life is cramping; it is a path choked with dust; to leave it is to come out into the open air. Settled in a house it is not easy to lead the Higher Life in its complete purity, polished like a conch-shell. Surely I should shave my head and beard, put on the yellow robe, and, leaving my home, go out into the homeless life."[199]

POSITION OF THE LAITY IN EARLY BUDDHISM

It is sometimes argued from the above passage, which occurs many times in the Buddhist scriptures, that the Buddha addressed his teaching entirely to recluses, prospective if not recluses already in fact. This is by no means the entire picture—it should be borne in mind that recluses were quite common in India in the Buddha's day. Precedent existed as far back as the *vaikhānasas* (see p. 13) and it would have been no particular distinction for any teacher that his students became recluses, at least for the period of study of his doctrine. It was, in fact, the least the student could do. The *samaṇas* (homeless wanderers), as a class, were permanent recluses, though they did not necessarily follow a particular method of teaching. The distinction for a teacher would lie in the appreciable number of people becoming recluses on account of his particular teaching, and this, according to the Vinaya text quoted above, occurred in Magadha with reference to the Buddha. But the most that could be argued from the circumstances is that the Buddha was more successful than other teachers; he did not lure men from their homes for unworthy reasons of self-aggrandizement or self-advertisement. As far as the daily necessities of life were concerned, householders were accustomed to recluses and to supplying them with food and clothing irrespective of their religious opinions; Buddhist recluses could rely on the householders for alms as much as any other recluses could.

With an increased following and the consequent necessity of an ordered progress for the bhikkhu, contacts with the laity increased as a matter of course. During the rainy season,[200] well-disposed householders attended specifically to the bhikkhus' wants, often taking them their food so that they did not need to make their daily round for it. This custom is still maintained even in countries where the three months' rainy season does not occur. At the end of the rains the householders made the bhikkhus gifts of robes. As would be expected, householders came to like and respect the bhikkhus, listened to their discourses on Uposatha days, and frequently declared themselves *upāsakas* or *upāsikās*. However, no more and no less than in any other religion did there exist anything spectacular for the laity to do. Buddhist teaching did not include any ceremony but, to the contrary, pointed out that belief in the efficacy of rites and ceremonies (*sīlabbataparāmāsa*) constituted a tie to the round of rebirths. But at the same time, no layman would ever have been permitted to participate in the Vedic or Brahmanic ceremonies, other than to the extent of helping provide an audience. Even such an apparently simple act as "holding up the sacrificial ladle"[201] was fraught with connotations and implied considerable previous study, while the chanting and reciting of hymns were, in the earlier Indian religions, the prerogative of the priests. Again, even in much later religions, the formal reading from a sacred text is rarely entrusted to laymen, though they offer certain arranged responses at prescribed intervals. The contribution of the Buddhist laity would then (as in the case of other religions and "ways of life" which are not supported by a national church or state grant) consist in studying the teaching, beginning with the keeping of the precepts, and helping to support the bhikkus or similar personages. But, as will be noticed latter in this chapter, no specific part of a layman's money is ever suggested for allocation to the Saṅgha.

Besides the *upāsakas* and *upāsikās*, the *Nikāyas* refer to *parisās* (literally, "company, association, assembly") as being also listeners to the Buddha's discourses. The range of *parisās* included the *samaṇa-parisā* and *parisās* of the deva worlds, while for the laity of the present world three classes were distinguished: the *Khattiya-parisā* (from the warrior class), the *Brāhmaṇa-parisā* (from the brahman or priestly class), and the *Gahapati-parisā* (from the householders). In these three cases the terms *mahāsālas* or *paṇḍitas* are employed as an alternative to *parisā*. In view of the grouping of *gahapati* together with *khattiya* and *brāhmaṇa*, it seems that *gahapati* is intended for "householders" of the upper classes, otherwise professional or business men and craftsmen. The only other one of the four classes considered as forerunners of the caste system, namely, the *suddas*, or servant class, is not mentioned in this connection, but it cannot be inferred that such a class was excluded from the Buddha's teaching. We have, in fact, the notable discourse in *Sāmaññaphala Sutta* which states at the outset: "A householder or householder's son, or one of some other clan, comes to hear the dhamma. Having heard it he gets confidence in the Tathāgata."[202] Of the three *parisās*, the *khattiya* produced the smallest number of followers of the Buddha, the *gahapatis* the largest, but in the towns suggested specifically to the Buddha as suitable places for his parinibbāna, namely, Campā, Rājagaha, Sāvatthi, Sāketa, Kosambi, Banaras, there were very appreciable numbers of all three *mahāsālās*.[203]

Of the numerous *vaggas* in the *Nikāyas* bearing the titles *Brāhmaṇavagga* and *Gahapativagga*, the term *brāhmaṇa* does not generally refer to members of the Brahman caste; "Brahman" is taken, in the titles, to signify the ideal type. The *Gahapativaggas*, on the other hand, invariably concern householders, professional men, and craftsmen. The extent of the instruction given to the gahapatis varied according to the capacity for understanding of the persons addressed; for example, in the first two *gahapativaggas* of *Saṃyutta Nikāya* the householder was told to observe the five sīlas, develop confidence in the Three Jewels (Buddha, Dhamma, and Saṅgha), and understand the law of causation, including the Four Noble Truths. *Saṃyutta Nikāya* gives the duties of a householder as maintaining one's parents, paying reverence to elders of the family, using gentle words, avoiding malicious talk, giving up miserliness, practicing generosity, speaking the truth, and avoiding anger. *Gahapativagga* of *Aṅguttara Nikāya* gives the special virtues of the householder as: firm confidence in the Three Jewels, charity and generosity, interest in religious discourses, lack of pride in spiritual advancement, and destruction of the five fetters of belief in personality, doubt, belief in the efficacy of rules and ritual, sensuous craving, and ill will. Householders were also expected to possess the virtues of confidence (*saddhā*), morality (*sīla*), modesty (*hiri*), shame (*ottappa*), much learning (*bahussuta*), charity (*cagā*), and knowledge (*paññā*).

These, however, involve a certain amount of understanding, or at least of Buddhist philosophical learning, and for the more strictly ethical teaching one turns to the *Dīgha Nikāya*. Here it is most concisely put in the *Mahāparinibbāna Suttanta* where the Buddha, on his final tour, was asked by the upāsakas of Pāṭaligāma to visit their local rest-house.[204] The Buddha did so and in his discourse to them addressed them as "Gahapatis." He gave five bad consequences to the offender against the moralities: falling into poverty by reason of indolence; acquiring an evil reputation; lack of confidence with which such a person approaches a company whether of the warrior caste, of brahmans, householders or samaṇas; fear at death; and rebirth in a state of suffering. The five good consequences of keeping the moralities were given in corresponding terms.

Lakkhaṇa Sutta of *Dīgha Nikāya,* describing the high standard of conduct maintained by the Buddha in his previous existences, still keeps to the strictly ethical side of that conduct, referring to the performance of good deeds; restraint in body, speech and thought; charitable actions; observances of the sīlas and Uposatha days; care for parents, samaṇas and brahmans; exertion for the good of others; and so on. *Sigālovā da Sutta,* explicitly prescribing the duties for the householder, gives: abstinence from killing, lying, stealing, and sexual offenses; avoiding offenses committed through impulse, hatred, delusion, or fear; abstinence from drinking, merrymaking, from attendance at fairs, and associating with bad companions; avoiding idleness; avoiding enemies posing as friends; and caring for parents, teachers, sons, wife, friends, and advisers, servants and workers, samaṇas and brahmans.[205] The goal held before the householder consisted in rebirth in one of the deva-worlds, but this conception was pre-Buddhistic and was endorsed by all opinions holding the doctrine of karma. The *Nikāyas* have many instances of good householders being reborn as devas. In an address delivered to Venerable Ānanda on the final tour, the Buddha stated that some of the most distinguished of his upāsaka followers had been reborn as *anāgāmi,* *sakadāgāmi* and *sotāpanna,* while others who had taken the Three Refuges and observed the moralities had been reborn among the devas of the *kāmāvacara.* But an advanced upāsaka would not wish for rebirth in any of the *lokas* or *āvacaras,* however exalted, since they were all conditioned by birth and death.

The question as to whether a gahapati could or could not become an arahat in this life and so avoid rebirth entirely was highly debatable and continued to be the subject of controversy. The view that the householder cannot attain to arahathood is, however, not supported by the early scriptures. Hence, it may be a postulated view which crept into Buddhist scholarship. Arahatship is a transcendental state beyond the states of bhikkhu, bhikkhunī, upāsaka, or upāsikā. According to the scriptures many householders have attained Nibbāna. Ananda K. Coomaraswamy rightly says: "It is true that the layman Arahant is not altogether unknown to Early Buddhism (twenty-one are mentioned in the *Anguttara Nikāya,* iii. 451, and Suddhodana, Gotama's father, is also specially mentioned), but the fulfillment of worldly duties, however selflessly, was never preached as a way of salvation."[206] The *Milindapañha* states that the householder who becomes an arahat "must enter the Order, else die."[207] This view is also not sanctioned by the early canonical works. It may be a contemporary Indian belief incorporated into his work by its author. It is obvious that a householder, after becoming an arahat, does not remain attached to his home or family.

The oldest of the Buddhist texts, such as *Dhammapada* and the first half of the *Dīgha Nikāya*, all stress the *āsavas*, representing their destruction as coinciding with realization of the Four Noble Truths; *Dhammapada* does not mention the fetters (*saṃyojana*), except in the general sense of bonds. Recollecting the Buddha's statement that his distinguished upāsakas and upāsikās were reborn as *sotāpannas, sakadāgāmīs* and *anāgāmīs*, it remains to be shown that they could expect, as upāsakas and upāsikās, to destroy the *āsavas* in this life and so become arahats. Taking the term with its full implications, we have the traditional Indian view that knowledge (*vidyā*) was "higher" (*parāvidyā*) or "lower" (*aparāvidyā*) according to whether it concerned Brahman as Absolute Reality, or *nāma-rūpa*, the things of common experience. *Parāvidyā* does not supply details of particular things but is an insight into the principle of being, and to those possessing the higher knowledge, the lower knowledge is not knowledge at all but merely a form of ignorance. Hence the alternative translation of *avijjā* (Skt. *avidyā*) as "ignorance" or "lack of the higher knowledge." But since the entire destruction of lack of the higher knowledge coincides with the realization of the Four Noble Truths, and since the Buddha stated this to be the ultimate reason why the bhikkhus led the religious life under him, it would appear that the householder could expect less chance to attain to arahat rank in the present life.

On the other hand, one is not entirely justified in maintaining that only those leading the homeless life could attain the ideal here in the present existence. In the account given in *Sāmaññaphala Sutta* of the Buddha's discourse to King Ajātasattu, when the king had risen and gone away the Buddha remarked that but for the murder of his father "the Eye of Truth would have arisen in him even as he sat there."[208] Again, the *Dhammapada* says: "Even though a person wears ornaments, if he conducts himself calmly, is constantly tranquil, controlled, leads a life of chastity, and has laid aside sticks in his dealings with other living beings, he is a brahman, he is a *samaṇa*, he is a bhikkhu."[209] And again: "A man is not a bhikkhu merely because he seeks alms from others. He is not a bhikkhu merely for having taken all the Rules of the Dhamma. He who, having gone beyond merit and evil, leads a life of chastity, walks in this world as though it were an appearance, that one is truly a bhikkhu."[210] The comprehensive view is perhaps most succinctly expressed in two *gāthās* peculiar to the *Dhammapada*: "There is no track in space; externally one is not a recluse. Mankind delights in manifoldness; Tathāgatas are without variety of expansion," and "There is no track in space; externally one is not a recluse. Conditioned things are not eternal; there is no instability in the Buddhas."[211]

If from these and similar quotations one wishes to infer that the terms *bhikkhu, brahman, samaṇa, householder,* or *worldling* have no difference other than that of states of mental development, one may support one's conclusion with a statement made by the Buddha at the end of the lengthy discourse on the nature of the self. He said: "But these are only designations, figures of speech, expressions, concepts, belonging to the world, and the Tathāgata makes use of them without being bound to, or holding onto, any of them."[212] They do, however, "belong to the world," and it was according to the standing and understanding of people of the world that he must declare his teaching in words. If the term *bhikkhu* had no mundane significance, why advocate the religious life? And if the religious life were to be advocated, must it not carry an advantage that would not accrue to those remaining in the world? The advantage lay in a formality of reserving the attainment of arahatship in the present life especially for those who had gone out into the homeless life. If those who did not so go out thought they could attain arahatship, there was nothing to prevent them making the effort.

With regard to observances arising after the parinibbāna of the Buddha, and of considerable interest in the present day, are those of visits or pilgrimages to Buddhist sacred places. Shrines, or *cetiyas*, were common in India long before the Buddha's day and generally consisted of a tree, stone, or small area of ground often believed to be inhabited by a good or evil spirit. *Vinaya* mentions two *cetiyas* at which the Buddha stayed,[213] while *Paṭika Suttanta* and *Mahāparinibbāna Suttanta* contain references to *cetiyas* near Vesāli.[214] The latter *suttanta* names also the *cetiyas* of Sārandada and Cāpālā at Vesāli,[215] Ānanda-cetiya in Bhoganagara, and Makuṭabandhana-cetiya of the Mallas at Kusinārā.[216] To the Buddha the Vesāli *cetiyas* would be attractive, no doubt, since they would lie away from the town and would constitute the type of lonely place suitable for meditation after the food collected as alms on the morning round had been eaten.[217]

The erection of mounds (*stūpas*) on the relics of persons distinguished for their social rank or outstanding spiritual attainment was also a custom of ancient India. According to *Mahāparinibbāna Suttanta,* the Buddha said that *stūpas* should be erected over the relics of a Tathāgata, a Pacceka Buddha, a Tathāgatasāvaka and a Rājā Cakkavatti. According to the same suttanta, a *stūpa* should be erected at the place where four highways meet, the direction following an account of the manner in which the Buddha's earthly remains should be cremated.[218]

Immediately preceding the instruction about visiting the earthly remains of the Buddha, the four places of pilgrimage are detailed. These were: the birthplace of the Buddha, the site of his enlightenment, the site of the preaching of the First Discourse, and the site of the parinibbāna. Persons who died in the course of such a pilgrimage would be reborn in a happy world. However, honoring of remains of the Tathāgata was to be left to *khattiya,* brahman, and *gahapati* paṇḍitas; the bhikkhus were to reserve their energies for their own spiritual development.[219] It is stated: "The bhikkhu or bhikkhum, *upāsaka* or *upāsikā,* who lives in conformity with the Dhamma, who has entered on and who walks in the proper course conforming to the Dhamma, he is the one who pays the highest and most excellent honor and reverence to the Tathāgata."[220]

The pilgrimages to the sacred places of Buddhism today are by no means confined to the laity. They are not undertaken in the conventional sense of "worship" but represent acts of extreme reverence.

THE BUDDHA'S APPROACH
TO TEACHING THE MORALITIES

Whatever the position assigned to the laity, whether in the Buddha's day or visualized to cover the centuries, the statement of the Four Noble Truths must determine the role which the layman should assume and play in the Buddhist life. In the characteristics of *anicca, dukkha,* and *anatta* (impermanence, suffering, and no self) lie the philosophy of Buddhism, and the layman must consider them early on as he strives to live according to the precepts. So we are brought again to the dictum: "Morality is washed all round with wisdom, and wisdom is washed all round with morality. Wherever there is morality there is wisdom, and wherever there is wisdom there is morality. From the observing of the moralities comes wisdom and from the observing of wisdom comes morality. Morality and wisdom together reveal the height of the world. It is just as if one should wash one hand with the other or one foot with the other; exactly so is morality washed round with wisdom and wisdom with morality."[221] Again, the *Dhammapada* statement: "Avoiding the doing of all evil, the accomplishing of good, purifying one's own mind: that is the teaching of the Buddhas" gives the logical procedure.[222] Further, the *Dhammapada's* "Cut down the forest, not only one tree; from the forest is born fear" points to the need for understanding the nature and extent of the "forest" and therefore to understanding the philosophical implications of the teaching.[223]

In the Buddha's day philosophical discussion was rife, and on occasion he set aside philosophy for a moment to consider the whole question of method or Path as starting from the general moralities. In such cases he confirmed the superiority of the Buddhist philosophical views by pointing to their effects on his own conduct and on that of his Saṅgha. A notable instance of this occurs in his conversation with Kassapa, the naked ascetic, and since this covers other important matters pertinent to the present consideration the conversation is quoted at length.[224]

At one time the Exalted One was staying in the Kaṇṇakatthala deer park at Ujuññā. Kassapa, a naked ascetic, came up to him and, after exchange of friendly and courteous greetings, stood to one side and said: "I have heard, Sir: 'The Samaṇa Gotama disapproves of all penance and religious austerities; all who practice them and lead a miserable life thereby he censures entirely.' Those who say thus, do they report you correctly, or do they accuse you falsely? Do they declare in conformity with your teaching, or does some co-religionist misinterpret you for contemptible reasons? Indeed we have no pleasure in representing you falsely, Sir."

"Those who spoke so, Kassapa, have not reported me correctly. They have accused me falsely from lack of mindfulness. With the purity of the Celestial Eye, beyond the human faculty of sight, I see these things: of those leading a miserable life of self-mortification in this world, at the destruction of the body at death some arising in states of wretchedness and suffering, and others arising in a happy and celestial world. Since I have come to know, as they really are in Absolute Truth, the coming and passing away of these ascetics, the consciousness disconnecting the present life and the re-uprising, how shall I disapprove of, or censure, all asceticism? How shall I reproach and condemn all who lead a miserable life practicing it?

"There are, Kassapa, certain samaṇas and brahmans, clever, skillful in disputation, experienced in controversy, hair-splitters, so to speak, who go about as if breaking into pieces by their 'wisdom' the speculations of their adversaries. Between them and myself there are some matters on which we agree and some on which we do not agree.

"I went to them and said: 'Friends, concerning those things in which we do not agree, let us leave them alone. For those in which we do agree, let the wise put questions and ask reasons—discuss the matter either with teachers or their followers in this way: Of those things that are bad or accounted as bad, reprehensible or accepted as such, undesirable of association, unsuited to the Noble Ones, evil or accepted as such, who exists with these things completely destroyed? The Samaṇa Gotama or other teachers with many followers?'

"It may be found, Kassapa, that the wise, from cross-questioning, from asking for reasons, conversing together, would say: 'These things that are bad, or accepted as bad, reprehensible or accepted as such, undesirable of association, unsuitable to the Noble Ones, evil or accepted as such, these the Samaṇa Gotama conducts himself as having destroyed without remainder. For the other teachers of many, that is not so.'

"And again: 'Concerning those things which are good, without blame, desirable of association, in keeping with the Noble Ones, pure or accounted pure, who exists having completely taken upon himself these conditions? The Samaṇa Gotama or other teachers with large followings?'"[225]

The Buddha pointed out that in such discussions it would transpire that he alone of all teachers had taken the conditions upon himself completely, and that his followers were more addicted to good and refrained more from what was considered evil than the followers of other teachers. He proceeded to instruct Kassapa in the Noble Eightfold Path.

The passage makes clear the following points. In the first place, the rigid austerity attributed to the Buddha's teaching by later generations was by no means fully endorsed by his contemporaries. In the second, the Buddha made clear that mere philosophic discussion was unlikely to lead to any appreciable results. Third, a discussion that would lead to useful results would be better begun with points of agreement than with differences. Fourth, these hopeful beginnings should deal with things accepted commonly by all shades of reputable opinion as definitely "good" or definitely "evil"; in other words, the starting points should be moral values. Fifth, the highest moral tone should be that of the persons with the soundest philosophical outlook.

If then the Buddha's teaching may be referred for re-appraisal back to the general morality, to the things that are good or bad or generally accepted as such, what were the general virtues recommended, what effect did they have on the individual, and how might they be utilized for the benefit of a community?

ADVICE TO THE INDIVIDUAL LAYMAN

Of the discourses addressed specifically to householders, the *Mahāparinibbāna Suttanta* was delivered to a group and *Sigālovāda* to an individual. The former has already been described in this chapter; the latter, which goes into much greater detail, is given under specific headings. The circumstances of delivery were as follows.

Sigāla, son of a householder who had recently died, had previously shown no interest in religion. At his father's death, however, he consented to observe the practice of paying devotion to the various quarters of the earth and sky immediately after his morning bath.[226] In such state he was found by the Buddha, who asked him what he was doing and proceeded to explain the real significance of those quarters and of Sigāla's actions in adoring them. The six quarters—east, south, west, north, the nadir, and the zenith—should be taken as representing parents, teachers, wife and children, friends and companions, servants and workpeople, and religious teachers and brahmans respectively. As a preface to this explanation, the Buddha spoke of the necessity of abandoning the evil actions arising from four motives and six practices leading to loss of property or wealth. He pointed out that the householder's son was a disciple of the Noble Ones insofar as he had abandoned the four impurities of conduct, did not act on the four conditions or causes of evildoing, and did not pursue the six practices bringing about loss of means. The four impurities of conduct consist in the violation of the precepts not to take life, not to take that which is not given, not to commit sensual offenses, and not to indulge in falsehood. The four motives on which one should not act are: impulse (uncontrolled or partially; *chanda*), hatred (*dosa*), fear (*bhaya*), and delusion (*moha*).[227]

However, the suttanta gives only the result of pursuit of evil motives, remarking that persons acting on them are brought to ruin just as the moon wanes with the passing month. More detailed treatment is given in various suttas of *Aṅguttara Nikāya*. Here, as advocating self-restraint in contrast to uncontrolled impulse, we have the story of two aged Brahmans who, fearing the approach of death, went to the Buddha for comfort.[228] They explained that they had performed no noble deeds or meritorious acts. The Buddha pointed out that the world is swept on by old age, sickness, and death, and that the only remedy lay in practice of self-restraint in body, speech, and thought. Such restraint would form a shelter, defense, resting-place, and support for one who goes beyond.[229]

For the second evil motive, hatred or enmity, the *Dhammapada* points out that these achieve nothing of advantage; that a person who even dabbles with them is playing with death since they are part and parcel of the realm of death.[230] The *Uragavarga* gives us: "Whatever a man may do in anger, whether he thinks it bad or good, once the anger has disappeared he feels a burn as if he has touched fire."[231] And again: "One should conquer anger by non-anger, conquer evil with good, avarice with generosity, lying with truth."[232] "From where should come anger to one who cannot be provoked to anger, who is controlled, leads a right life, who is set free through right knowledge? For that one anger does not exist."[233]

Concerning delusion, this quality may be considered strictly as *moha*, one of the three evil roots (*hetus*) of action, the other two being greed (*lobha*) and hatred (*dosa*). *Dosa* is mentioned specifically among the present four motives from which no action should be committed; but *moha* is often considered to be a synonym of *avijjā*, "ignorance," and in that connection has a much more extensive significance than "delusion." The wider meaning seems necessary here in order to cover *lobha* which is not synonymous with *chanda* ("impulse"), but since consideration of *avijjā* would take us beyond the advice to the householder's son in *Sigālovāda Suttanta*, we point out here merely the two qualities typical of the ignorant man's lack of investigation (*ananuvicca*) and lack of understanding or lack of having penetrated (*apariyogāhetvā*), in contrast to those of the wise man who accomplishes both investigation and penetration. "Having investigated, having penetrated (the wise man), speaks blame of one who should be blamed, and praise of one who should be praised."[234] Such a person therefore gives a considered and reliable judgment.

The fourth motive from which no action should spring is fear. This may be of four varieties: fear of self-reproach (*attavādanubhaya*), fear of the reproach of others (*paravādanubhaya*), fear of punishment (*daṇḍabhaya*), and fear of bad results in the life to come (*duggatibhaya*).[235] Such fears act as a deterrent, but if one disregards them and commits an evil action, one is considered to have acted *from* fear rather than *in spite of* fear.

The fears are analogous to moral shame and dread (*hiri-ottappa*), which are two mental concomitants present in types of good consciousness, while awareness of fright (*bhayatūpaṭṭhāna*) comprises knowledge of the fact that the conditions and continuity of existence appear to oneself as fear, or fright. Whoever recognizes the impermanence of existence sees the karma formations (*saṅkhāra*) as fear, since they drive on to death. To one who believes the *saṅkhāra* is a misery, the continuity of existence appears as fear in that it is oppressive. Whoever believes the *saṅkhāra* is impersonal, these, as well as the continuity of existence, appear as fear, like an empty village or a mirage. Such is one of the eight kinds of knowledge that are free from defilements, are following the right process, and are considered to be insight.

In the more popular sense, *hiri* and *ottappa* are considered the "bright" states that protect the world, for without them there would exist no differentiation between mother and mother's sister, uncle's wife, teacher's wife, or wife of an honorable man, and the world would come to a condition of promiscuity such as exists among animals.[236] *Hiri* is also numbered among the four good qualities praised by virtuous men and leading to the realm of the devas.[237]

The six courses mentioned in *Sigālovāda Suttanta* as being conducive to loss of property and wealth are: indulgence in intoxicants, sauntering in the streets at unseemly hours, frequenting entertainments, gambling, associating with evil companions, and idleness. The first of these leads not only to loss of wealth but fosters quarrels and increases liability to disease, acquiring an evil reputation, indecent exposure, and impaired intelligence. The frequenting of the streets at unseemly hours results in a man's leaving his wife and family alone, and his property unprotected. Addiction to entertainment leaves him directing his thoughts constantly to locating such entertainment, while gambling, in addition to the loss of wealth, leads to grieving for that wealth and hatred towards the winner. No reliance is placed on the gambler's word in a court of law; he is despised by his friends and associates, and no one will consider him as a possible husband since he is obviously unfit to look after a wife. Association with evil companions may involve association with any gambler, any libertine, any drunkard, swindler, cheat, or man of violence. The lazy person does not work, excusing himself on the ground that it is too cold, too hot, too late, too early, that he is very hungry, or has eaten too much. In the meantime, what he should do remains undone, and any wealth he already possesses dwindles away.

However, laziness may be considered in more extensive form than in *Sigālovāda Suttanta* for, under the synonyms of torpor and languor (*thīna-middha*), it represents one of the five hindrances to mental development and vision and constitutes an immoral factor of consciousness. In this connection laziness would not mean merely doing nothing at all, but failing to put forth one's maximum efforts for good on whatever occasion. Contrasting laziness with its opposite, vigilance, we get the *Dhammapada* chapter *Appamāda Vagga*, with the characteristic verses: "Vigilance is the way leading to the deathless state; negligence is the road to death. Those who are vigilant do not die; those who are negligent are as if dead already."[238] "By means of energy, vigilance, control, self-mastery, the wise man builds an island which the flood does not overwhelm."[239]

This teaching relates explicitly to the individual, and before considering his relationship to his associates we may consider the effect in general of the good man on his surroundings. *Aṅguttara Nikāya* uses the simile of the scent whose savor spreads both in the direction of the wind and against it.[240] Here the Buddha says that recluses and brahmans, devas and nonhumans, all praise the man who takes the Three Refuges, keeps the five precepts, is virtuous and of lovely nature, settles in the household life with heart free from stinginess, is open-handed and delights in giving, is one of whom one would ask a favor, and is one who delights in sharing gifts with others. The effect of such virtues is also likened to the defense enlisted by a king for his country and the effect of a good supply of rain on crops.[241]

6

THE LAYMAN'S DUTIES
TO HIS ASSOCIATES

CHILDREN AND PARENTS

THE DUTIES OF CHILDREN to their parents were stressed in India from a very early date. *Rukkhadhamma Jātaka* expressed the value of the solidarity of a family, using the simile of the trees of a forest; these are able to withstand the force of the wind whereas a solitary tree, however large, is not.[242] The Buddha confirmed and emphasized family relationship, exhorting all persons who decided to remain in the worldly life to maintain family ties together with the honor and dignity of the family as a social unit. The Asoka *Edicts* concern themselves very much with the duties of children to parents; we have, for example: "Meritorious is obedience to mother and father";[243] "Right conduct to mother and father is obedience";[244] "Obey mother and father";[245] "Listen to mother and father."[246] These are, however, modifications of the Upanisadic dictum: "Be one to whom mother is a god. Be one to whom father is a god."[247]

Aṅguttara Nikāya records that great approval is accorded to families in which parents are held in high respect. Such families, said the Buddha, counted as belonging to the Brahma rank (*sabrahmakāni*) and with the early great teachers (*sapubbacariyakāni*); they were "worthy of offerings" (*āhuṇeyya*),[248] an expression indicating great distinction since it was used also by the Buddha in reference to the members of the Saṅgha. He pointed out that parents do much for their children, bringing them up (*āpādaka*), taking care of them (*posakā*), introducing them to the world (*lokassa dassetāro*).[249] The duty of supporting one's parents is included in the three good things proclaimed by the wise, the other two being the practice of charity (*dāna*) and going forth into the homeless life (*pabbajjā*). The debt to one's parents is, in general, impossible to repay; it can be discharged only in a case where the child arouses in his parents confidence in the Dhamma, settles and establishes them in morality, replaces their meanness by generosity,or dispelling their foolishness, settles and establishes them in wisdom.[250] *Sigālovāda Suttanta* gives five ways in which a child should minister to his parents. He should maintain: I will support my parents since they at one time support-ed me, I shall take upon myself the duties incumbent on them, I shall establish a succession, I shall follow a method of inheritance, and I shall make gifts in due course to the dead. In return, the parents should show their love for their children by restraining them from vice, exhorting them to virtue, training them for a profession, arranging a suitable marriage for them, and in due course handing over to them their inheritance.[251]

An occasion is recorded when certain sons fulfilled none of the duties prescribed; rather they followed the course taken by the children of Shakespeare's Lear. The story is told in *Saṃyutta Nikāya* where an elderly and once wealthy brahman, coarsely dressed and very weary, visited the Buddha at Sāvatthi. He stated that he had four sons who, with their wives, had put him out of their houses. The Buddha advised him to recite the following verses when the populace had assembled in their local hall:

Those in whose birth I took delight,
For whose existence I had longed,
They now together with their wives,
Reject me as one would a hog.

Wicked, contemptible are these
Who spoke familiarly like sons,
Yet far from filial care of me
Now leave me, aged and alone.

Just as a worn-out horse is forced
Away from food and driven from his shelter,
So do these children drive away their father
To beg for alms at other people's doors.

Better a stick, I say, would be
Than disloyal sons estranging me;
At least it keeps away an ox
Or drives away a pariah dog.

Yet—once bewildered, in the dark,
Now I have gained a solid hold.

Supported firmly by the hold,
Though once I stumbled, now I stand.[252]

The aged brahman followed the Buddha's advice and his sons amended their behavior.

For reward for keeping the rules of conduct, there is given the case of Sakka, ruler of the devas. Sakka, when a man, declared he would observe the following seven conditions: he would maintain his parents; revere the head of the family; use gentle language; speak no slander; with a mind free from stain conduct himself in his home with generosity, delighting in renunciation, be willing to listen to petitions, and delight in sharing gifts; speak the truth; and not give way to anger; if anger should arise in him he would repress it quickly. As a result of so living and conducting himself, the Tāvatimsa devas conferred on him the name "Good man" (*sappurisa*) and in due course he became the ruler of the devas.[253]

HUSBAND AND WIFE

Of the more advanced type of advice given to householders, much was of necessity directed to the relationship between husband and wife, since they were to be considered by their children as devas. The story of Nakula's parents is a case in point.[254] Here the father lay ill, and the mother, reminding him that death with a worried mind was followed by bad results, reassured him on these points: that she could support the children and maintain the household by spinning cotton and carding wool; that since she and the father had led a good life together for sixteen years she would not remarry; that she would welcome the Exalted One and members of the Saṅgha even more warmly than before; that as long as there existed any upāsikās she would keep the moralities in full, would acquire calmness of mind, become established in the dhamma and discipline (*dhammavinaya*), put an end to doubt, abolish indecision, be self-confident, not rely on others, and live in the Teacher's teaching. The reassurance was sufficient to heal her husband. He rose from his bed and not long after, with the aid of a stick, visited the Buddha. The Buddha remarked on his great gain in having such a wife as Nakula's mother, compassionate and solicitous for her husband's welfare, for a counselor and teacher, and said that as long as he had any women lay disciples at all she should be one of them.

For interpretation of *Sigālovāda's* adoration to the direction of the west, the *suttanta* gives five ways in which a husband should minister to his wife: by being courteous to her, by not despising her, by being faithful to her, by handing over authority to her, and by providing her with necessary adornments. In return, the wife should minister to her husband: by ordering the household well, by hospitality to their relatives, by fidelity, by taking care of his wealth, and by her industry.[255] *Aṅguttara Nikāya* takes into account the case of the wife who fulfills her task perfectly, and here the Buddha enumerates the four qualities by which woman wins power in this world and has this world in her grasp.[256] These are as follows:

She is capable in her work; whatever her husband's home industries, whether in wool or cotton, she is skillful, gifted with an inquiring mind into the work, and able to carry it out. She is able to manage her servants, knowing the duties of each and seeing these are carried out; further, she knows something of sickness and is able to allot the food suitably. She studies the approval of her husband and keeps safe whatever money, corn, silver, or gold he brings home. With these qualities, said the Buddha, "she wins power and this world is within her grasp."[257]

This, however, does not establish her ultimate limitation. She may win power in the world beyond, have the world beyond in her grasp. By what means? By establishment in confidence, virtue, charity, and wisdom. For confidence she knows the arising of a Tathāgata and such and such is so (see note 91). She is accomplished in virtue by keeping the five precepts. She is accomplished in charity, living at home with thought free from avarice, delighting in almsgiving. She is wise in the penetration into the rise and fall of things and in the complete destruction of suffering. With these four qualities she wins power and has the world beyond in her grasp.[258] Yet though these last four qualities contain realization of the destruction of suffering, her reward is only formally acknowledged as rebirth in the deva worlds.

Instructions to girls about to marry are recorded in *Aṅguttara Nikāya* as given by the Buddha at the invitation of a man whose daughters were shortly going to their husbands. The Buddha advised them to rise early, work willingly, order their affairs smoothly, and cultivate gentle voices. They should honor and respect all persons honored and respected by their husbands, whether parents or recluses, and on the arrival of these should offer them a seat and water. Other instructions were similar to those given to wives, namely, skill in the various handicrafts, care of servants and sick people, and care of the wealth brought home by the husbands.²⁵⁹

A further point raised by the Buddha concerned appreciation of the trials of women who, in addition to the disabilities of their sex, were called upon to leave their own families and to live with their husbands' families.²⁶⁰ From that time on, the wife was cut off from her former associates and was entirely dependent for her happiness on the new conditions and surroundings. While the Buddha speaks of ill-assorted couples, and of couples in which both the husband and wife are bad or good,²⁶¹ a particular address dealing with what would appear to be a form of frustration is also extant. The persons concerned were Anāthapiṇḍika, owner of the famous park, and his daughter-in-law, Sujātā.²⁶² The Buddha, going one morning to the house of Anāthapiṇḍika, heard a great noise therein; likening it to that of fishermen who had just made a haul of fish, he inquired the reason for it. Anāthapiṇḍika replied that the commotion was due to Sujātā who was rich and had been brought from a wealthy family; she took no notice of her parents-in-law or of her husband, nor did she respect the Buddha himself. The Buddha called to her and she came and sat down by his side. He said that there were seven kinds of wives, one like an executioner inflicting punishment, one like a thief, one like a mistress, one like a mother, one like a sister, one like a companion, and one like a slave. When the Buddha asked which of the seven she herself was, Sujātā replied that she did not understand, he had put the matter too briefly; but would he teach her the Dhamma so that she might understand? The Buddha expounded. The executioner wife was pitiless and corrupt, a prostitute. The thief robbed her husband of his gains. The lazy gossip and shrew with loud voice was a mistress. The mother-wife cared for her husband and his possessions as she would for an only son. The sister-wife behaved like a younger sister to an elder. The companion-wife behaved as the term would indicate, as a companion. The slave-wife endured all things, remaining calm and pure in heart, and obedient. The last four kinds of wife would, at death, wander in a heavenly world. Sujātā said that she would be the seventh kind. Exactly what she had in mind is left to the interpretation of the reader, but the fact that she found herself in a responsible position in a Buddhist household could hardly have been independent of an inner awareness of the nature of life and therefore of a subconscious desire for knowledge of the Dhamma. The Buddha did not refuse her request to be taught.

FRIENDS

If selection of the family into which one is born in the present existence is closely connected with the karmic effects of previous lives, the selection of one's friends is clearly more directly associated with the circumstances and acts of the current life. Physiologically, the world is perpetuated by the family relationship, but the Buddha has also given the quality of making friends as one which is instrumental in "making the world go round." "The person who is kindly, who makes friends, makes welcome, is free from avarice, is understanding, is a conciliator, such a one obtains good repute. Generosity, kindly speech, doing good to whatever person, fairness in all things, everywhere, as is fit and proper, these are indeed the means on which the world turns, just as a chariot moves on quickly depending on the pin of a wheel axle."[263]

Concerning the selection of one's friends, and the including of oneself in their selections, the following observations are made. One makes friends with a person who gives what is hard to give, does what is hard to do, and is forbearing when it is hard to be so.[264] A person who is inferior to oneself in morality, concentration and one-pointedness of mind, and wisdom, should not be followed, served, or honored except for reasons of compassion. A person who is one's equal in them should be followed, since one's conversation with him would be on these subjects and so conducive to mutual profit and comfort. A person who is one's superior in them should be followed, served, and honored with reverence since one would increase one's own virtue and understanding thereby. One should not be angry with an ungrateful person but merely avoid him,[265] while a wise enemy is better than a foolish friend. One should not loiter among enemies; a night or two nights with such brings suffering.[266] One may recognize a potential enemy in that he will not smile at the sight of one, will not show a welcome, but will deliberately turn his eyes away.[267]

When a mutual friendship is already established, certain duties are incurred. Loyalty to one's friends brings service and support, freedom from enemies, a welcome home after one's travels, and success in one's undertakings.[268] One should live up to one's promises[269] and should regard with friendliness any object or person that has done one a service. For example, one should not break a branch of a tree that has sheltered one; if one has accepted hospitality for a night and taken food and drink from a person, one should never entertain unfriendly thoughts of him or contemplate any unkind act towards him.[270] If one hears gossip concerning a friend, one should examine the matter carefully before accepting it as true; a chance word of a stranger should never separate friends.[271]

Returning to the simile of the quarters, *Sigālovāda Suttanta*, giving as the northern quarter the ministrations of friends, asserts the following.[272] A genuine friend is one who is a help and support, is the same in happiness and sorrow, who advises for one's welfare, and who is sympathetic. As a help and support he guards his friend when he is negligent, protects his property when he neglects it, is a refuge in anxiety, and on occasion, undertakes twice the amount of service needed. As one who is the same in happiness and sorrow, he does not withhold confidences, does not forsake his friend in distress, and even sacrifices his life for his friend's welfare. Advising his friend for his welfare, he prevents him from doing evil, establishes him in good, tells him what he has not heard, and points out to him the road to happiness. As one who is sympathetic, a genuine friend does not rejoice in his friend's mishaps but rejoices in his successes; he restrains a person from speaking disapprovingly of his friend and commends a person who speaks in praise of him. A wise person should recognize such a friend and be thoroughly devoted to him. As opposed to a genuine friend, an enemy posing as a friend may be recognized by his greed, his superfluity of words as compared with his acts, his flattery and spendthrift habits. Such a person appropriates one's possessions, expects much from little, does his duty through fear, and gets all he can for himself out of anything. Again, he makes vain protestations regarding the past and future, but when an opportunity for service arises he does nothing about it. A flatterer consents to do wrong and avoids doing right; speaking in praise of one to one's face, he speaks ill of one in one's absence. A spendthrift is a willing companion in indulging in intoxicants, sauntering the streets at unseemly hours, frequenting entertainments, and gambling. Such friends are to be avoided as one would avoid a dangerous road.[273] It is therefore incumbent on a person to conduct himself toward his true friends with generosity and courteous speech, acting in their interests, treating them as he treats himself, and living up to his word. In return, friends protect him from negligence, including negligence of his belongings; are a refuge in anxiety; do not forsake him in his distress; and show honor to his family. So does a person minister to his friends and associates as the northern quarter.[274]

However, the selection of friends is not always a matter for entirely free choice, for besides the people one would try to cultivate as friends are those to whom one gravitates through similarity of character and those who are thrust upon one. "He who strikes finds another who strikes; the enemy finds enmity; the injurious find the injurious and the angry find the angry."[275] "Breakers of bones, takers of life, thieves of oxen, of horses, riches, and even revilers of kingdoms, between them there is always unity. Between you, how should there not be, you who know the Dharma?"[276] The sentiment is expressed succinctly in the Western proverb, "Birds of a feather flock together."

Only a person's own improvement will disembarrass him of the undesirables toward whom he may gravitate, while for those who have undesirables thrust upon them the advice and assertions given above should be followed. There are, however, potential associates whom it is difficult to avoid, namely, the matters presented by the radio and television set. These are thrust upon us to an extent to which one human being could not thrust himself upon another, for their stream is continuous and, under some circumstances, often wears down a person's resistance. In making one's selection of program one may bear in mind the following: "Whatever a friend does, whatever he practices, by association with him one becomes of such quality."[277]

It is frequently pointed out in the Buddhist texts that one's estimates should not be the result of superficial or hasty observation; the dictum holds also with regard to friends. "Not by the texture of his skin is a man known. Not in a passing glance should one put trust. The unrestrained wander about the world disguised as the well-restrained."[278] A person's morality should be assessed with consideration over a long period; similarly with regard to his purity, strength in distress, and wisdom in conversation. A person's actions may prove, over a spell of time, to be inconsistent in character. Intimacy with a person may lead one to see that he behaves in one way with some persons and in quite another with others. Again, a person afflicted with misfortune, loss of wealth, of relatives, of property, may come to reflect thus: One is born, lives in the world, acquires a personality, insofar as that in being born, living in the world and acquiring a personality, eight things of the world keep the world turning and the world keeps turning on eight things. These are: getting and losing, disrepute and fame, blame and praise, happiness and suffering. In his affliction a man may be overwhelmed with distress and utterly bewildered; on the other hand, a person so afflicted may not grieve or become confused. Further, by conversation with a man one comes to know his uncertainty or resolution. One sees whether or not he utters profound, calming words, beyond the realm of logic and reasoning. Concerning his conversation on the Dhamma one comes to know whether he is able to offer explanations, analyses, clarification of matters: consequently one is able to gauge his wisdom.[279]

One may summarize the foregoing in the words of the scriptures: "If a man finds a companion well-versed, always comporting himself well in the world, overcoming all obstacles, he should walk with him with mind receptive and reflective. If a man does not find a companion with experience, always conducting himself well in the world, like a king leaving his lost kingdom, let him walk alone and commit no evil. And if, in walking, you do not meet a companion who might be your equal and be suitable for you, continue resolutely your solitary walk. A fool is not company. The solitary walk is more worthwhile; a fool is no companion. Walk alone and do not do evil, having few desires, like an elephant in the forest."[280]

TEACHER AND PUPIL

Since ignorance (*avijjā*) is considered the greatest impurity,[281] and since considerable sympathy and understanding are necessary to help someone himself of this impurity, the relationship between teacher and pupil is very highly valued in Buddhism. Considering the teacher the southerly direction, *Sigālovāda Suttanta* gives five ways in which a pupil should conduct himself toward the teacher and five in which the teacher should conduct himself toward the pupil.

The five devolving on the pupil are stated in Pali terms which may be construed both literally and figuratively. In the literal sense, the pupil should rise from his seat in salutation, wait on the teacher, desire to hear him, render him personal service, and honor him by reception. Figuratively these may be taken as displaying energy, understanding the teacher, paying attention, showing obedience, and preparing the work thoroughly.[282]

The teacher should show his compassion, or love, for the pupils by teaching and training them well and happily, seeing that they grasp all the arts and crafts equally and thoroughly, teaching them in the respectful manner he adopts towards friends, and making them secure in every way, including the knowledge of their duties to persons represented by the other directions.[283]

Aṅguttara Nikāya recognizes five ways of growth: growth in confidence based on knowledge and personal experience (*saddhā*), in morality (*sīla*), in learning (*suta*), in the practice of giving up things or generosity (*cāga*), and in wisdom (*paññā*).[284]

The foregoing shows a considerable advance on the attitude adopted by the Brahman guru. According to McKenzie, "It is characteristic of the Indian guru that he imparts the highest instruction very reluctantly and as a profound secret, only to those whom he considers fit to receive it."[285] Again, "A father may therefore tell that doctrine of Brahman to his eldest son, or to a worthy pupil. But no one should tell it to anybody else, even if he gave him the whole sea-girt earth, full of treasure, for this doctrine is worth more than that; yea, it is worth more."[286] According to Muller, the teaching by the father was superseded by the teaching by *ācariyas*, or professional teachers, and already in *Chāndogya Upaniṣad* we have the story of Svetaketu, who, having studied for twelve years under a teacher, guru, or *ācariya*, returned to his father "conceited, considering himself well-read." His father inquired if he had ever asked for that instruction by which "we hear what cannot be heard, by which we perceive what cannot be perceived, by which we know what cannot be known." After some preliminary remarks by his father, Svetaketu said: "Surely those venerable men (my teachers) do not know that. For if they had known it, why should they not have told me? Do you, Sir, therefore tell me that?" "Be it so," said the father.[287] There is, however, nowhere any suggestion of a free discussion of doctrine among friends conducted for their mutual advantage (see p. 105 and note 279).

SERVANTS AND WORKPEOPLE

According to *Sigālovāda Suttanta*, a gentleman (*ayirakena*)[288] should conduct himself towards his servants and employees in these ways: by arranging their work according to their strength and capabilities, by providing them with food and salaries, by looking after them when they are sick, by sharing occasional good things with them, and by giving them leave at times. In return, the employees so treated should rise before the master rises, go to rest after he has done so, take what is given them, work well, and establish a good reputation for him.[289] Many of the *Rock Edicts* bear out this advice: "Now in this practice lies great fruit, namely in the practice of dhamma, in which is included right conduct towards employees."[290] Or again: "Right conduct towards servants and employees."[291]

The sentiment of this advice was in marked contrast to that historically maintained. According to passages in *Rgveda*, misdeeds were classified as those committed "against the gods, our friend, and our house's chieftain,"[292] and again as actions against "the man who loves . . . a brother, friend or comrade, the neighbor ever with us or a stranger."[293] Toward the aboriginal inhabitants of India, who were always contrasted with the "noble Aryans," no special duties were recognized.[294]

DUTIES CONNECTED WITH MEANS OF LIVELIHOOD

It is clear from the preceding account that a high standard of duty is expected regarding one's family, friends, and associates; if one remains in the household life, one must fulfill those duties. No less demand is made in the conduct and management of one's professional or business affairs and, moreover, it is recognized that a moral person should expect and achieve success in his ventures. The Buddha gave five reasons why a moral person should desire to be possessed of means. Firstly, by his work, diligence and clear-sightedness he could make happy himself, his parents, wife and children, servants and workpeople. Secondly, he could make happy his friends and companions. Thirdly, he would be able to keep his property from the depredations of fire, water, rulers, robbers, enemies, and heirs. Fourthly, he would be able to make suitable offerings to his kin, guests, deceased (*petas*), kings and devas.[295] Fifthly, he would be able to institute, over a period, offerings to recluses and others who abstain from pride and negligence, who are established in patience and gentleness, and who are engaged in every way in perfecting themselves. At the same time, whether his wealth increases or whether it does not, he should not be disturbed in his mind if he knows that his reasons for trying to amass it were good. In the meantime the householder successfully amassing wealth by lawful and honorable means, by his own energy and effort, enjoys ownership, well-being, independence in the sense that he does not run into debt, and blamelessness.[296] His parents, wife and children, servants and workpeople, honor him, as do also the recluses and priests to whom he is accustomed to give alms and make charitable gifts. All of these wish him long life and protection, and by reason of his virtue it may be expected that he will not go into decline.[297]

There are, however, certain trades and pursuits that the householder should not follow since these are not in accord with the precepts. These are trade in weapons, human beings, flesh, intoxicants, and poison.[298] Apart from these, a shopkeeper is recommended to be alert, capable, and dependable. His clear-sightedness consists in judging the possibility of sale and amount to be obtained thereby, and in his capability in sales technique. That he becomes a dependable person will be evident from the willingness of people to invest their money in his ventures.[299] It is possible to start business in a small way; according to a simile employed in the *Cullaseṭṭhi Jātaka:* "By means of accumulation of small money, the wise man establishes himself even as by skillful application small particles are fanned to a fire."[300]

Having attained some success, it is necessary to make it enduring. Four reasons are given for failure to do so: failing to seek what has been lost, not repairing what is decayed, eating and drinking to excess, and putting immoral and unreliable men or women in responsible positions.[301]

Having acquired and consolidated one's wealth, one should distribute it suitably. No benefit accrues to the miser who hoards it, or to the person who uses it entirely for selfish ends. Of the miser it is said: "At no time whatever does he get himself clothing, food, garlands or perfumes, nor does he give any to his relatives. He guards them, crying: 'Mine! Mine!' Then rulers, thieves, his heirs, having taken his wealth, go away in disgust. Yet still he cries: 'Mine! Mine!' as before. The wise man, having acquired wealth, helps his relatives and gains their respect; after death he rejoices in a heavenly region."[302]

The Buddha was once visited by Pasenadi, king of Kosala, at the unusual hour of noon.[303] The king explained that there had just died a wealthy man who had left no instructions regarding the disposal of his property; therefore Pasenadi had ordered that the goods should be brought to the royal residence. Vast quantities had arrived, gold and silver. Yet the deceased had always dressed in very poor garments and had been in the habit of eating only sour husk-gruel. He had gone about in a wretched little chariot with only a leaf awning. Since this man had not utilized his wealth properly, either on his own account or on that of his parents, wife, children, workpeople, friends, samaṇas, or brahmans, it would be confiscated by ruler or robbers, destroyed by fire or water, or appropriated by heirs for whom he had had no regard. The Buddha confirmed that this would have been the natural order of events, and that in the opposite circumstances, when the wealthy man would have allocated his wealth properly, he would have been happier himself, would have made others happy, and his charitable deeds and almsgiving would have been productive of a happy future state. His riches would not then have been wasted.

Both the squandering and hoarding of wealth are therefore deplored.

The ideal disposition lies in a division into four parts: one part should be used by the householder for his own ease and convenience, two parts for his business or occupation, and the fourth should be saved in case of adversity.[304] No mention is made here of charitable contributions, and it is believed that the omission was intended since the amount of these is always left to the discretion and inclination of the giver.

Advice to one agricultural worker is less detailed, but it is stated that his fields should be well plowed and well prepared, that sowing and watering should take place at the proper time, and that the worker should be quick at his work.[305] But whatever the nature of one's occupation, one must be diligent. Any man leading the life of a householder who is prudent and possesses the qualities of truth, self-control, firmness, and liberality, will escape affliction in his next existence.[306]

It is clear that no blame attached to the householder as such; he was merely advised that, as a householder, he must try to make a success of his chosen work. To achieve this he must exercise all the moral and physical effort of which he is capable, and if at times he is unsuccessful he must take for consolation the thought that he acted rightly as far as such action could be judged under the circumstances. On such occasions he should not give way to distress but should turn immediately to consider: "How shall I use my strength in the present situation?"[307] He was told to use his wealth, not only for others but to some extent on his own behalf. He was even told to live in a suitable locality.[308] But, in the end, of course, the wealth must be left behind. Therefore the wise man, discerning this, should enjoy and share his benefits. Blameless, he would attain rebirth in a happy place.[309]

There were, of course, many people who thought often of the final parting with their belongings and so looked for something more durable than wealth to which they could devote their energies. King Pasenadi once asked the Buddha if there were anything of profit attainable in the things of the present world which would also be of value in the world beyond. The Buddha replied simply: "Vigilance (appamāda)."[310]

On one occasion when the Buddha was staying at the market town of Kakkarapatta, he was approached by one Dīghajānu who, remarking that he and other householders were absorbed in the affairs of the present world, suggested that the Buddha should preach the Dhamma to people like them. They wished to know the things that would be of advantage to them in the future world. The Buddha gave the four things leading to happiness in the present world as attainment of energy (*uṭṭhānasampadā*), attainment of watchfulness (*ārakkhasampadā*), association with people of high moral standing (*kalyāṇamittatā*), and leading a balanced life (*samajīvikatā*).[311] Whatever one's occupation, whether farming, trading, cattle herding, archery, civil service, or crafts, one should be skillful and industrious, be possessed of an inquiring mind, and able to do and to arrange the work; these qualities constitute attainment of energy. The second item necessary for happiness, attainment of watchfulness, should be interpreted as care of one's possessions, so that they would not be stolen or taken from one or come to any harm. By associating with friends of high moral standing one should emulate the virtues of confidence (*saddhā*), morality (*sīla*), charity (*cāga*) and wisdom (*paññā*) displayed by the best of one's associates. As for leading a balanced life, whether one is experiencing an easy or difficult time, one should neither be unduly elated nor depressed; further, one should order one's affairs according to one's income.

The four things leading to welfare and happiness in the world beyond were given by the Buddha as confidence based on understanding and experience, morality, generosity or charity, and wisdom; these are also the four that the layman should seek in his associates. Here "confidence" is the certainty of the qualities of the Buddha, such as his enlightenment.[312] Achievement in the moralities lies in keeping the precepts, while achievement in generosity and charity lies in freeing thought from avarice and the practicing of giving up things. Achievement in wisdom lies "in the rise of that wisdom leading to welfare, to the penetration of the noble way leading to total destruction of suffering."[313] The Buddha concluded his address with the following *gāthās:*

> From rising and taking action, arranging his matters with care,
> He who is vigilant orders his living, guards and protects his wares.
> With confident understanding, moral and willing to hear,
> Free from the taint of the niggard, he clears a continuous road
> Leading to things that are excellent, things of the world beyond.
> By one who is named the "Truth" there are declared eight things
> To bring the understanding layman present joy
> And joy in future worlds. For increased merit
> Let him be generous, happy to make a gift.[314]

To Ugga, the King's chief minister, the Buddha gave seven states that are not subject to fire, theft and other such damage:

The riches of confidence, riches of morals, of shame and fear of
        wrong-doing,
The riches of listening, of charity, wisdom are seven.
Of whom is possessed these riches, or woman or man,
That one is invincible either to devas or men.
Because confidence, morals, are brightness, the vision of Truth,
Give yourselves up, wise one, to remembering
That which the Buddha has taught.[315]

Such were the ethics prescribed for the householder and those states to which the practice of these ethics led.

7

THE LAYMAN'S RELATION
TO THE STATE

IT MIGHT HAVE BEEN EXPECTED that, with the attention given to the conduct of the laity and the frequency of his advice in social matters, the Buddha would at some time have sketched the political construction of an ideal state: yet no thought of any reform in the existing political setup is apparent. The warrior class (*khattiyas*), priestly class (*brāhmaṇas*), householders (*gahapatis*), merchants *(seṭṭhis)*, servants (*suddas*), all occupied a definite status and there is no suggestion in the Buddha's Discourses that this distribution would be modified, except in cases of reference to a general promiscuity resulting from the collapse of morality.[316] Nor does it seem that the Buddha felt the need for any such change, since his teaching was designed for, and addressed to, "a householder, or householder's son, or son of some other clan."[317] It seems that he attributed the success of a system to the morals of the people working it rather than to any virtue inherent in the system itself. This, surely, is sound enough, if it is taken that a community develops a system according to its own understanding of life and improves on it as that understanding improves, always assuming that no other system is forced on it from the outside against its will. The thesis of this book, however, was set forth in comparison with the study of ethics as inaugurated by Aristotle, since his predecessor at the Academy, Plato, who flourished only a short while after the Buddha, did in fact produce the *Republic,* a full-scale work envisaging a political system. And because Socratic and Platonic thought largely forms the foundation of modern Western thought, one may with advantage compare the conditions in India and Greece which made outlining a political system seem necessary to Greek thought but not to Indian Buddhist thought.

It has been said that Socratic inquiry "implied a standard of truth and good, undiscovered but endlessly discoverable, and to be approached inductively."[318] Plato, however, was explicit in identifying virtue with knowledge as an "art of measurement"[319] and in the vision of an absolute object of desire.[320] He would not break with experience, and in his *Dialogues* often contrasts what ought to be with what is, that is, the principles of truth and

right with the practices of man. His basic aim is always virtue and the fur-
therance of virtue. But good has more than one aspect, and the beautiful or
noble when realized in action constitute the just, and closely allied to the
consideration of justice is that of the political state. The trial of Socrates had
represented merely a show of justice in which clever rhetoric played a large
part, and Socrates, maintaining that his real "trial" would take place before
the judge of the world, showed no fear of death since he knew he had done
no wrong. Inspired by the wisdom and courage of Socrates, Plato showed
that the more clearly he appreciated the qualities of Socrates the more clearly he saw this philosophic idealism to be separated from the everyday world.
In Plato's case the world was that of the restored Athenian democracy, which
alloted no place for philosophers. In the *Republic* all governing power rests
with the philosophers, since the remainder of the community is unable by
its ignorance to prosecute virtue.[321] Yet the philosopher, in so governing, is
making a sacrifice.[322] He has a special, advanced education which enables
him to perform his duties as a ruler, and these duties must supersede all private ties and interests. That in the process the individuality of the subjects
would be lost to sight was of no particular consequence since the aim lay in
educating the people to virtue.[323] Excellent educational systems, which, inci-
dentally, included in their curricula music and gymnastics, were devised to
that end. Even the existence of the state was of value only insofar as it constituted the sole means of preserving virtue and controlling that preservation. It was believed that a state that represented merely a collection of people was not worthy of consideration.

But the state must be defended from without, and therefore a second, if
much lower, section of the community must be formed. This consisted of
naval and military personnel. The third section was composed of farmers,
peasants, and people following trades and professions, so that obviously
something of a caste system must shortly evolve.

The *Republic* was not merely a politico-economic treatise since, though
it contained many inconsistencies of which Plato may or may not have been
aware, he was clearly more confident concerning moral than political matters. At the same time, he believed that man could attain the state he
designed and that it represented man's highest development. The work contains ten sections, the first of which raised the main question of justice; the
next three outlined the perfect state, including the education of the
"Guardians" and the definition of justice in the state as well as in the indi-

vidual. Sections 5, 6 and 7, thought by some to be additions to, and by others to be the kernel of, the whole production, provide for a community and for the education of the philosopher-rulers. Sections 8 and 9 show the decline, through four stages, of the state and the individual, terminating in the complete injustice which is tyranny. The final section, number 10, reviews some of the previous matter and ends with a vision of judgment.

Though the Buddha left no "Republic," the attitude expressed in the *Nikāyas* is clear enough to be compared with Plato's. We may first consider a point common to Socrates, Plato, and the Buddha: that one's first duty lies toward oneself and only in the second to the community.[324] This combines with the idea that there is no place for the philosopher in the everyday world; moreover, one must increase one's own virtue in order to be able to do anything for others, for one cannot teach that which one does not know. The *Dhammapada* says: "Let each one establish himself in that which is proper; then he should advise others, and not become impure."[325] And again: "Let no one neglect his own good for the sake of another's, however great. Let it be that, having understood the ideal, he engages himself in it."[326]

Returning to the comparison, if for "philosophers" we may take the samaṇas who wished to live apart from the world, preferring always the life of the mind, the Buddha never envisaged that these should attempt to "govern" the rest of the community. They were there for guidance and advice if they were asked for it, but from the Buddha's teaching of suffering no perfect state could be possible here in the present world. The caste system, potential in the *Republic,* was already established in India to the extent that the brahmans represented the thinkers and educated portion of the population, the *kshatriyas* the warrior class, the gahapatis the householders and professional men, and the *sudras* the servants and workpeople. These did not attempt to follow each others' callings, but with the advent of the recluses any member of the four classes could leave his calling and aspire to the most select rank. Within the Saṅgha, rank was determined solely by length of membership. The Buddha took the line that, with the cultivation of the moralities, any person of any social rank could improve, be successful in the mundane sense, and, if he took the Refuges and kept the precepts, be certain of an improved status in future lives. Finally, with the understanding that he would acquire in conjunction with keeping the moralities, he could rise entirely above the world.

Regarding the formulation of a definite scheme of government which would last indefinitely, producing always satisfactory results solely by reason of its own excellence, it seems unlikely that any person of vision, or even any thinking person, would ever have embarked on the task. In the last two thousand years, Western Europe has worked out many types of governments, but in the main they present a series of checks and modifications tending towards one side or the other of the principle for which the Greeks of the fifth century B.C.E. fought the Persians at Marathon and Salamis: freedom of individual thought versus regimentation of thought. To some extent it might be believed that Plato was advocating the latter, but there is no question that the Buddha entirely advocated the former. In forming an estimate, however, it is necessary to bear in mind the conditions under which the schemes worked or were to work. Life in Greece was always hard; riches as understood by contemporary Indians would have been to them fabulous. With the Greeks, austerity was largely a matter of necessity, and housing was a major problem. In the sense that a wealthy Indian might leave the household life to devote himself to meditation, the average Greek had much less to leave. Where the Indian was constantly exhorted to lead a moral life, to the Greeks sex was already contemptible. Devoting a certain space to such a comparison may be justified by the fact that the alleged Christianity on which the Western world has supported itself for so long has a large Greek philosophical component, and it is this, not the Hebraic or Zoroastrian components, that has furnished its outlook on and general conduct of life. The Western ideal has always been physical fitness, simplicity of living, reasoning, "doing beautifully whatever needs to be done"(*aretê*);[327] these are entirely Greek concepts. If, therefore, faith in the mythical and mystical side of Christianity having given way to Greek reasoning, one comes to see the basic qualities of the Westerners as those which the Buddha gave as "extolled by the wise," one understands the present Western interest in the Buddha's teachings.

Because of the importance the Buddha assigned to man's moral standards and outlook, then, one must look for a description of the qualities of the people who will operate a scheme rather than for any intrinsic virtue in the scheme itself. If the scheme is an autocracy such as prevailed in the Buddha's day, then one must look for political teaching that will render that autocracy benevolent; this will consist in injunctions to the kings and their proclaimed duties to their peoples. Of such we have several examples.

The leader of a community should realize that by his integrity and foresight will be constructed the course which his people will naturally follow. The case is compared to that of a bull crossing fields by a devious route with the cows straggling in disorderly fashion behind him. When the ruler keeps to righteous ways, his people will be righteous also and peace will reign in the realm.[328] A fool in an exalted station causes great trouble.[329] When kings are evilly disposed, so are their ministers, brahmans, and householders. Seasons become disordered, the rains and winds occur at the wrong times, and the crops are deficient. The people are weak and sickly. If, however, the king is a good man, the people are like him and the kingdom is a happy one.[330] To enlist a following, a gift, a kindly word, a good turn, or equality of treatment, according to the nature of the person desired as a follower, may be counted as advisable means.[331]

Two suttas describe at length the conditions of a kingdom. In *Cakkavatti-Sihanāda Suttanta* we have the story of Daḷhanemi, a universal monarch.[332] After a very long reign he commanded a certain man to let him know if the celestial wheel should at any time move back or lag.[333] In due course the wheel did so and the king was informed. Inferring from this that he had not much longer to live, he handed over his domain to his son and went out into the homeless life to devote his remaining years to contemplation of celestial joys. Seven days later the wheel disappeared. The son went lamenting to his father, who explained: "The Celestial Jewel of the wheel is not an inheritance passing from father to son. See, my dear! By means of the service in the noble duty of the universal monarch, a place exists in that duty in which you are functioning. At Uposatha, once in every fifteen days, if the leader, having bathed and having observed the Eight Precepts, goes to the upper story of his palace, there will become manifest before him the Jewel of the Celestial Wheel with a thousand spokes, rim and hub, complete for working." The son asked: "What, then, Sir, is this noble duty of the Universal Monarch?"

> The King replied: That duty consists in one's support in honoring the Dhamma, paying reverential homage to it, being one who reveres it, is a symbol and banner of it, one to whom the Dhamma is the overlord, a righteous screen and protection in arranging for the family units, army, nobles (Khattiyas), subordinates, Brahmans, householders, country people and people of the market-towns,

samaṇas, and brahmans, animals and birds. Do not, my dear, in
your kingdom set going or continue wrong action. Whoever in the
kingdom should be without means, to him should be handed some.
Whoever in the kingdom, samaṇas and brahmans who, having from
vigilance abstained from sensual attachments and become established in patience and gentleness, such a one training himself, calming himself, bringing himself to approach final rebirth, if coming to
you from time to time should inquire: "What, Sir, is good and what
is not good? What is to be censured and what not censured? What
should be made use of and what should not? What over a long period will be valueless and painful to one, and what over a long period
will be beneficial and of happiness to me?" then, having heard, you
should make them avoid and get rid of evil, and take up that which
is good. This, surely, my dear, is the noble duty of the Universal
Monarch.[334]

The son followed his father's advice and to him was manifested the celestial wheel. Desiring to become a world monarch, he confirmed the wish by
taking in his left hand a pitcher, and with his right sprinkling water from it
over the wheel. With the wheel always before him, he traveled with his
armies, horses and chariots, elephants and men, all over the world. The
rulers of the regions through which he passed welcomed him and asked him
to teach them; he did so by declaring the five precepts, not to kill any living
thing, not to take that which is not given, not to commit sexual offenses, not
to lie, and not to drink intoxicants. He concluded his teaching with the
injunction to enjoy their possessions as they had always done, and then
passed on, leaving them willing vassals.

The same events occurred with many succeeding rulers until at length
there arose one who, on the disappearance of the wheel, did not consult his
hermit father. Instead he ruled according to his own ideas. The results being
unsuccessful, nobles, officials, councillors, ministers, courtiers, and reciters
of verses went to him complaining. They suggested that he should consult
with the many persons in the kingdom who knew the noble duty of a great
ruler, and that he should govern on those lines. In accordance with their rec-
ommendation he provided the necessary protection for the well-to-do but
did not attend to the poorer people. Poverty became widespread and a case
of theft occurred. The thief, being brought before the king, gave as his rea-

son for the theft his entire lack of means of subsistence, whereupon the king made him a gift. A second case occurred with similar result. Many persons taking to thieving, the king decided to put a stop to the whole matter by making an example of one culprit. The man was drummed around the town and executed at one of the main gateways. Thieves now began to conduct their operations with violence, and murder became common. The physical appearance of people deteriorated and the span of life declined from a former eighty thousand years to forty thousand. Lying became common, and with the spread of this and other evils the life span declined to twenty thousand years. The suttanta then records the case of a thief who was denounced by a certain man; this denunciation was considered yet another evil in that it involved the speaking of evil of another person. The life span declined to ten thousand years. Physical appearance deteriorated to the extent that many persons were ugly; these, coveting the more beautiful, misconducted themselves towards other men's wives. A further succession of evils arose: immorality, abusive speech, trivial talk, covetousness and ill will, false opinions, lust, and poisonous greed. Consequent on these the respect previously shown to mother, father, samaṇas, brahmans, and the elders of the clan decreased continuously. By this time the span of life declined to a hundred years.

Before proceeding to the description of further deplorable states provided in the sutta, one may consider some of the points so far advanced. The idea that man has descended to his present state from some higher life appears to have been widespread among the early peoples, and attached to it is the notion that he enjoyed a much longer span of life than he now knows. Modern research has put the length of time since the first civilization at some eight thousand years, but recent employment of the isotope carbon 14 in excavation work in Asia Minor indicates figures in the region of twenty thousand years. Viewing the question from another standpoint, the "king-lists," schematic lists of kings drawn up by Sumerian scribes about 2000 B.C.E. as a framework for a history of Sumer, give reigns of many centuries each, the ten antediluvian kings accounting for 432,000 years between them. Excavations at Ur and Kish have yielded elaborate palaces and much grave-furniture containing material of which the nearest source of supply must have been the west coast of India and, in the case of lapis lazuli, the Pamirs. One can hardly fail to attribute this and similar facts to a close association with the people of the ancient Indus cities and to at least some similarity of ideas. It is known that by 3500 B.C.E. Sumer had attained a standard of architec-

ture—employment of the arch, dome, colonnade construction and so on—
which the Western world did not achieve for many centuries, while a notable
feature of important Sumerian buildings consisted in an elaborate flight of
steps leading to the pillared entrance. This is the subject of a simile well
known in the Buddhist suttas. Again, the port at the mouth of the Narbuda
River, Broach, known to Ptolemy as Barygaza, is mentioned in the *Jātakas* as
a very ancient port from which trading was conducted with the
Mesopotamian countries.

Though the estimate of a very long life was not peculiar to Indian
thought, it is by no means suggested that Buddhism flourished in either
Sumer or the Indus cities; to the contrary, these and other civilizations ultimately fell because they failed to develop the higher levels of thought. The
extent to which such thought does develop should determine the persistence
and improvement of the race; once this ceases to develop the race would
decline. In the case of Sumer, beyond an ethical code and the high degree of
civilization, nothing was achieved but interminable works on magic.
Regarding any suggestion of Buddhist thought, one may turn to the
Buddha's declaration: "I shall go to Banaras; I shall beat the drum of the
Deathless State; I shall make turn the Wheel of the Law which in this world
has not yet been turned." But this does not preclude the existence of earlier
phases of man's occupation of the earth, for according to the account given
in *Mahāpadāna Suttanta*, Vipassi Buddha was the first of the six Buddhas
who flourished in previous eons. Still, whatever interpretation one decides to
put on the length of eons or the possibility of a human life ever extending to
eighty thousand years, or even if one abandons the estimates as wholly ficti-
tious or legendary, there are two points involved which the present generation has seen proved in its own experience. They consist in the fate of a race
whose higher thought has stagnated either due to indifference or weight of
dogma; and the source and progression of evils that will reduce a state, and
finally the entire world, to anarchy and destruction.

So far the decline may be taken to have originated in an initial poverty,
and it is noticeable that the list of evils, as contrasted with those given
according to the precepts or at other places in the Buddhist texts,[335] is now
arranged with the first three components as stealing, violence, and killing. In
the instructions given to householders, the theme is largely success in one's
professional or business undertakings, and little is said of poverty apart from
the aspect of dissipation of wealth, while the observations apply to the indi-

vidual person. The present homily deals with the danger of increasing individual poverty as regards the state, and we learn here that if rulers do not prevent the spread of poverty in their domains they not only induce disorder therein but create disrespect for all recognized forms of authority, so contributing to the deterioration of the human race. We have, moreover, further stress on the interrelation of physical conditions, collective as well as individual, with morality. The present generation is, of course, all too familiar with such a state of affairs, and stands in no doubt regarding the dangers of mass poverty.

From a life span of a century the suttanta goes on to consider a reduction to ten years.[336] In these circumstances the marriageable age will be five years. The tastes of ghee (*sappi*), fresh butter (*navanīta*), oil (*tela*), honey (*madhu*), molasses (*phānita*) and salt (*loṇa*) will disappear, and the highest kind of food will be the grain *kudrūsaka*.[337] The ten moral ways of action will have disappeared and the ten immoral ways will be very much in evidence.[338] The word *good* will no longer exist; whence, then, a doer of good? Honor and respect will be paid to the evildoer, just as at present they are paid to a doer of good. The world will become lawless as with goats, sheep, and such animals. Enmity will be the rule, until a period of general slaughter occurs. After seven days, some persons will decide to abandon the killing and will take refuge in dens, rocks, and holes in trees, living on the produce of the jungle. Emerging after another seven days, people will feel well disposed towards each other, will rejoice to find that someone else is left alive, and will comfort each other. Tracing their heavy losses of kin to their former conduct they will distinguish between good and bad, and will cease to take life. Working up through the range of virtues they will come back to their life span of eighty thousand years, when they will have regained their beautiful appearance. In that condition the marriageable age will be five hundred years. There will be only three kinds of affliction: desire, fasting, and old age.[339] India will be rich and prosperous, with cities and towns so close to each other that a cock could walk from one to another; the population will be enormous. The city of Vārāṇasi will be called Ketumatī, will be crowded with well-fed, prosperous people, and will be the chief of the 84,000 towns of the country. Here will arise Saṅkha, a universal monarch who has conquered the world not by the sword but by goodness. The Buddha Metteyya will then arise, and Saṅkha, having raised up the palace built long ago by

King Mahāpanāda,[340] will give up his possessions and go forth into the homeless life under the Buddha Metteyya.[341]

The *Kūṭadanta Sutta* discusses a similar subject, though in a rather more circumscribed manner. Here we have the story of a king of a distant date, by name Mahāvijita, who, finding himself possessed of great wealth, his treasure houses and storehouses full, felt that he should perform a great sacrifice to show his gratitude.[342] He consulted with his religious adviser, who said:

> Sir, it is remarked that the king's territory is oppressed with murderous attacks, the sacking of villages, market-towns and cities, with ambush and robbery. If now the king would uproot this oppression by imposing a tax, he would not be fulfilling his duty. It may be that the esteemed king feels: "I should put an end to that robbery-trouble by punishment, imprisonment, fine, or by making an example of somebody, or by exile"; but it is not by that means that violence is rightly exterminated. Those who survive cause fresh difficulties. But by adopting this method the robbery-trouble is rightly exterminated. In this case, to those in the king's territory who work on the land, cultivating and farming, let him distribute food and seeds; to those who are traders let him make a grant; to those who are in his service let him consider food and wages. These men, attached to their own work, will not make trouble; they will help in the raising of revenue and the country will be free from oppression. People will be pleased and happy, and, rejoicing in the rearing of their children, will surely dwell with their houses open.[343]

The king, following the advice, found that his territory became secure and peaceful, his people happy and loyal. The religious adviser was now called to prepare a great sacrifice and to instruct the king concerning the procedure. Accordingly, notable personages were invited, representatives of the *khattiyas*, ministers of state, brahmans and householders, all of whom brought much wealth which they offered to the king. He declined it since he had already sufficient revenue and possessions, and the gifts were funded to constitute a perpetual charity. The sacrifice consisted entirely of ghee, oil, butter, milk, honey, and molasses, and to it the king himself brought his personal gifts of wealth and power, his confidence and understanding, and his intelligence. His religious adviser brought his scholarship, virtue, and wisdom.

That such an underlying spirit will bring peace and happiness to a country is evident from the report of Fa-hsien, the first of the Chinese Buddhist pilgrims whose records are still extant. Passing through central India some eight centuries after the parinibbāna of the Buddha, Fa-hsien writes: "Of all the countries of Central India, this (i.e. Magadha) has the largest cities and towns. Its people are rich and thriving and emulate one another in practicing charity of heart and duty to one's neighbor. Regularly every year, on the eighth day of the second moon, they have a procession of images . . . .There may be some twenty cars, all beautifully ornamented and different from one another. On the above-mentioned day all the ecclesiastics and laymen in the district assemble; they have singing and high class music, and make offerings of flowers and incense . . . the elders and gentry of these countries have instituted in their capitals free hospitals, and hither come all poor or helpless patients, orphans, widowers and cripples. They are well taken care of, a doctor attends them, food and medicine being supplied according to their needs. They are all made quite comfortable, and when they are cured they go away."[344]

It cannot, of course, be assumed that the peace and prosperity of Magadha had continued without interruption over the centuries. King Bimbisāra, mentioned frequently in the *Nikāyas* as being favorably disposed towards the teachings of the Buddha, was an ambitious ruler who by conquest and matrimonial alliances added appreciably to his dominions. His son and successor, Ajātasattu, continued the policy and less than a year before the parinibbāna of the Buddha was projecting an attack on the powerful Vajjians. The chief minister of Magadha was sent to the Buddha with the information and with instructions to find out as far as possible the chances of success. Venerable Ānanda, who was present at the interview, confirmed to the Buddha that the Vajjians had followed advice the Buddha had given them sometime previously regarding their conduct, and from this the minister inferred that Ajātasattu would be definitely the loser. The advice given had been that the people should: attend habitually the formal assemblies; assemble in a spirit of unity and harmony, pass the time there harmoniously, and do what had to be done harmoniously; not make new laws or abolish old ones but continue in the old Vajjian manner; honor and respect their elders, paying heed to them; not detain by force women or girls of their clans; honor the Vajjian shrines in their country and continue with their former religious offerings; and protect and provide for the arahats among them and admit new ones. If the Vajjians would fulfill these conditions, said the

Buddha, they might be expected to prosper and not to decline.[345]

It is not known whether the particular attack intended did take place within the near future, but at length Ajātasattu gained control of Kosala and Vaisāli; his son and successor, Udayana, continued the tradition. The program of expansion seems to have been halted by a succession of weak rulers until the usurper Sisunāga annihilated the only outstanding rival state, Avanti. In this building up of a Magadha empire it was inevitable that Buddhist interests should have been adversely affected, and it seems hardly strange that the earliest Buddhist scriptures, whether they were ever written down or not, should have disappeared as a collection. We have evidence for them only in the *Dhammapada* and the oldest of the *Sutta* and *Vinaya* texts, but it seems possible that the major groups of Buddhists, though these need not necessarily have been representative of different sects, each possessed its compendium, if only for purposes of reference for teaching. The *Mahāvastu* would be a case in point. Though it carries as its full title "The *Vinaya Piṭaka* according to the text of the *Lokuttaravādins*"[346] belonging to the Mahāsāṇghikas,[347] in the form in which we know the compilation at present there is practically no *Vinaya* material. The contents do include narratives, poems, *Jātakas*, early versions of the *Mahāgovinda Sutta*[348] and others of the well-known Pali suttas, the whole of the *Sahassavagga* of the *Dhammapada*, the *Khuddakapāṭha* (see note 139), and suttas of the *Sutta Nipāta*. That a concentrated effort was made at some time to reassemble the early scriptures is clear from the compilation of the *Āgamas* and the *Nikāyas*, for these were drawn from a common source which apparently represented a stage intermediate between the very early texts and the *Āgamas* and *Nikāyas* as we know them at present. One fact at least is outstanding, namely, that the compilers of the *Nikāyas* were unaware of the origin of the texts they incorporated in the *Khuddaka Nikāya*, to the extent that these *Khuddaka* texts were already survivors of a complete and larger collection.

However, the fact that groups of Buddhists attempted to hold collections of texts, and also when more favorable conditions prevailed to reassemble or reconstruct the whole body of scriptures, bears witness to upsurges of Buddhism in parts of India even to the level of that described in Magadha by Fa-hsien. The efforts of some of the sections of the community to follow the Buddha's instructions to the Vajjians were therefore not made in vain.

Still we have no indication that among these earlier works was ever included a formal treatise of the nature of Plato's *Republic*. As always, the

Buddha stressed the thought behind a thing, and if the happiness and well-being of a state were dependent on the moral quality of its rulers, we have to recognize, also according to the advice given to the Vajjians, that the duties of the populace were to attend and cooperate in the public gatherings where the discussion of legislation took place. Moral responsibility lay not only with the rulers but also with the masses; there was no question of a dictatorship. In short, each person should share in the responsibility of making decisions, and, in the working out, the community should present a united front. Here, obviously, the moral character of the individual must be a factor of primary importance.

8

■ THE ULTIMATE GOAL ■

STATEMENTS OF THE AIM

THE ULTIMATE AIM of the Buddha's teaching is, without question, the attainment of Nibbāna with the realization of the Four Noble Truths. Various aspects of the goal may be presented in the course of dissertation and various terms employed which are intended to convey a similar meaning, but these are all tributary to the statement that the goal consists in the realization of the Truths. The standards of moral conduct must therefore always be those conducive to this realization; perfection in sīla, samādhi, and paññā must always represent the means of accomplishment. It is never sufficient to say merely that the goal, by whatever name it may be called, is not of the order of logical deduction (*atakkāvacara*), and so hint that in order to attain it one has only to wait for some kind of supernatural revelation. For the Fourth Noble Truth is that of the Way to the cessation of suffering (*dukkha-nirodha-gāminī paṭipadā*) which, we are told, must be followed continuously and diligently throughout the present life. In support of this statement we will now consider the goal according to two well-known aspects, first the one indicated by the popular term *Nirvāṇa* or *Nibbāna*, and second according to the Buddha's description of the goal as freeing of mind and freeing of insight (*ceto-vimutti paññāvimuti*).

NIRVĀṆA, NIBBĀNA

For etymology we have the Vedic association of *nirvāṇa* as *nir* plus *vā*, "to blow," the suggestion being "to make cool by blowing"; later this came to connect with *vr*, "to cover," the sense then associating with the extinguishing of fire. The Buddha frequently used the imagery of flame and fire found in the early *Upaniṣads,* while the nature of the residue of the fire, if any, has long been a matter of consideration. However, before embarking on the question of residue, we will consider the general statements found in the Buddhist texts concerning Nirvāṇa or Nibbāna.

The Pali *Dhammapada* gives the following information regarding Nibbāna. It makes the general statement: "The Buddhas declare Nibbāna to be the highest of all things."[349] For comparison we have: "Hunger is the most extreme of afflictions; the conditioned state is the utmost suffering. Having understood this according to absolute truth, Nibbāna is the extreme of happiness."[350] Or again: "Health is the greatest of gifts; one's own contentment is the greatest wealth. Confidence (intimacy) is the most excellent of relationships; Nibbāna is the highest happiness."[351] But more specifically we have: "For those who maintain vigilance, who study day and night, who strive for Nibbāna, their *āsavas* disappear."[352] In this case the Sanskrit text contains the variation "who strive for deathlessness."[353] Again: "Those wise ones who meditate constantly and with strong effort touch Nibbāna, the unsurpassed release from attachments."[354] But the key to the situation lies in the *gātha:* "Cut out the love of self as you would an autumn-lily with the hand. Develop the way to Nibbāna, taught by the Happy One".

The first of these quotations occurs also in *Mahāpadāna Suttanta* as part of a *Pātimokha* spoken by Vipassi Buddha to the assembly of bhikkhus who had just returned to Bandhumatī after seven years of teaching the Dhamma in distant places.[355] The full context is: "Patient endurance is the extreme austerity; the Buddhas declare Nibbāna to be the highest. One who injures is not a recluse; the *samaṇa* does not harm others. Avoiding the doing of all evil, the accomplishing of good, purifying one's own mind: that is the teaching of the Buddhas. Not blaming, not injuring, restraint according to the *pātimokkha* rules, moderation in food, walking, sleeping, and sitting, exertion in the concentration of the mind: that is the teaching of the Buddhas."[356]

In the second of the *Dhammapada* quotations given above we have the contrast between the extreme suffering of the conditioned state and, by inference, the extreme happiness of the unconditioned state brought about by realization of the nature of suffering. Recalling the three characteristics of existence (impermanence, suffering, and no-self; see p. 23-26) in which all *saṅkhāras* are impermanent and imbued with suffering, while all things, whether conditioned or unconditioned, are without substratum, the present *Dhammapada* verse is amplified by the words: "This is the road to purity." According to the *Sarvāstivāda* philosophy, the *asaṃskṛta* dharmas[357] are space (*ākāśa*), extinction through intellectual power (*pratisaṅkhya-nirodha*), and extinction due to lack of a cause (*apratisaṅkhyā-nirodha*), which is to say, not by any type of knowledge but by nature. *Sautrāntika*[358] is also in agreement with this view. *Vijñānavāda* adds three other such dharmas: extinction by a motionless state of heavenly meditation (*āniñjya*), extinction by the stoppage of idea and sensation (*saṃjña vedayita-nirodha*) as achieved by an arahat, and Tathāgata. Nirvāṇa is considered an example of extinction through intellectual power. Examination of the reasons why space is classed as an unconditioned *asaṃskṛta* dharma suggests for the inclusion in the class of the other dharmas; the reasons are that space gives no hindrance, penetrates through any hindrance freely, and manifests no change. With no interference of any kind, one may think of Nirvāṇa as being essentially calm, therefore happy, as contrasted with the constant commotion in a conditioned state.

Two important instances are extant wherein the Buddha employed the terms *conditioned* and *unconditioned* (*saṅkhata* and *asaṅkhata*). He put the question: "What is the *asaṅkhata*?" and himself replied: "That which is the destruction of lust, hatred and delusion, bhikkhus, is called *asaṅkhata*."[359] Again he said: "Whatever the thing, whether *saṅkhata* or *asaṅkhata*, that which is declared the highest is dispassionateness, absence of desire which is to say: the subduing of pride, the removal of thirst, the uprooting of desire or attachment, the breaking of the cycle of rebirth, the destruction of craving, dispassionateness, cessation, Nibbāna."[360]

Deferring for a moment further consideration of happiness, or the "highest happiness" as mentioned in the third of the *Dhammapada* quotations given above, we turn to the fourth quotation, in which the attainment of Nirvāṇa is connected with the removal of certain conditions. Venerable Sāriputta once stated: "That which is the destruction of lust, hatred and delusion is said to be Nibbāna."[361] He proceeded to declare that the way to accomplish these destructions was to follow the Noble Eightfold Path. Destruction of the three evil roots (*hetus*), and with them the *āsavas*, is a means of attaining the goal. Asked by a certain bhikkhu what the removal of the three bad *hetus* implied, the Buddha answered: "The expression 'removal of lust, hatred, and delusion,' because it means the destruction of the *āsavas*, is called the sphere of Nibbāna." Asked further by the same bhikkhu, "What is the deathless state (*amata*)?" the Buddha replied: "That which is the destruction of lust, hatred, and delusion is called the 'deathless state.' The way to it is the Noble Eightfold Path."[362]

The destruction of the *āsavas* covers that of the three evil *hetus*. The realization of the Four Noble Truths and therefore attainment of Nibbāna is contingent on destroying the *āsavas*. At the end of the discourse recounted in *Sāmaññaphala Sutta* we have the following words of the Buddha: "He comes to know what, according to absolute truth, are suffering, the origin of suffering, the cessation of suffering, and the way to the cessation of suffering. He comes to know, according to absolute truth, the *āsavas*, the origin of the *āsavas*, the cessation of the *āsavas*, and the way of their cessation. From knowing and seeing thus, his mind is freed from the *āsava* of sense-desires, from the *āsava* of craving for existence, and from the *āsava* of lack of the Higher Knowledge. In this freedom he knows: Exhausted is birth, the Higher Life has come to perfection, that which should be done has been done, there will be no more to be done for the present state (*nāparaṃ itthattāyā ti*)."[363] Attainment of Nibbāna must therefore be understood as the destruction of sense desires, craving for the process of life, and ignorance, so that Nibbāna will then imply a cessation of the processes that constitute life, and also the acquisition of a perfect knowledge and vision, that is, seeing according to absolute truth (*yathā bhūtaṃ*).

Regarding the *āsava* of sense desires, a conversation is recorded between Venerable Sāriputta and Venerable Udāyi[364] in which the former, addressing a gathering of bhikkhus, stated that Nibbāna is happiness. Venerable Udayi asked what is the happiness in Nibbāna which is not that of the senses. Venerable Sāriputta replied to the effect that the happiness of Nibbāna is just that which is not recorded by the five physical senses; the well-being arising from the five senses is merely sensuous happiness. With the improvement of understanding, the forms of happiness become of an order higher than that of the senses. That which was happiness, or ease, at one mental level becomes a dis-ease as one attains a higher level. Tracing the refinements of mentality according to the jhānic states, he at length reached the highest jhāna; with perception and feeling ended, and with the *āsavas* destroyed, genuine happiness is attained.[365] It should be noted, however, that in this dissertation Venerable Sāriputta included all the jhānic states, *rūpa* and *arūpa* (see pp. 8–9), whereas in the *Sāmaññaphala* discourse the Buddha did not include the *arūpa* jhānas. The principle of elimination is, however, the same in both cases.

Regarding the second *āsava*, that of love of the process of life, the *Nikāyas* contain many statements that the ceasing of the process is Nibbāna.[366] From this it has been mistakenly inferred that, since there is no basic substratum to a personality, Nibbāna must be total annihilation. The Buddha's verdict on the soul theories, as also on annihilation, have been set forth in chapter 2, but we have also his dictum that Nibbāna is impossible to define, as recorded in the following incident.

A statement was once made by a brahman and endorsed by the Buddha that the five senses have each their particular "pasture" or "roaming-ground" (*gocara*), and do not interfere with each other, but that mind is the repository for all of them. The brahman put a series of questions and the Buddha replied to each of them. He said that the repository of mind is mindfulness, that of mindfulness is release or deliverance, and that of deliverance is Nibbāna. For the repository of Nibbāna he said: "Taking the question to the limit it is transcendental, not to be directly observed. Living the religious life is the approach to Nibbāna; its end and perfection is Nibbāna."[367] That the religious life is not to be taken merely as a form of asceticism is clear from the following. Venerable Ānanda once remarked to the Buddha that half of the religious life (*brahmacariya*) is friendship and intimacy with that which is lovely. To this the Buddha replied: "It is the whole, not the half, of the religious life. Of a bhikkhu who is a friend, an associate, of that which is lovely, morally good, is intimate with it, it may be expected that he will develop and progress according to the Noble Eightfold Path."[368] It may be taken, therefore, that constant association and intimacy with the lovely, the morally good, is a means of progress to Nirvāna.

Regarding the third *āsava*, that of ignorance (*avijjā*), it is necessary to recall the type of knowledge of which *avijjā* indicates a lack. *Avijjā* is the lack of the higher knowledge; besides the *āsava* aspect, it inevitably represents a component of the paṭiccasamuppāda, instrumental in maintaining the round of rebirths. It is also the last of the ten fetters binding one to the round of rebirths. "But the superlative impurity, greater than all others, is ignorance; having struck down that impurity, bhikkhus, be pure."[369] Ignorance is considered to be the origin of lust and hatred and, in fact, all evil states of mind are bound up with it, while ignorance in the sense of blindness is an unconscious state, a remainder from death, a remainder consisting of the effect of deeds performed in the previous life or lives. Such ignorance is not merely lack of knowledge, since it includes both knowing and not-knowing. It is the characteristic of the blind mind, leading to a blind activity, which in turn, has its effect in the will to live, the strongest characteristic of living beings. Again, cutting off obstructions caused by lust or desire, or even the production of a cessation of consciousness, is by no means Nirvāna; both represent merely a return to the *avijjā* which is termed "blindness." Only complete enlightenment destroys this blindness.

We may now consider the alternative reading of "deathlessness" (*amṛtam*) as employed in the corresponding verse of the Sanskrit (see note 353). At death the consciousness normal to a person during his life becomes reduced to an infraconsciousness that persists to form the basis of a rebuilding in the coming life. Then, if a state of deathlessness is not to occur, either consciousness must never so sink down, or alternatively, some entity must be present or have been realized whereby the former normal consciousness will be entirely superseded. There will, in fact, be no basis on which another normal consciousness could build up. With the blind consciousness absent there will be no will to live, consequently there will be no further life, that is, there will be "no more to be done for the present state."[370] The view taken by some of the brahmans, such as the Gotama's early teacher Udraka Rāmaputra (see note 48), that the "neither-perception-nor-non-perception" (*nevasaññā-nāsaññāyatana*) stage of *arūpa* jhāna is tantamount to Nirvāṇa is understandable if one could relate the cessation of normal consciousness to entire exhaustion of the infraconsciousness, but this is not possible. As in the case of death, the normal consciousness is only temporarily suspended, so that the cessation is comparable only to a type of blindness. We have therefore to take it that a deathless state represents complete abrogation of the life that consists in an assembly of processes and processing.

The definition of Nibbāna according to the fifth quotation given from the *Dhammapada* consists in "the unsurpassed release from attachments." Here the term *yoga* for "attachment" is synonymous with *āsava*.[371] Four *yogas* are recognized,[372] three of them identical with the *āsavas* already considered, while the fourth, attachment to wrong views or speculative theory, is also sometimes taken as a fourth *āsava*. Since, however, the term *ignorance* covers false views and speculative theory, the *āsavas* are very often limited to three. Taking remarks applying to the *āsavas* to hold also for the *yogas*, in the sense in which *yoga* is here employed, we may proceed to the last of the six *Dhammapada* quotations under review.

"Cut out the love of self as one would an autumn water-lily with the hand. Develop the way to Nibbāna, taught by the Happy One" (see note 43). Attention has already been drawn to the Buddha's repudiation of the idea of a permanent indwelling self, to his expositions on the identification of feeling with the self (see notes 59–61), to the attainment of final release from the self (see note 63), and to the fact that all dhammas are without a self (see note 65). Regarding the release from the self, it is essential to be clear on the point that the Pali *attā* is by no means identical with the Sanskrit *ātman. Atman*, having a much longer history than *attā*, has many connotations which could not apply to *attā*. Prior to the personification of Brahman, the Absolute Reality of the *Upaniṣads*, *ātman* represented a far more profound concept than soul, and in some respects signified the nonself rather than the self. Nearer to the soul, self, or *attā*, was *jīva*, which was the transmigrating portion of the being. When Brahman was personified, with the *saprapañca* aspect some distinction could still be drawn between the *ātman* and the *jīva*, but with the *nisprapañca* aspect (see notes 18 and 19) *ātman* and *jīva* are inextricably confused. But as though to disclaim any relationship between the Tathāgata of Buddhism and the aspects of Absolute Brahman or Brahma we have the statements already quoted: "Mankind delights in manifoldness; the Tathāgatas are without variety of expansion,"[373] and "There is no movement with the Buddhas."[374] The *Nikāyas* do not indicate whether the brahmans as a body inclined to the *saprapañca* ideal; *Brahman* appears merely as *Brahmā*; therefore the question so frequently put to the Buddha: "Is the *jīva* the same thing as the body, or is the *jīva* one thing and the body another?"[375] represented no idle inquiry but was the result of much disputation and hairsplitting over the philosophical problems presented by the personification of Brahman. Sometimes the Buddha refused to reply, in conformity with the reasons given to Poṭṭhapāda (see pp. 38–39); at other times, as in the case of Maṇḍissa and Jāliya, he adopted the procedure of describing the training of a bhikkhu and then asking if to such a person the question would be even intelligent.[376] Any quotations regarding *ātman* should therefore be treated with circumspection before applying their content to the *anattā* of Buddhism. The Buddhist *anattā* is always the absence of a permanent indwelling self or essence of any kind; this is confirmed in the presentation of life as a stream of consciousness.

Burning (*āditta*)

The employment of the simile of burning (*āditta*)[377] with regard to the life of a living being may be extended to a comparison well beyond the field of poetic imagery. In fact, the details of burning correspond to many details of the basis of progress of an existence and of the passing from one existence to another. In the usual sense of the term, however, *burning* is so common that few people have paused to consider what happens exactly when a thing is burned. Primitive man produced a fire by rubbing two sticks together until sparks appeared and the sticks caught light, thereby supplying directly from himself the energy necessary to start the process going. It was not until the third century C.E. that it was recognized that the presence of air was essential for burning, and fourteen more centuries elapsed before the suggestion was advanced that respiration and burning are similar processes. At the time the idea seemed fantastic, but after another century there was liberated from the atmosphere a gas which was found to be essential to both processes. This gas was oxygen (from the Greek *oxus*, sharp and *genes*, produced), and the processes were found to be those of oxidation. Three conditions are necessary to burning: something to burn, the oxygen in which to burn it, and the application of some form of energy that will raise the temperature of the surroundings sufficiently to start the activity. Similarly, for respiration are needed something that can breathe, some oxygen for it to breathe, and a supply of energy to start the process going. Failing any one of these specific conditions, we have neither burning nor breathing, neither combustion nor respiration.

If burning or breathing is active, in order to halt it one of the three conditions must be withdrawn. If the fire has been allowed to burn itself out, in other words if all the wood—assuming this to be the sticks of primitive man—that would burn at the temperature supplied has now burned, there remains ash, which might or might not be rekindled if a higher temperature were available. The energy supplied to start the reaction has been converted into the heat and light of the flame; these have dissipated and one must look for them somewhere in the universe. According to older Indian thought they have returned to a universal stock of such forms of energy; but in any case they cannot be recovered in the form in which they were previously expended. If we take the parallel of human life, the removal of one of the three conditions for breathing would result in the cessation of breathing and therefore in the death of the individual concerned. The physical body disintegrates, and, in the words of Hamlet: "Why may not imagination trace the noble dust of Alexander till he find it stopping a bung-hole?" But we have the dictum: "This is my body, possessing material qualities, formed of the four great elements, produced by mother and father, an accumulation of rice and fluid, a thing by its nature impermanent, fragile, perishable, and subject to total destruction; and this is my consciousness, bound up with and dependent on it."[378] What becomes of the consciousness?

At death the mentality is reduced to the level of infraconsciousness, which continues, without a break, as the first form of prenatal consciousness of a new existence. In terms of the burning wood one may say that, given sufficient incentive, the ash is ready to break again into' fire; in terms of the human being the infraconsciousness continues as the potential to be energized into a new existence. In the term *Nirvāṇa* we have the implication of the dying out of fire, but since *Nirvāṇa* is, literally, "making cool by blowing," we have to reckon that the extinguishing is due to deliberate effort to remove the condition that makes any further reaction possible, whether or not the equivalent of the ash remains. That any potential should remain at death is impossible if the person has become enlightened during the present life. It could be taken, however, that sufficient potential remains to carry him through the remainder of his present life in the everyday world, and that in this remainder he is merely carrying on in conformity with his antecedents. In this connection the Buddha used the simile of a mango branch.[379] Such a branch, though severed from its parent plant, continues to maintain its previous appearance and habits and to produce mangoes of the same type as the fruit of the parent tree until it finally dies, then subsiding into complete decay. There remains nothing to be re-energized.

Taking the attaining of Nibbāna to be synonymous with becoming enlightened, we may recognize two kinds of Nibbāna, that with substrata remaining, and that with no substrata remaining. The Buddha once considered the case of a bhikkhu who had destroyed the *āsavas*—had done what ought to be done, had laid down his burdens, attained good welfare, destroyed the fetters of existence, and was emancipated by perfect knowledge.[380] If he rejoices in his feelings, he has a remaining substratum and the Nibbāna is *saupādisesa*; if he does not rejoice in his feelings, these will burn out and no substrata will remain. This is the *anupādisesa* condition of Nibbāna. The extinction of human passion is therefore called the "Nibbāna with the condition of being still remaining," or, more literally, the "Nibbāna with the *upadhi* remnant," where *upadhi* is the material and immaterial condition of being. This would represent a person without passion while yet alive. The total extinction of the conditions of being, as well as extinction of passion, represents the Nibbāna without any remainder, the complete and perfect freedom.

But though with the final disappearance of the potential to live there will be no more of the present state, a situation of an entirely different kind from that previously known has transpired. We have the parallel in the case of splitting the atom when, though no new material substance was found within the atom, there did transpire what is now referred to as a microworld. Here the problems of the macroworld for the most part ceased to exist; there is no similarity in the factors creating them. The everyday world's laws of time and space do not govern the microworld in the same way, and in place of substantial bodies we have something more of the nature of fields of force or spheres of influence. It is by no means suggested that Nirvāṇa is a microworld with the present as a macroworld, but that, in researching one type of situation or solving one set of problems, one may arrive at some novel state which is quite unpredictable from the viewpoint of the former state. But regarding living beings, what passes on from one life to another is at least the potential of the past life or lives, whatever the visible surroundings may be. What exists at attainment of Nibbāna may be perfected and true vision, but there is no content that we recognize from the present state. Hence it was logical that, though after the parinibbāna of the Buddha neither man nor devas would perceive his body,[381] it would be incorrect to say that after death the Tathāgata exists, does not exist, both exists and does not exist, or neither exists nor does not exist.

The position taken up by the commentators Buddhaghosa and Upatissa consists largely in agreement that "the Blessed One preached about the Cessation of Suffering by way of the Origin of Suffering."[382] Upatissa does not directly describe Nibbāna but Buddhaghosa treats it in *Visuddhimagga*,[383] where he recognizes eleven kinds of fire: lust, hatred, delusion, sickness, decay or old age, death, grief, lamentation, suffering, melancholy, and tribulation.[384] On the other hand Buddhaghosa does not comment on the word *dhamma,* but Upatissa says of it: "Thus is the Dhamma, Nibbāna, and the way of progress to Nibbāna. What is that way of progress? The Four Applications of Mindfulness, the Four Right Efforts, the Four Roads to Power, the Five Guiding Faculties, the Five Forces, the Seven Factors of Enlightenment, and the Noble Eightfold Path. This is called the Way of Progress leading to Nibbāna."[385] This is exactly the enumeration given by the Buddha when addressing bhikkhus shortly before his parinibbāna. He put the question: "What are the things I have taught you? What are the Truths I have perceived, that you, having thoroughly learnt them, should practice them, cultivate them, take them up seriously, so that the religious life, lasting a long time, may be perpetuated, that it may be for the good of the many, for the happiness of the many, for compassion for the world, for the sake of the welfare and happiness of *devas* and men."[386] He then gave the list of the things he had taught, as quoted immediately above.

Other statements concerning Nibbāna

Other statements made by the Buddhas concerning Nibbāna include the following. Speaking of his own parinibbāna the Buddha said: "On the night the Tathāgata attains to the Highest Perfect Wisdom, and on the night in which he attains to the Final Release, to the state without substratum, the natural condition of Nibbāna, on these two occasions the skin of the Tathāgata is of complete purity and perfection." Again, when Vipassi Buddha had discerned the second and third of the Four Noble Truths and had been freed from the *āsavas*, he considered preaching the Dhamma; then decided: "This generation is attached to pleasure and delights in the attachment and because of this it is difficult for it to understand the matters, namely this Causation and the Law of 'This arises depending on That.' These too are matters difficult to understand, namely, the calming of all mental concomitants, the forsaking of all substrata of rebirth, the destruction of craving, dispassionateness, no prevention, no obstruction, Nibbāna."[387] The latter part of this quotation, "the calming of all mental concomitants" and onwards, is given elsewhere in the *Nikāyas* as a definition of Nibbāna.[388]

According to the paṭiccasamuppāda the cessation of consciousness is contingent on cessation of the *saṅkhāra*, and the cessation of the *saṅkhāra* is contingent on cessation of ignorance (*avijjā*), and vice versa. The associations of the *saṅkhāra* have already been considered, so that we may now examine the question of craving, or thirst (*taṇhā*).

Craving, Thirst (Taṇhā)

It has been stated that ignorance is the greatest impurity (see note 369). By reason of this ignorance one mistakes the true nature of life, and because of the sustained and intensified effort to hold on to the present existence, one brings on oneself all manner of ills. As a result of ignorance comes the blind will to live—the thirst, not merely for incidental things, but for the whole process of life.

"What is the Noble Truth of the Origin of Suffering? It is the craving, leading to rebirth, that is connected with impassioned delight, rejoicing first in one place then in another, namely: the sensual craving, the craving for the process of life, and the craving for the negation of the process of life."[389]

Here craving for existence is intended to cover not only existence in the present world but also that in the fine-material (*rūpāvacara*) and nonmaterial (*arūpāvacara*) realm . All such forms are condemned as "craving," as is also the desire for annihilation. The verdict is given frequently in the Buddhist texts, for example: "Beings held in the bonds of craving, with minds infatuated with existence and non-existence, who are harnessed to the yoke of Māra and have fear of the bonds, so difficult to avoid in this world, are pursued by birth and death. But he who abandons craving, is without craving for existence or non-existence; a bhikkhu without craving, who has destroyed craving, attains to *Parinirvāṇa*."[390]

These verses occur in the *Udānavarga* chapter on craving (*tṛṣṇāvarga*) and are followed by others (occurring also in the *Dhammapada* and other Pali texts), which appear to be part of a discourse delivered by the Buddha. They run: "Whoever is subject to that contemptible craving, so difficult to overcome in this world, for him sorrows increase like the *bīrana* grass after rain. But he who overcomes this contemptible craving, difficult to pass over in this world, from him sorrows fall off like drops of water from a lotus. I tell you this good thing: as many of you as are assembled here, dig up the root of craving as one digs up the *bīrana* to find the fragrant root of *usīra*."[391]

The *Udānavarga* proceeds to stress nonexistence: "A man who has associated with craving for a long time, again and again follows the road of birth and death; again and again without ceasing he submits to the process of life, in this way or that, coming and going.[392] But abandoning craving he is without craving for existence or non-existence; he is not subject to rebirth, indeed to him craving does not exist."[393] But peculiar to the Pali texts is the employment of the word *vāṇa*, "craving," for which there is no corresponding Sanskrit, and which is used in connection with *taṇhā* and *nibbāna*. We have, for example, *vāṇa saṅkhātāya taṇhāya nikkhantattā nibbānaṃ*—"the departure from craving is called nibbāna."

For the remainder of the definition of Nibbāna quoted above (see note 360) we have *virāgo, nirodho, nibbānam*. *Virāgo*, signifying "dispassionateness, without color, without passion," is often considered to be synonymous with *nibbāna*. *Nirodho*, if interpreted as "extinction," can be misleading, yet taken as *ni* plus *rodho*, "no prevention," or "no obstruction," we have an aspect of the goal that is rarely presented and which is in keeping with the statement "There is no movement (instability) with the Buddhas" (see note

374) and with the classification as an *asaṃskṛta dharma* (see note 359).

Recognizing that the basic obstruction to realization of Nibbāna lies in craving, therefore in ignorance, and that until these are removed the vision to perceive Nibbāna is obscured, we turn to the consideration of "freeing of mind, freeing of insight."

FREEING OF MIND, FREEING OF INSIGHT (*CETO-VIMUTTI PAÑÑĀVIMUTTI*)

When the Buddha was asked by Mahāli if the bhikkhus led the religious life under him in order to cultivate samādhi, he replied that they did not, that there were other things, higher and more excellent, that they sought to realize (see notes 148–49). He then described the stages of the Path, the highest occurring with the destruction of the *āsavas*. Then he continued: "The bhikkhu, having come to understand thoroughly and to experience for himself, freeing of mind and freeing of insight, here amongst things as seen in the present world, having attained therein continues."[394] The destruction of the *āsavas* coinciding with the attainment of the goal, one may take it that this attainment consists in freeing of mind and freeing of insight in the present life. In this passage from *Mahāli Sutta*, the Buddha states that the way to reach such understanding was to follow the Noble Eightfold Path, but here the terms *ceto-vimutti paññā-vimutti* are not expressly mentioned. We will therefore examine their associations according to other parts of the Buddhist texts.

The assumption that *ceto-vimutti* and *paññā-vimutti* are synonymous is incorrect, while the statements that *ceto-vimutti* is always with *paññā-vimutti*, and *paññā-vimutti* is always paired with *ceto-vimutti* are also not accurate.[395] For example, *ceto-vimuttiya* occurs alone in *Tevijja Sutta*, *Dīgha Nikāya* XIII, where an account is given of the states known as the *Brahmavihāras*, which lead to *ceto-vimutti*. The discourse was delivered when a young Brahman, Vāseṭṭha, inquired of the way to "Union with Brahma."[396] The Buddha described the moralities and samādhi in the terms of the *Sāmaññaphala* address (see pp. 40–42), up to and including the abolition of the five hindrances and the consequent joy, but instead of proceeding to the description of the jhānic states he continued as follows: "From his thought imbued with loving-kindness (*mettā*), the bhikkhu suffuses with loving-kindness one quarter of the world and so continues. Then he suffuses a second, a third, a fourth quarter. Above, below, across, everywhere, the entire world, he suffuses with loving-kindness from the mind, extensive, becoming unlimited, without ill-will or trace of hurt, and so remains. Just as, Vāseṭṭha, a powerful trumpeter reaches with little difficulty to the four quarters of the world, so with the freeing of the mind by loving-kindness he who fulfills this example will not remain standing there. This, Vāseṭṭha, is the way to union with Brahma."[397] The Buddha then describes how the bhikkhu imbues his thought with compassion (*karuṇā*), sympathy for the welfare of others (*muditā*), and equanimity (*upekkhā*). In each case he uses the simile of the trumpeter, and, emphasizing that one who follows this example "will not remain stationary, or standing, there," states that this is the way to union with Brahmā. In striving to effect the union, or as the Buddhist teaching enunciates the projected result *ceto-vimutti*, all four *Brahmavihāras* must be taken into account; too frequently, and probably because the Western translations of the text give in full only that for *mettā*—as has been done here— there is a tendency to overlook the practices of *karuṇā, muditā,* and *upekkhā.* This, of course is not legitimate. It must further be established that there is no identity between the Brahmanic goal and any stage on the Buddhist *magga* (Path); Vāseṭṭha used the expression "Union with Brahma" and the Buddha accordingly continued with it during the conversation.

The *Brahmavihāras* were already familiar to Indian thought before the Buddha's day; so also were the jhānic states whose position according to the *Sāmaññaphala* discourse is, in *Tevijja Sutta,* taken by the *Brahmavihāras.* But whereas in the *Sāmaññaphala* the jhānic states—and it must be remembered that only the *rūpa* jhānas are there described—are followed by the section comprising *paññā*, with the *Brahmavihāra* in the *Tevijja* we have only the assurance that the person practicing them does not "stand" there. Notably, in both cases the highest point reached is that of *upekkhā*, "equanimity"; it may therefore be considered that the study and development of *paññā* is the natural sequence also in both cases.

Regarding a mention of *paññā-vimutti* without the accompaniment of *ceto-vimutti*, in *Mahānidāna Suttanta*,[398] the Buddha described the seven stages of sentient beings and two spheres of consciousness as follows. The first stage, in which there is a variety of bodily states and states of intelligence, as in the case of men, certain devas, and certain people born in miserable states; the second stage, in which there are beings with a variety of bodily states but with uniform intelligence, like the devas of the company of Brahmā having attained rebirth in the Brahma world for the first time; the

third stage, in which beings have one kind of body but diversity of intelligence as in the case of the Ābhassara devas; the fourth stage, in which are
beings with uniform body and uniform intelligence, like the Subhakiṇha
devas;[399] the fifth stage, in which are beings who, from passing beyond perception of form, from setting down perception of the opposing nature of
objects, and from nonattention to discriminating between the diversity of
objects (such as "Space is infinite"), attain the field of consciousness on
which arises the consciousness of the infinity of space; the sixth stage, in
which beings attain the consciousness dwelling on the infinity of consciousness; the seventh, in which consciousness dwells on "nothingness." The
sphere of beings without consciousness is the first. Where consciousness is so
subtle that it barely exists, if it exists at all, is the second sphere of consciousness. The last four of those stages will be recognized as stages of consciousness of the formless, or arūpa consciousnesses, already mentioned. The
Buddha, having enumerated these stages, and having pointed out that it
would not be fitting that a person who had come to know them, their origin, passing away, satisfaction and disadvantages, and the way of departure
therefrom should take any delight in them, continued: "From the time the
bhikkhu has found out, according to the Truth, the origin of these seven stages
and two spheres, their passing away, their satisfaction and disadvantages, and
the way of departure from them, then he is said to be freed by insight."[400]

The Buddha then enumerated eight stages of deliverance, known generally as the eight freedoms (vimokkhas), but these do not correspond throughout to the stages described in the previous paragraph. The first three of the
vimokkhas are given in a very condensed form of Pali, while the remaining
five, which represent the four arūpajhānas and the final cessation, are in
more academic Pali, in the standard form in which they appear in both the
Pali and Sanskrit texts. The vimokkhas are: (1) the seeing of material compositions as being material qualities; (2) having oneself perception of form-
lessness one sees material compositions as exterior (without intrinsic nature);
(3) that "pleasantness" is one's inclination to a thing; and (4–8) the
arūpajhānas and the cessation of consciousness.[401] It is not until the Buddha
has added to these stages the destruction of the āsavas that he employs the
terms ceto-vimutti and paññā-vimutti in conjunction. He concludes:
"Having understood and experienced for himself the freeing of mind and
freeing of insight, here amongst things as seen in the present world, and having attained therein continues, then it is said that the bhikkhu has attained

freedom by both ways; further or more excellent freedom than this does not exist."[402]

ORIGIN OF ATTAINMENT

The essential condition for attaining Nibbāna being therefore a freeing of insight, *paññā-vimutti*, we turn to consider the *paññā* of *paññā-vimutti* in relation to the Noble Eightfold Path. The components of the Path have already been stated: right view and right aspiration constituting paññā; right speech, right action and right livelihood constituting sīla, and right effort, eight mindfulness and right concentration or one-pointedness of mind constituting samādhi. Here we are reminded of the main groups into which the Buddha divided his teaching, namely, sīla, samādhi, and paññā, and also of the simplest form in which he described his teaching: "Avoiding the doing of all evil, the accomplishing of good, the purifying of one's own mind."[403] In the latter case the samādhi and paññā components may be combined under the heading of purification of the mind; in the Noble Eightfold Path the components are interrelated but certain qualities are common to them all. Just as it was possible to point to the existence of ignorance or craving as the essence of the bonds tying one to the rounds of rebirth, so it is also possible to point to certain radical features as providing the means of attaining the Goal. These features are investigation (*vīmaṃsā*) and vigilance (*appamāda*).

In the instructions given to householders it was clear that the qualities they were advised to cultivate were exactly those that they would need throughout their journey along the Path, the Road (*magga*). There was never any question of arguing that the householder, whether formally he could or could not attain Nibbāna in the present life, need not exert himself in current affairs. There was no pseudo-puritanism to the effect that he should welcome poverty or live meanly; on the contrary, he was expected to be successful, live in a suitable locality, dress himself suitably, and conduct himself in a hospitable manner towards his associates. He was, in fact, to use all his possessions, material and nonmaterial, to the utmost advantage for good. The difference between the training for the householder and for the recluse lay not in the faculties employed but in the specific ends to which they were directed. Therefore, when in the course of time a householder came to see an unworthiness in his specific objects and to look for something better and higher, he had already acquired the habits of virtue he would need to use.

Moreover, it was in practicing these virtues that he would have come to a better understanding and mental vision that would lead to a quest for the higher life. If the objects on which, as a householder, he had concentrated his energies were among the toys of his mental childhood, they had not been unserviceable, for in the lawful pursuit of them he had come to search for others more worthy of his attention.

Regarding *vīmaṃsā* (investigation), even the housewife was told to go about her duties in a skillful, able, energetic manner and with a spirit of investigation (*dakkhā analasā tatrupāyaya vīmaṃsāya*). In the conversation with Vyagghapajja the Koḷiyan, the Buddha gave four qualities for alertness: "By whatever activity he makes a living, whether by cultivation of the soil, by trading, by cattlerearing, by archery, in government service, by whatever craft, he is skillful, energetic, able, and of an investigating mind, able to carry out his work satisfactorily. This is called the origin of attainment."[404] In the *Kālāma Sutta* the Kālāmas were told to investigate every doctrine before adopting it.[405] Finally, this spirit of investigation is one of the four ways to *iddhi* (originally, "potential, possession of latent power; later "wonder, an extraordinary happening").

The Buddha enumerated three kinds of *iddhis*: mystic wonders (*iddhi*), prophecy (*ādesāna*), and instruction (*anusāsanī*).[406] The first two, by reason of their misuse, he said "distressed, vexed, and disgusted" him, but the third was to him the genuine wonder. It was attained by cultivation of the four essential conditions for the striving for concentration and one-pointedness of mind, namely: the impulse to strive, the energy to strive, the consciousness of the procedure, and the investigation of it.[407] According to *Visuddhimagga*, the "roads to power" (*iddhipāda*) are so called "for they, as guides, are indicating the road to power connected therewith and because they are forming, by way of preparation, the roads to power constituting the fruition of the Path."[408] He who has reached the four roads to power has reached the right Path leading to the cessation of suffering. Hence the importance of the investigating mind, and the emphasis on cultivating it from the commonplace of life and onwards.

Concerning vigilance, one recalls the occasion on which King Pasenadi asked the Buddha if there were anything profitable in the things of the present world which would be of value in the world beyond. The Buddha replied in one word: "Vigilance."[409] The *Dhammapada* chapter on vigilance (*appamāda*) has already been referred to, and *gāthās* concerning the connection of vigilance with the deathless state have been quoted (see note 124), but the final reference to vigilance is contained in the Buddha's last instructions. *Mahāparinibbāna Suttanta* gives the following: "Now, bhikkhus, I call upon you: Conditioned things are things of decay; with vigilance try to accomplish." These were the last words of the Tathāgata.[410]

If the qualities of the investigating mind and vigilance are to be understood as the basic and irreducible minimum for following the Path throughout its entire length, one may ask why, in cultivating them, it should have been necessary to introduce such matters as the deva-worlds, jhānic states, and so forth. It must be appreciated, however, that the Buddha addressed a community of people who had themselves evolved these ideas over a period of many centuries, and that the ideas were therefore the very alphabet of their thinking. Having stated his principle of the Four Noble Truths, he had the choice of denouncing the current concepts in their entirety or of employing existing terminology and remodeling and restating the concepts that lay behind it. The first alternative he was not always disposed to adopt, as, for instance, in the matter of asceticism. When the naked ascetic Kassapa asked him if it were correct that he condemned all ascetic practices,[411] the Buddha asked Kassapa, how, since he knew the coming and passing away of the ascetics, the consciousness disconnecting the present life and the re-uprising, he should censure all asceticism. Though he had had his own severe experiences of asceticism and had found that ascetic practices were, of themselves, by no means instrumental in bringing about development of vision, he was aware that a person adopting such practices might improve or might not improve. Concerning the use of current terminology, it is often remarked that the Buddha took over the beliefs in the brahman devas, gods, devils, and other features. In the sense that he made use of the range of worlds as commonly accepted in his day, the statement contains an element of truth. But the idea that either the worlds or the devas furnishing them formed an integral and indispensable part of his teaching is not correct, since he made it clear that beings superior to men were still subject to birth and death and therefore to a measure of suffering. The Four Noble Truths were therefore unaffected by either the presence or absence of devas and contingent worlds. That the devas were instrumental, or the worlds applicable, in regard to the fact that better conditions of life awaited persons who maintained a high morality and developed their insight in the present life, is a logical enough outcome of the karma doctrine. But that the devas and worlds contributed to the question of the final state of excellence of the Tathāgata after death was clearly impossible. They were therefore unavailing in the actual development of the main Buddhist theme, and it was with this development and its expounding that the Buddha naturally concerned himself to the exclusion of all other themes. Throughout his teaching this dictum holds true: "But these are only designations, figures of speech, concepts, belonging to the world, and the Tathāgata makes use of them without being bound to, or holding on to, any of them."[412]

Similarly with the jhānic states. These were of extreme use and provided a valuable practice; the Buddha quoted them on many occasions. But he also names them among the theories which, if adhered to, would help to constitute the net of opinions tying one to the round of rebirths.[413] We get, moreover, his definite pronouncement on his two early teachers, Ārāda Kālāma and Udraka Rāmaputra: that their teachings, culminating in the third and fourth *arūpa jhānas* respectively, did not satisfy him (see note 48). He does not mention the jhānic states when describing his attainment of enlightenment under the Bodhi tree, but states definitely that he and all the Buddhas came to their enlightenment by way of the reasoning of the *paṭiccasamuppāda*.[414] It may be that the *arūpāvacara jhānas*, being held in such high regard by the brahmans themselves, were interpolated on many occasions, suitable and unsuitable, by ex-brahman converts to Buddhism who compiled or commented on Buddhist texts, and here the case of the *vimokkhas* immediately suggests itself by reason of the types of phraseology employed. It is noteworthy that the jhānic states are not mentioned explicitly in the *Dhammapada*, nor, as far as is known at present, in any other of the *Dharmapadas*.

Further, concerning the use of current terminology, perhaps the most difficult case to appreciate is that of the word *brahman* in the sense employed by the Buddha in the famous set of *gāthās* in the *Brāhmaṇavagga* of the *Dhammapada* and in the *Mahāvagga* of *Sutta Nipāta*. Here each *gāthā* ends with the sentence: *Tam aham brumi brāhmaṇam*: "That one I call a brahman." If, as is often intimated, the brahmans as a class were the natural antagonists of the Buddha, why should he employ such a sentence in recounting, as he does in the *gāthās*, the salient qualities of the Buddhist of the highest attainments? One may infer that in the general course of events it would have been a brahman by caste who would have been the seeker after truth, but whether he ranked as *brāhmana*, *samana*, or was known by any other title, he must, as a genuine seeker after truth, fulfill certain conditions. The technical title must be immaterial. Since the conditions cover the Buddhist teaching, we consider them in detail, taking the block in the *Sutta Nipāta* as being entirely representative of the particular *gāthās* and the most conveniently arranged for the present purpose.[415]

620. I do not call a man a brahman because of his ancestry; if he is with possessions he is a *bhovādi*.[416] He who is without possessions and does not seize any, that one I call a brahman.

621. Having cut all fetters, he who has no longing for anything, does not cling to anything, is detached, that one I call a brahman.

622. Having cut off pleasure, the strap and chains and all that goes with them, lifted up the cross-bar, become enlightened, that one I call a brahman.

623. He who, though guiltless, strongly equipped with the power of patience, endures insults, ill-treatment and bonds, that one I call a brahman.

624. He who is observant of religious duties and the moralities who is without attributes, is controlled, bearing his final body, that one I call a brahman.

625. As water does not smear a lotus leaf, or a mustard seed the point of an awl, he who similarly is not smeared by lusts that one I call a brahman.

626. He who comes to know, here in the present existence, destruction of suffering, who has put down the burden of self, who is unyoked from the world, that one I call a brahman.

627. A man of profound insight, with possession of right wisdom regarding the Path and Not-Path, a man who has attained to the topmost height, that one I call a brahman.

628. One who does not associate with either householders or non-householders, is houseless and is satisfied with little, that one I call a brahman.

629. One who, having laid aside the stick, does not injure or destroy living beings, movable or immovable, that one I call a brahman.

630. One who amongst hostility is not hostile, who is peaceful in the midst of violence, who amongst people attached to the world is not grasping, that one I call a brahman.

631. One whose greed, hatred, pride, depreciation of others, fall off like a mustard seed from the point of an awl, that one I call a brahman.

632. One who does not speak harshly, speaks clearly and truthfully, by whose speech no one is offended, that one I call a brahman.

633. One who does not take that which in this world is not given, whether long or short, fine or coarse, pleasant or unpleasant, that one I call a brahman.

634. One who has no wishes in this or any other world, who does not rely on outward things, is detached, that one I call a brahman.

635. One of whom through understanding there does not exist any resting-place for doubt or uncertainty, who has attained to the deep conception of Immortality, that one I call a brahman.

636. One who in this present existence has overcome attachment both to merit and evil, is without grief, stainless, and pure, that one I call a brahman.

637. One who is unstained, clean, bright as the moon, undisturbed, who has surmounted the state of existence dominated by lust, that one I call a brahman.

638. One who, from the passing away of the delusion of repeated existences, has crossed over this path beset with obstacles, difficult of access, has reached to the end, who meditates, is free from lusts, is without doubts, without grasping, and who has finished with movement, that one I call a brahman.

639. One who in this world, having beaten down lusts, is homeless, having in a wanderer's life surmounted the plane of sensuous existence, that one I call a brahman.

640. One who in this world having overcome craving, is homeless, having in a wanderer's life surmounted the plane of existence where is craving, that one I call a brahman.

641. One who, having cast off human bonds, having overcome celestial bonds, is detached from all bonds, that one I call a brahman.

642. One who, having cast off attachment and lack of attachment, is calmed, without substratum for further rebirth, conqueror of all the worlds, a hero, that one I call a brahman.

643. One who has found out in every respect the passing-away and uprising of beings, is non-attached, happy, enlightened, that one I call a brahman.

644. The one whose way neither gods nor *gandhabbas*[417] nor men know, who has destroyed the *āsavas*, the arahant, that one I call a brahman.

645. One to whom "before," "afterwards," "between," do not exist, are nothing, who does not take anything on to himself, that one I call a Brahman.

646. The man of great strength, noble, heroic, a great sage, one who has conquered, who is free from lusts, not a slave to them, that one I call a brahman.

647. He who recognizes his former abodes, perceiving happiness and misery therein, and has attained to destruction of birth, that one I call a brahman.

The above *gāthās* show the "brahman" at various stages along his path. In *gāthās* like 629, 632, 633, he is shown as keeping the precepts of noninjury (629), speaking truthfully (632), and not taking that which is not given (633). He is patient (623) and is peaceful in the midst of violence (630). He overcomes greed, hatred, pride (631), and is unaffected by lusts (625). He attains a state of no longing (621), no doubts (635), no craving (640), has no bonds of any kind, human or otherwise (641), even attachment to merit or evil (631), and he suffers no delusion about repeated existences (638). Here his achievements approach their highest, for he comes to know the destruction of suffering (626). He has put down the burden of self (626), has no attributes (624), and for him time does not exist (643). Having attained the conception of no-change, with no attachment or lack of attachment, he is entirely calm (642).

In conclusion, I draw attention to two remarks made by the Buddha concerning his own teaching. At the outset, as in the case of Vipassi Buddha, he refused to preach the Dhamma for the sake of the few but consented to do so for the sake of mankind at large.[418] The second allusion concerns the Buddha's conversation with Venerable Ānanda when he was recovering from his last illness. The circumstances were as follows. Venerable Ānanda, distraught with anxiety, had tried to comfort himself with the thought: The Exalted One will not go to his Parinibbāna until he has spoken something about the Saṅgha of bhikkhus. The Buddha replied: "But what, then, does the Saṅgha expect of me? I have expounded the Dhamma throughout, in its entirety; the Tathāgata has not the closed fist of a teacher who holds back something of his doctrine. If there is anyone who thinks: 'I should look after the Saṅgha,' 'It is mine to arrange a program for the Saṅgha,' he it is who should speak something."[419] But the Buddha had already taught his Dhamma in full, to mankind at large, as he had promised he would. It began with the most elementary of the moralities, and proceeded without a break to the realization of the ultimate goal: the attainment of Nibbāna with the realization of the Four Noble Truths.

NOTES

ABBREVIATIONS

(PTS indicates issues of the Pali Text Society)

A. *Aṅguttaranikāya,* vol. I, ed. R. Morris, 2nd edn., 1961, vol. II, ed. R. Morris, reprint, 1956, vol. III, IV, V, ed. E. Hardy, reprint, 1959, PTS.

Ap. Apadāna, vol. I, ed. M. E. Lilley, 1925, vol. II, ed. M. E. Lilley, 1927, PTS.

Ndii. *Cūlaniddesa,* ed. W. Stede, 1918, PTS.

Dh. *Dhammapada,* ed. Sūriyagoḍa Sumangala, 1914, PTS.

Dhs.A. *Dhammasaṅganī Aṭṭhakathā* = Atthasālinī , ed. E. Müller, 1897, PTS.

D. *Dīghanikāya,* vol. I, ed. T. W. Rhys Davids, J. E. Carpenter, reprint, 1947, vol. III, ed. Carpenter, 1960, PTS.

Dvy. *Divyāvadāna,* ed. E. B. Cowell and R. A. Neil, Cambridge, 1886.

J. *Jātaka,* vol. I, ed. V. Fausböll, reprint, 1962, vols. II, III, ed. Fausböll, reprint, 1963, vols. IV, V, VI, ed. Fausböll, reprint, 1964, PTS.

Kkvt. *Kaṅkhāvitaranī,* ed. D. A. L. Maskell (née Stede), 1956, PTS.

Kvu. *Kathāvatthu,* vol. I, II, ed. A. C. Taylor, 1894, 1897, PTS.

Khp. *Khuddakapāṭha,* ed. Helmer Smith, reprint, 1959, PTS.

Lal. *Lalitavistara,* ed. S. Lefmann, Halle, 1902.

MNid. *Mahāniddesa,* vols. I, II, ed. L. de la Vallée Poussin, E. J. Thomas, 1916, 1917, PTS.

MV. *Mahāvastu,* ed. É. Senart, 3 vols., Paris, 1882–97.

MN. *Majjhimanikāya,* vol. I, ed. V. Trenckner, reprint, 1964, vols. II, III, ed. R. Chalmers, reprint, 1960, PTS.

Miln. *Milindapañha,* ed. V. Trenckner, reprint, 1963, PTS.

Ps. *Paṭisambhidāmagga,* vols. I, II, ed. A. C. Taylor, 1905, 1907, PTS.

Pv. *Petavatthu,* ed. J. Minayeff, 1889, PTS.

Sdhp. *Saddhammopāyana,* ed. Richard Morris, PTS, 1887.

S. *Saṃyuttanikāya,* vols. I–V, ed. L. Feer, reprint, 1960, PTS.

Su. *Suttāgame,* ed. Puppha Bhikkhu, Sūtrāgamaprakāśaka Samiti, Gurgaon Cantt. East Punjab, vol. I, 1953, vol. II, 1954.

Sn. *Suttanipāta,* ed. Dines Andersen, Helmer Smith, reprint, 1948.

Tkg. *Telakaṭāhagāthā,* ed. E. R. Gooneratne, PTS, 1884.

Thag. *Theragāthā,* ed. H. Oldenberg, R. Pischel, 1883, PTS.

Ud. *Udāna,* ed. P. Steinthal, reprint, 1948, PTS.

Uv. *Udānavarga* (= Skt. *Dharmapada),* ed. N. P. Chakravarti, Paris, 1930.

UC. *Upāsakajanālankāra,* ed. H. Saddhatissa, 1965, PTS.

INTRODUCTION

1   A bibliography of Ven. Saddhatissa's writings, along with a more detailed biography, can be found in the felicitation volume published in his honor: Gatare Dhammapala, Richard Gombrich, and K.R. Norman, eds., *Buddhist Studies in Honour of Hammalawa Saddhātissa*, (Nugegoda: University of Jayawardenapura, 1984).

2   H. Saddhatisa, "The Way to Health and Happiness," in *In Memoriam: Venerable Dr. Hammalawa Saddātissa* (London: International Buddhist Center, 1990), p. 5.

3   The significance of Ven. Saddhatisa's point has been elaborated and gently challenged by John Ross Carter in "'Beyond 'Beyond Good and Evil'" in *Buddhist Studies in Honour of Hammalawa Saddhātissa*, 41-55.

4   Dhammapada vs. 183; *The Dhammapada*, translated by John Ross Carter and Mahinda Palihawadana (New York: Oxford University Press, 1987), 243.

CHAPTER 1

5   *Odhams Dictionary of the English Language Illustrated*, Odhams Ltd, 1946; The *Elements of Ethics*, H. John Muirhead, London, 1910, p. 4; *A Manual of Ethics*, S. John Mackenzie, London, 1929, p. 1.

6   *Principia Ethica*, G. E. Moore, Cambridge University Press; Reprint 1954, p. 2.

7   *Encyclopaedia Britannica*, 1926 ed., Vol. 9, p. 809. Article: *Ethics*. Rev. H. H. Williams.

8   *Encyclopaedia of Religion and Ethics*, ed. James Hastings, Edinburgh. T. and T. Clark; New York, Charles Scribner's Sons, 1908–26. Vol. 5, p. 414. Article on *ethics*: by J. H. Muirhead.

9   Dh. v. 118: *sukho puññassa uccayo*—Happiness is the accumulation of merit.

10   *Encyclopaedia Britannica*, 1926 ed., Vol. 2, p. 512; article on Aristotle by Thomas Case.

11   D. I. 124.

12   *Ibid*, and substantially in all *Dīgha suttas*.

13   *Encyclopaedia Britannica*, 1926 ed., Vol. 2, p. 513; article on Aristotle by Thomas Case.

14   *Encyclopaedia Britannica*, 1951 ed., Vol. 8, p. 757; article on *Ethics* by Abraham Wolf.

15   D. I. 222.

16   *Ibid*, I. 223.

17   D. I. 223; M. I. 329.

18   *nisprapañca*: from *nis* plus *prapañca*; *niṣ*, "free from"; *pra* plus *pañc*, "to spread out," i.e., "expansion, diffusion, manifoldness." Therefore, *nisprapañca*: "free from diffusion."

19   *saprapañca*: *sa* plus *pañc*. Therefore, *saprapañca*: "with diffusion, with manifoldness," etc.

20   *prathama-ja*, the "first-embodied." Prajāpati occupies the first place in the *Brāhmaṇas*. *Śatapatha Brāhmana v.i.* 2, 10, and 13 state that there are thirty-three gods and that Prajāpati is the thirty-fourth including them all.

21 · *Bṛhadāraṇyaka Upaniṣad*. I. vi. 1. "Verily this is a triad, name, form, and work." *The Upaniṣads*. Tr. by F. Max Muller, Oxford, 1900. Part II, p. 99. (The Sanskrit term here translated as "work" is *karma*.)

22   *vedanā, saññā, saṅkhāra, viññāṇa*, respectively.

23   The *rūpakkhandha* consists of the four *mahābhūtas*, or "great" elements, namely, earth, water, fire, and air. A similar classification of elements was made in ancient Greece.

24   Modern Pali-English dictionaries are quite clear on this point, but standard translations of Buddhist texts, many of which were made in the closing decades of the nineteenth century, use *nāma-rūpa* only for "name and form," thereby imposing an unwarranted limitation which often obscures the meaning of the text.

25   *Ṛgveda*, VII. 64. 2.

26   *Ṛgveda*, X. 117. 6: *sa kevalāgho bhavati kevalādi.*

27   Dh. v. 255.

28   According to Louis Renou some material was taken over from Dravidian (or pre-Dravidian) religion into Vedic religion. The doctrine of rebirth or *saṃsāra* was fully formulated in the earliest *Upaniṣads*. Even the word *saṃsāra* does not appear before the *Kaṭhopaniṣad*. Referring to karma Renou says: "The doctrine did not attain acceptance, however, without the influence of its ethical element: reward and punishment for merit and sin. The same word, *karman*, which meant 'ritual act' now receives the meaning of moral act and the result of action." *Vedic India* (Classical India Vol. 3), Louis Renou, Calcutta, 1957, see pp. 37, 57, and 89.

29   A. II. 415: *Cetanā'haṃ bhikkhave kammaṃ vadāmi. Cetayitvā kammaṃ karoti kāyena, vācā, manasā.*

30   Dh. v. 1; v. 2.

31   *Ibid.* v. 140.

32   *Piyavagga*: This is the ch. XVI which contains 12 verses from 209–20.

33   Dh. vv. 219, 220.

34   S. I. 72; Uv. v.v. 22: *Tasmāt kuruta puṇyānām nicayaṃ sāmparāyikam puṇyāni paraloke hi praitiṣṭhā prāṇinām hi sā.*

35   Dh. v. 136; Uv. IX. v. 12.

36   *Ibid.* vv. 5, 6; see also Uv. XIV. v. II.

37   *Ibid.* vv. 1, 2.

38   *Ibid.* v. 33; Uv. XXI. i; *Gāndharī Dharmapada*, ed. J. Brough, London 1962. VIII. v. 136.

39   Cunningham's Bharhut Plates, XLIV. 2.

40   See *Mahājanaka Jātaka*, J. (No. 539), Vol. VI, pp. 30–68.

41   D. I. 187–93.

42   D. II, 33.

43   Dh. v. 285; Uv. XVIII. v. 5; J. I. 183.

CHAPTER 2

44   *Tathāgata*: The name used by the Buddha when referring to himself. No satisfactory derivation of the word has been established and the commentaries, suggesting a variety of definitions, are obviously uncertain about its meaning. Since, however, the accepted meaning of *Tathāgata* is "One who is Enlightened" or "One who has attained to the Truth," it seems the derivation of the word might be from *tathā*, "reality, truth," and *gata*, "gone, arrived at, having come to." Thus *Tathāgata* means "One who arrived at Truth" or "One who discovered Truth."

45   D. II. 100: *Desito Ānanda mayā dhammo anantaraṃ karitvā; na tatth' Ānanda Tathāgatassa dhammesu ācariyamuṭṭhi.* Rhys Davis has translated the first sentence: "I have preached the truth without making any distinction between exoteric and esoteric doctrine" (*Dialogues of the Buddha*, Part II, p. 107); but there is no justification for the terms *exoteric* and *esoteric*. Rather the sense would be "having made not-inside and not-outside." The only esoteric school claiming to be Buddhist is the Shingon, which dates from about the seventh century C.E., over a thousand years after the *parinibbāna* of the Buddha. But *Shingon* is a Japanese translation of the Sanskrit term *mantra*; hence, perhaps, the confusion with *antaraṃ*. See *Essentials of Buddhist Philosophy*, J. Takakusu, University of Hawaii, 2nd ed. 1949, reprint, 1956, pp. 142–48.

46   D. I. 84.

47   See M. I. 91 f.; J. I. 57.

48   The two generally mentioned in the Buddhist texts are Ārāda Kālāma and Udraka Rāmaputra. According to *Lalitavistara* (Ch. XVI, XVII) the former could not teach beyond the third *arūpāvacara jhāna* and the latter not beyond the fourth. Gotama, having soon absorbed all that Ārāda Kālāma could teach him, went to Pāṇḍava Hill close to Rājagṛha where King Bimbisāra saw him on an alms round. Struck with the brilliance of his appearance, the king made offers which Gotama refused; he did, however, promise that if he ever attained the highest truth he would teach it to Bimbisāra. Under Udraka Rāmaputra, Gotama soon attained to the fourth *arūpāvacara jhāna*, then, lacking a teacher who could teach him anything more, he set out on his own wanderings, pursuing the course of asceticism.

49   Ud. pp. 1–3.

50   *Paṭiccasamuppāda: paṭicca*—"on account of, because of, concerning"; *samuppāda: saṃ* and *uppāda*—"coming into existence, appearing, rising"; (Skt. *sama*, "even the same"; *samā*, "in the same way"; *sa* [Pāli and Skt.] "together"). *Visuddhimagga* (p. 521) gives *sammā* or *saha uppajjati* as equivalent to *samuppāda* (*sammā* [Skt. *samyak*] "correctly" or towards one point." Therefore, *paṭicca* or *pratītya*, "together," and *samuppāda* or *samutpāda* "appearance" means "coming into existence together, in the same way, and to one end." The expression *hetuppaccayasāmaggi* has precise and direct reference to the causal relation of things as explained by *paṭiccasamuppāda*. See Uj. p. 23.

51   *nidāna*: source, cause, origin.

52   D. II. 55–71.

53   *Ibid.* II. 31–35.

54   *Ibid.* II. 55.

55   *Conception of Buddhist Nirvāṇa* by Th. Stcherbatsky, Leningrad, 1927, p. 91.

56   *Tattvasaṃgraha*, Vol. I, ed. Embar Krishnamacharya, General Library, Baroda, 1926, p. 1.

57   M. II. p. 32.

58   *Conception of Buddhist Nirvāṇa*, op. cit., p. 122; *Prasannapāda*, ed. La Vallée Poussin, Bibliotheca Buddhica, St. Petersburg, 1913, p. 38.

59   In each case the word *small* refers to the theory that the self is composed of atoms very much finer than those of material substances such as the body.

60 D. II. 66.

61 *Ibid.*

62 D. II. 66 ff.

63 *Ibid.* II. 68.

64 *Ibid.*

65 Dh. vv. 277, 278, 279.

66 *The Central Conception of Buddhism and the Meaning of the Word 'Dharma',* Th. Stcherbatsky, publ. Royal Asiatic Society, London, 1923, p. 30.

67 *Odhams Dictionary of the English Language Illustrated.*

68 D. I. 51.

69 *Pali Text Society's Pali-English Dictionary,* p. 336.

70 *Sarvāstivāda Literature,* Anukul Chandra Banerjee. Publ. D. Banerjee, Calcutta, 1957, pp. 52, 65.

71 *Sarvāstivāda:* the most extensive of the early Buddhist schools. *Vijñaptimātravāda:* the school holding that nothing exists apart from consciousness; it is also known as *Vijñānavāda* or *Yogācāra.*

72 D. II. 305; Vin. I. 10.

73 D. I. 3.

74 *Buddha: His Life, His Doctrine, His Order,* Hermann Oldenberg, Edinburgh, 1882, p. 381.

75 D. II. 35 f.

76 *Ibid.* II. 39.

77 D. II. 39.

CHAPTER 3

78 Monier Williams: *Sanskrit-English Dictionary,* p. 994.

79 *Pali Text Society's Pali-English Dictionary.*

80 *Concise Pali-English Dictionary.* A. P. Buddhadatta Mahāthera. U. Chandradasa de Silva, Ahangama, Ceylon, 1949; See Uj., pp. 6 ff., 124 ff.

81 A. I. 189 f.

82 *Tattvasaṅgraha,* Vol. II, Gaekward's Oriental Series, No. xxxi, Baroda, 926, V. 3588: *Tāpāc chedāc ca nikaṣā suvarṇam iva paṇḍtaih parīkṣya bhikṣavo grāhyam madvaco na tu gauravāt.*

83 Sn. 182; Uv. X. v. 3.

84 *Bhagavatgītā,* XVIII. v. 66: *Sarvadharmāṃ parityajya mām ekaṃ śaraṇaṃ vraja ahaṃ tvām sarvapāpebhyo mokṣayiṣyāmi mā śucah.*

85 Dh. vv. 188–92. Attention is drawn to the slight variation made here in the wording of the Four Noble Truths. These are generally stated as in note 42, and the associated text. See also D. I. 189; M. I. 431 f.

86 There are four pairs of saints who realize the paths (*magga*) and fruitions (*phala*) of the following stages: stream-winning (*sotāpatti*); once-return (*sakadāgāmi*); never-return (*anāgami*); and perfection (*arahatta*).

87 D. II. 93.

88 Dh. v. 165.

89   Dh. v. 290; Uv. XXX v. 30; *Cf. Mahābhārata*, XII. 174.46; 177.51; 276.7.

90   *Pūjemi Buddhaṃ kusumen' anena*
      puññena-m-etena ca hotu mokkhaṃ,
      pupphaṃ, milāyāti yathā idam me
      kāyo thathā yāti vināsabhāvaṃ.

      For this and similar verses (*gāthā*) see *Handbook of Buddhists* by H. Saddhatissa, Mahabodhi Society of India, Sarnath, Banaras, 1956 (this v. p. 24).

91   Vin. I. 35, 242, II, 1; D. I. 49, 87, 224, II. 93 and *passim* throughout the scriptures.

92   D. II. 138.

93   S. III. 120; *yo kho Vakkali dhammaṃ, passati so maṃ, passati, yo maṃ, passati so dhammaṃ, passati.* Cf. Ap. 467.

94   D. I. 13.

95   *rūpāvacara.* See p. 8.

96   D. I. 18; 190.

97   *Ibid.* I. 21.

98   *Ibid.* I. 36.

99   *Ibid.* I. 45.

100   Dh. vv. 153, 154; Uv. XXXI. v. 6, 7; J. I. (*Nidāna*), p. 76; cf. Thag. 78, 183 f.

101   Queen Mallikā was a wife of Pasenadi, king of Kosala. See J. III. 403; IV. 437. The hall was one of many such, donated together with parks and resthouses by the civil authorities or by distinguished persons for holding religious and philosophical discussions.

102   D. I. 178–89.

103   *Ibid.* I. 187; M. I. 431.

104   *Ibid.* I. 188; M. I. 431.

105   *Ibid.* I. 189; M. I. 431.

106   *Ibid.* I. 189; M. I. 431 f.

107   M. I. 426–32.

108   S. II. 178–93 ff., III. 149–51, v. 226, 441; Nd. ii. 273; Kvu. 29.

109   D. II. 122.

110   *Ibid.* I. 47–86.

111   *Dialogues of the Buddha*, Part I, translated by T. W. Rhys Davids from Pali (*Dīgha Nikāya*, I.), London, reprint, 1956, p. 59.

112   Four sublime states of mental development, i.e., loving kindness (*mettā*); compassion (*karuṇā*); sympathetic joy (*muditā*); and equanimity (*upekkhā*) are called *Brahmavihāra* or boundless states (*appamaññā*). *Brahmavihāra*: Brahma-like (*Brahmasamo*) abodes (*Vihāra*). See D. I. 254; *The Path of Purification* (*Visuddhimagga*) translated by Bhikkhu Nāṇamoli, Lake House, Colombo, 1956, Ch. IX; *The Path to Deliverance* by Nyāṇatiloka, Lake House, Colombo, pp. 97–118.

113   See D. I. 215, 233.

114   See D. I. 63 f.

115   *Ibid.* I. 70–76.

116   See the five hindrances, (*pañcanīvaraṇa*), p. 8.

117   D. I. 76.

118 *Ibid.* I. 83.

119 D. I. 206; 208; 209.

120 See D. I. 124.

121 D. I. 124; *Sīlaparidhotā hi paññā paridhotā hi sīlaṃ.* Cf. *Viśeṣāva-śyakabhāṣya* on *Avāśyakaniryukti,* ed. D. Malvania, Lalbhai Dalpatbhai Series, Ahmadabad, 1966, vv. 1127, 1155, 1156, 1162.

122 Dh. v. 259; Uv. IV. v. 21.

123 *Ibid.* v. 327; *ibid.* IV. v. 27.

124 Dh. v. 21; Uv. IV. v. 1; cf. *Ācārāṅga Sūtra* (in Su. Vol. I, 1953) 1. 3. 1. 165; 1. 5. 2. 277; *Sūyagaḍa,* 1. 8. 3; *Uttarajjhayana* (in Su. Vol. II.), Ch. IV. 6, Ch. XI.

125 Vin. I 10 ff. S. v. 420 ff.

126 Vin. I . 10; *ibid.* v. 240.

127 A. IV. 14.

128 D. I. 110, 180; M. III. 280; S. IV. 47, 107, v. 4, 23 *passim.*

129 *A Catalogue of the Chinese Translation of the Buddhist Tripiṭaka,* compiled by Bunyiu Nanjio, Oxford, 1882.

130 Examples of the common origin occur in the cases of the *Āgamas* and *Dharmapadas.*

131 *Brahmajāla Sutta,* for example, is *Dīgha Nikāya* I in the Pali, *Dīrghāgama* 21 in the *Āgamas,* but is also a Sanskrit Vinaya text. The last was translated into French by J. J. M. de Groot: *Le Code du Mahāyāna en Chine.* Publ. Johannes Nuker, Amsterdam, 1893.

132 See *Sarvāstivāda Literature.* A. C. Banerjee. Publ. D. Banerjee, Calcutta, 1957.

133 This is a Pali work entitled *Vimuttimagga* written by Arahat Upatissa. See *Vimuttimagga and Visuddhimagga,* P. V. Bapat, Poona, 1937, p. 66. *Vimuttimagga,* translated from Chinese by Rev. N. R. M. Ehara, Soma Thera and Kheminda Thera, Colombo, 1961. The original Pali work was discovered recently in Ceylon, ed. Siri Ratanajoti and Siri Ratanapāla, publ. Department of Cultural Affairs, Government of Ceylon, Colombo, 1963.

134 On the first day of the half-month (*pātimokkha*) bhikkhus are assembled to recite the code of rules for the purpose of purge.

135 These occupy the first two subsections of the *Cullavagga.*

136 The First Council at Rājagaha was convened by Mahā-Kassapa with the assistance of King Ajātasattu shortly after the parinibbāna of the Buddha. It consisted of five hundred of the Buddha's foremost disciples and at it were recited Discourses of the Buddha and the rules of discipline. The Second Council was held at Vesāli, some one hundred years after the Buddha's parinibbāna, with a view to reconciling differences of opinion regarding Vinaya rules.

137 In the Long Discourses of the *Nikāyas* the suttas work up from contemporary views and the Buddha's own teaching to the parinibbāna recounted in no. 16, the remaining suttas from 17–34 containing varied matter; the Sanskrit Long Discourses begin with a *Nidāna Sūtra* and the *Mahāparinirvāṇa Sūtra,* but the titles corresponding to the first thirteen of the Pali, with the exception of Nos. 6, 7, and 10 *(Mahāli, Jāliya,* and *Subha Suttas)* which are not represented, are consigned to the last places in the Sanskrit.

138 Dh. vv. 44, 45; Uv. XVIII. vv. 1, 2; *Gāndhāri Dharmapada, op. cit.*, vv. 301, 302.

139 They are: *Khuddakapātha, Udāna, Itivuttaka, Sutta Nipāta, Vimānavatthu, Petavatthu, Theragātha, Therīgātha, Jātaka, Niddesa, Paṭisambhidāmagga, Apadāna, Buddhavaṃsa,* and *Cariyāpiṭaka.* These are described respectively as: Nine short texts for neophytes; A series of stories with maxims; A collection of pieces, many very old; Narratives in verse showing the working of karma (applying to both Vatthus); Poems by bhikkhus; Poems by bhikkhunīs; Tales of former existences of the Buddha; Commentary on part of Sutta Nipāta; Scholastic notes on the Path of Sacred Knowledge; Biographies and legends; Versified narrative of previous births of the Buddha.

140 D. I. 178–203; D. II. 55–71; D. III. 207–71.

141 Vin. II. 285; *handa mayam āvuso dhammaṃ ca vinayaṃ ca saṅgāyāma pure adhammo dippati dhammo paṭibāhīyati avinayo dippati vinayo paṭibāhīyati.*

142 Vin. I. 4.

143 "The group of five bhikkhus" (*pañca vaggiye bhikkhū*). They are: Aññakoṇḍañña, Bhaddiya, Vappa, Mahānāma, Assaji. See Vin. I. 10; S. v. 420 ff.

144 Vin. I. 15–18.

145 Those who have attained the four supramundane paths (*magga*) and fruitions (*phala*). See also note 82.

146 *Indian Philosophy,* Radhakrishnan, London, 1923, Vol. I, p. 437.

147 Kkvt. p. 2 f.

148 D. I. 156.

149 D. III. 234; M. I. 432; S. v. 61; A. I. 63 f., IV. 459; v. 16 f.; Vbh. 377, 391.

150 *āsava:* The term has been translated as "deadly flood, intoxicants, bias, depravity, evil," etc. The Sanskrit term *āsrava* derives from *ā* plus *sru,* meaning "that which flows, discharge from a sore." According to the Majjhima Commentary (*Papañcasūdan,* Part I. p. 61: *Ciraparivāsikaṭṭhena madirādayo āsavā viyā ti pi āsavā*) the meaning extends to "intoxicants," and it is used in a psychological sense, hence "influxes" is reasonable. Since, however, these terms do not convey entirely the idea of a constant flow, it is better to retain, without translation, the Pali or Sanskrit term which suggests the basic misconceptions of the nature of life to which all the suffering of mankind is due. The *āsavas* are: sense-desire (*kāmāsava*), desire for the process of life (*bhavāsava*), and lack of higher knowledge or ignorance (*avijjāsava*). A fourth is sometimes included, namely *āsava* of views (*diṭṭhāsava*), but this is generally considered to be covered by *avijjāsava.* Lack of "higher knowledge" is taken as lack of understanding of the truth, as contrasted with a lack of empirical knowledge.

151 D. I. 156.

152 *Ibid.* I. 156 f.

CHAPTER 4

153 Dh. v. 130; Uv. v. 19; cf. *Ācārāṅga Sūtra, op. cit.*, 1, 2, 3, 92, 93; *Sūyagaḍa, op. cit.*, 1, 11, 9, 10, 169.

154 See D. I. 128 f.

155 *Ibid.* I. 143–46.

156 Sn. 394.

157 Dhs. A. 129; Sdhp. v. 58; Kkvt. 50; Uj. 62; cf. *Sūyagaḍa, op. cit.*, I. 1, 2.24–29.

158 Dhs. A. 129; Kkvt. 30.

159 Tkg. v. 78:

Sabbopabhogadhanadhaññavisesalābhī
rūpena bho sa makaraddhajasannibho pi
yo yobbane pi maraṇaṃ labhate akāmaṃ
kāmaṃ parattha parapāṇaharo naro hi.

Makaraddhaja mentioned in the second line of the stanza is the Sanskrit equivalent of the Greek Adonis, in the sense that he possesses youth, beauty, grace, and all the good things of life.

160 Vbh. 272.

161 Ps. II. 130.

162 Sn. v. 145.

163 Fixing of thought on the object, especially of the attainment of absorption.

164 M. I. 129.

165 A. III. 185.

166 Vism. 308; Trn. adapted from the *Path of Purification* by Bhikkhu Nāṇamoli, Colombo, 1956, p. 326.

167 See A. III. 186.

168 S. II. 189.

169 D. I. 250; Vbh. 272.

170 D. I. 4.

171 Dhs. A. 130.

172 For details see Kkvt. 26–30.

173 Sn. v. 395.

174 Uv. VI. vv. 8, 19.

175 Dhs. A. 130; Sdhp. v. 61; see Uj. 60 f.

176 Tkg. v. 79; Sdhp. v. 78.

177 Sn. v. 396.

178 Dh. vv. 13, 14; Uv. XXXI. vv. II, 17; Thag. 133, 134.

179 *Ibid.* v. 42; XXXI. v. 9.

180 D. II. 300; M. I. 60.

181 See Sdhp. v. 79; Tkg. v. 80.

182 Dhs. A. 130.

183 Vin. I. 349; Ud. 61; cf. Uv. XV. v. 9.

184 S. I. 189, Sn. v. 458; Thag. 1229; cf. Uv. VIII. v. 14.

185 Dhs. A. 131; Sdhp. v. 65; See Uj. 61.

186 See Kkvt. 16; cf. *Upāsakadaśāṅga*, ed. Kanhaiyalal, Rajkot, 1961, I. 46: writing false statements (*kūṭalekhakaraṇa*).

187 Dh. v. 224; Uv. XX. v. 16; cf. *Dasaveyāliya*, in Su. Ch. IV. p. 950, Ch. VII. vv. II, 54.

188 Sn. vv. 398, 399.

189 *Pañcasīlapañcadhamma*, published in commemoration of the Third Cycle of the Birthday Anniversary of H. M. King Bhumibol Adulyadej by the Mahāmakuta

Educational Council, the Buddhist University, Thailand, December 2506 (1963).

190 *Uposatha*: Vedic *upavasatha*, the eve of the Soma sacrifice during which day it is prepared. With the advent of Buddhism the word had come to mean the four stages of the lunar month's waxing and waning, namely, 1st, 8th, 15th and 23rd. The Buddhists adopted this day as their weekly sacred day (equivalent to the Sabbath).

191 See Vin. I. 83, IV. 274; D. I. 5; A. I. 212, II. 209; Sn. v. 400; cf. *Dasaveyāliya, op. cit.*, Ch. IV., p. 950, Ch. VIII, p. 28.

192 Vism. 12.

CHAPTER 5

193 Dh. v. 353; Sn. v. 211; M. I. 171; S. II. 284; Vin. I. 8; Uv. XXI. v. 1, etc.

194 Uv. XXI. v. 6: cf. Vin. I. 8; Mtn. 327; Lal. 406.

195 Dh. v. 275; Ndi. 59.

196 See Ndi. 59; cf. *Samavāya*, in Su. Vol. I. 318.

197 See pp. 52-53.

198 Vin. I. 43: *aputtakāya paṭipanno samaṇo Gotamo vedhavyāya paṭipanno samaṇo Gotamo kulūpacchedāya paṭipanno samaṇo Gotamo.*

199 D. I. 63.

200 This is called "sojourn of rainy season" (*vassāvāsa*), similar to keeping Lent. See Vin. III. 10; Mtn. 16, 8.

201 D. I. 120: Soṇadaṇḍa brahman, having enumerated the qualities of a true brahman as those of high birth, high scholarship, commanding physical appearance and high morality, concludes: "He is a wise man and a sage, the first or the second to hold up the sacrificial ladle."

202 D. I. 62 f.

203 D. II. 146.

204 *Ibid.* II. 85.

205 D. III. 142–79; 180–93.

206 *Buddha and the Gospel of Buddhism* by Ananda K. Coomaraswamy, Harper & Row, New York, 1964, p. 212. Jains also accepted the liberation (*siddhi* or *mokkha*) of householder. See *Paṇṇavaṇā*, in Su., *op. cit.*, Vol. II 272.

207 Miln. 264 ff.

208 D. I. 86.

209 Dh. v. 142.

210 *Ibid.* Dh. vv. 266, 267; Uv. XXXII. vv. 18, 19.

211 *Ibid.* vv. 254, 255.

212 D. I. 202.

213 Supatiṭṭha-cetiya and Aggālava-cetiya at Ālavi near Rājagaha, Vin. I. 37; II. 172.

214 Udena-cetiya to the east of Vesāli, Gotamaka to the south, Sattamba to the west, and Bahuputta-cetiya to the north. D. III. 9; also II. 10.

215 *Ibid.* II. 107. The Buddha commented on the beauty of Vesāli and its six *cetiyas* when, with Venerable Ānanda, he had gone to spend the day at the Cāpāla-cetiya.

216 *Ibid.* II. 123 and II. 163, respectively.

217 *Ibid.* I. 71.

218   *Ibid.* II. 142.
219   *Ibid.* II. 140, 141.
220   *Ibid.* II. 138.
221   D. I. 124.
222   Dh. v. 183.
223   *Ibid.* v. 283; Uv. XVIII. v. 3.
224   D. I. 159–63.
225   D. I. 162 f.
226   "In the *Śatapatha Brāhmana (Sacred Books of the East,* XII, 283; XI.III, 277, 314) five, and also seven *disās* as well as four are mentioned in rites. In the *Grihya Sūtras* (S.B.E. XXIX, 320, cf. 232; XXX, 171, 194, 213, 278. These *Sūtras* contain the rules of Vedic domestic ceremonies. (Grihya means 'houseness') the four quarters are to be worshipped in connection with certain rites. And so much self-anointing or contact with water is enjoined that the lay celebrant may well have had both hair and garments wet as Sigāla had." *Dialogues of the Buddha,* Part III by T. W. and C. A. F. Rhys Davids, Pali Text Society, London, 1965, p. 170; also see pp. 168–72. For further information on the quarter-worshippers (*disāpokkhiyas*) see the *Bhagavatī,* in Su., *op cit.,* Vol. I. *śataka,* 11, *uddesaka,* 9.
227   D. III. 181; 182.
228   A. I. 155.
229   Cf. note 31; *Thāna,* in Su., Vol. I. 204.
230   Cf. note 33.
231   Uv. XX. v. 4.
232   Dh. v. 223; J. II. 4; Uv. XX. v. 19; cf. *Dasaveyāliya, op. cit.,* Ch. VII. vv. 38, 39.
233   S. I. 162; Thag. 441; Uv. XX. v. 20.
234   A. I. 89.
235   A. II. 121 ff.
236   A. I. 51.
237   *Ibid.* IV. 236; Uv. X. v. I.
238   Dh. v. 21; Uv. IV. v. 1.
239   *Ibid.* v. 23; *ibid.* IV. v. 3.
240   A. I. 225 f.
241   J. I. 280; J. IV. 244–45.

CHAPTER 6

242   J. I. 329: *Sādhu sambahulā ñāti api rukkhā araññajā, vāto vahati ekaṭṭhaṃ brahantam pi vanaspatiṃ.*
243   *Rock Edict,* Girnar, III. line 4: *sādhu mātari ca pitari ca susūsā.*
244   *Ibid.* XI. line 2: *samyapatipaī mātari pitari sādhu sususā.*
245   *Ibid.* XIII. line 3: *mata pitri suṣushā.*
246   *Pillar Edict,* Delhi Topra, VII. line 29: *mātāpitisu sususāyā* (for the above references see *Corpus Inscriptionum Indicarum,* Vol. I. ed. by E. Hultzsch, London, 1925).
247   *Taittirīyopaniṣad,* I. ii. 2: *mātṛ devo bhava pitṛ devo bhava.*
248   A. I. 132; It. 109 f.

249 A. I. 62, 132; It. 110.

250 *Ibid.* I. 151.

251 D. III. 180. See A. I. 61 f.; Uj. 270; cf. *Thāna* in Su., Vol. I. 260.

252 S. I. 175–77.

253 S. I. 228.

254 A. III. 295–98.

255 D. III. 190.

256 A. IV. 269.

257 A. IV. 270: *mātugāmo idhalokavijayāya paṭipanno hoti, ayaṃ sa loko āraddho hoti.*

258 A. IV. 271: *mātugāmo idhalokavijayāya paṭipanno hoti, ayaṃ sa loko āraddho hoti.*

259 *Ibid.* III. 26–28.

260 S. IV. 239.

261 A. II. 57–59.

262 *Ibid.* IV. 91–94.

263 D. III. 192.

264 A. I. 286.

265 *Ibid.* III. 124 f.; 27.

266 *Ibid.* I. 247; 413.

267 *Ibid.* II. 131.

268 J. VI. 22.

269 *Ibid.* III. 253.

270 Pv. 23; UJ. 299.

271 J. III. 192.

272 D. III. 187; UJ. 268 ff.

273 D. III. 185 f.; *ibid.* 267.

274 *Ibid.* III. 190; *ibid.* 267.

275 S. I. 85; Uv. XIV. v. 3.

276 M. III. 154; Uv. XIV. v. 6.

277 It. 67 f.

278 S. I. 79.

279 A. III. 187 ff.

280 Vin. I. 350; M. III. 154; Dh. vv. 328–30; Uv. XIV. vv. 13–16. Cf. *Dasaveliya op. cit.,* *cūliā* 2nd v. 10.

281 A. IV. 195; Dh. v. 243: *avijjā paramaṃ malaṃ.*

282 D. III. 189; UJ. 274.

283 *Ibid.*

284 A. III. 80.

285 *Hindu Ethics,* John Mackenzie, Oxford, 1922, p. 83.

286 *Chāndogya Upaniṣad,* III. II. 5. See The *Upanishads. Sacred Books of the East.* I. Max Muller's translation, Oxford, 1900, p. 44.

287 *Ibid.* VI. I. 5–7. See Muller's translation, pp. 92, 93.

288 *ayiraka, ayira, ayya:* nobleman, gentleman, man of letters, man of culture.

289 D. III. 190 f.; UJ. 275 f.

290 *Rock Edict,* Girnar, IX. line 4: *ayaṃ tu mahāphale maṃgale ya dhamma-maṃgale tata*

dāsabhatakamhi samyapatipati.

291   *Rock Edict,* Kalsi XI. line 4: *dāsabhaṭakaṣi samyāpaṭipati.* For both the references 52 and
       53 see *Corpus Inscriptionum Indicarum,* Vol. I. ed. by E. Hultzsch, London, 1925.

292   *Ṛgveda,* I. 185. 8.

293   *Ibid.* V. 85. 7.

294   *Ibid.* I. 51. 8.

295   A. III. 45 f. The gift of *petas* entioned here consists in donations made with the object
       of perpetuating the memory of deceased persons. This act of goodwill and gratitude
       is called the "ransference of merit" (*pattidāna*) which is the sixth of tenfold meritori-
       ous deeds (*dasakusala*). See UJ. 12 ff., 305; Sdhp. vv. 497, 500.

296   *Ibid.* II. 69 f.

297   *Ibid.* III. 75–78.

298   A. III. 208.

299   *Ibid.* I. 116 f.

300   J. I. 122: *Appakena pi medhāvī pābhatena vicakkhaṇo samuṭṭhāpetiattānaṃ aṇuṃ
       aggiṃ'va sandhamaṃ.*

301   A. II. 249.

302   J. III. 302.

303   S. I. 89 ff.

304   D. III. 188; cf. *Uvāsagadasāo* in Su., Vol. I. 1127.

305   A. I. 239 f.

306   Sn. vv. 187, 188.

307   A. III. 56: *kammaṃ daḷhaṃ kin ti koromi dāni.*

308   Sn. v. 260; A. II. 32.

309   S. I. 31.

310   *Ibid.* I. 87.

311   A. IV. 281–85.

312   See also D. I. 62.

313   D. III. 237, 268; M. I. 356. II. 95, 128; S. V. 197, 199, 392 and *passim: udayatthagāminiyā
       paññāya samannāgato ariyāya nibbedhikāya sammādukkhakkayagāminiyā.*

314   A. IV. 285.

315   A. IV. 6 f.: *Saddhādhanam sīladhanaṃ hiri-ottappiyaṃ dhanaṃ
       sutadhanañ ca cāgo ca paññā 'me sattamaṃ dhanaṃ
       Yassa ete dhanā atthi itthiyā purisassa vā,
       sa ve mahaddhano loke ajeyyo devamānuse.
       Tasmā saddhañ ca sīlañ ca pasādaṃ dhammadassanaṃ
       anuyuñjetha medhāvī saraṃ Buddhānasāsanaṃ.*
       See also A. IV. 4 f.

CHAPTER 7

316   A state foreshadowed if no fear of shame or wrongdoing (*hiri-ottappa*) existed. See A.
       I. 51.

317   D. I. 62 f.

318   *Encyclopaedia Britannica,* 13th ed. 1926, p. 815, article on Plato by Lewis Campbell.

319   *Protagoras.* B. Jowett's translation, extensively revised by Martin Ostwald, New York, Liberal Arts Press, 1956. For definition of the "art of measurement" see Plato's *Gorgias*; translated with an introduction by W. C. Helmbold, New York, Liberal Arts Press, 1952, and *Philebus*, Plato's examination of pleasure; a translation of the Philebus, with introduction and commentary by R. Hackforth, Cambridge, the University Press, 1945. The extent to which virtue can be taught, and the distinction between transcendental and commonly acquired knowledge, are debated in various aspects in many of the *Dialogues*, the types of knowledge being comparable to the *parāvidyā* and *aparāvidyā* of early Indian thought.

320   "Lysis". In *Phaedrus, Lysis, and Protagoras*, translated by J. Wright, London, Macmillan, 1888.

321   *Politicus* 293A. In Lewis Campbell's *The Sophistes and Politicus of Plato*, Oxford at the Clarendon Press, 1867; *The Republic, with an English translation* 428D, by Paul Shorey, London, W. Heinemann, 1937.

322   *Ibid.* 519.

323   *Gorgias* 464. In W. R. Lamb's *Plato with an English translation*, London, W. Heinemann, 1932; *The Republic with an English translation* 500, by Paul Shorey, London, W. Heinemann, 1937.

324   *Symposium*, 216A. In W. R. M. Lamb's *Plato with an English translation: Lysis, Symposium, Gorgias*, London, W. Heinemann, 1932.

325   Dh. v. 158. *Attānam eva paṭhamaṃ patirūpe nivesaye ath'aññam anusāseyya na kilisseyya paṇḍito.*

326   *Ibid.* v. 166.
       Attadatthaṃ paratthena bahunā pi na hāpaye
       atthadattham abhiññāya sadatthapasuto siyā.

327   *aretē*: sometimes translated as "virtue." To the Greeks it combined all the moral and social qualities which make the perfect man and citizen.

328   J. III. 3.

329   *Ibid.* I. 445.

330   A. II. 74 ff.

331   *Ibid.* IV. 216, 218.

332   D. III. 58 f.

333   According to a very old Indian tradition, the Celestial Wheel was the first of seven treasures belonging to a great ruler at whose birth it had been foretold that he would become either a universal monarch or, if he went out into the homeless life, "an arahat, fully enlightened, who removes the veil from the eyes of the world." (*Sace kho pana agārasmā anagāriyaṃ pabbajati arahaṃ hoti Sammāsambuddho loke vivattacchaddo*). D. I. 89.

334   *Ibid.* III. 60-61.

335   According to D. I. 3 f. the order would be: taking of life, stealing, sexual intercourse, lying, slander and gossip, harsh speech, frivolous talk.

336   D. III. 71 f.

337   A coarse type of grain resembling rye.

338   See Vbh. 391. The "ways" are practically those given in the present sutta.

339 D. III. 75: *asītivassasahassāyukesu manussesu tayo ābādhā bhavissanti icchā anasanaṃ jarā.*
340 See Thag. 130.
341 D. III. 75 ff.
342 *Ibid.* I. 134–42. See also ch. 3 of the present work.
343 *Ibid.* I. 135.
344 *The Travels of Fa-hsien* or *Record of the Buddhistic Kingdoms,* trans. H. A. Giles, Routledge & Kegan Paul, Second impression 1956, p. 47.
345 D. II. 72–76.
346 Transcendentalists. They believed that the Buddha was not a human being but was raised far above the life of the present world.
347 An early sect of Buddhists which tended to raise the Buddha above the human level and to identify his personality with that of former Buddhas.
348 D. II. 220–52.

CHAPTER 8

349 Dh. v. 184:
Nibbānaṃ paramaṃ vadanti Buddhā.
350 *Ibid.* v. 203:
Jigacchā paramā rogā saṅkhāra paramā dukhā
etam ñatvā yathābhūtaṃ nibbānaṃ paramaṃ sukhaṃ.
351 *Ibid.* v. 204:
Ārogyaparamā lābhā saṃtuṭṭhīparamam dhanaṃ
vissāsaparamā ñāti nibbānaṃ paramaṃ sukhaṃ.
352 *Ibid.* v. 226:
Sadā jāgaramānānam ahorattānusikkhinaṃ
nibbānaṃ adhimuttānaṃ attaṃ gacchanti āsavā.
353 Uv. XV. v. 8:
Jāgaryam anuyuktasya ahorātrānusikṣinaḥ
amṛtam anuyuktasya astaṃ gacchanti āśravāḥ.
354 Dh. v. 23; Uv. IV. v. 3:
Te jhāyino sātatikā niccaṃ daḷhaparakkamā
phusanti dhtrā nibbānaṃ yogakkhemaṃ anuttaraṃ.
355 D. II. 38 f. The incident referred to here occurred after Vipassi Buddha had acquired a large following and had sent out bhikkhus to teach.
356 *Ibid.* II. 49 f.; Dh. vv. 183–5.
357 See the *Central Conception of Buddhism* by Th. Stcherbatsky, 3rd ed., Calcutta, 1961, p. 334.
358 An early school of Buddhist thought which claimed that nothing, either matter or mind, exists at all. See Kvu. 3, 5. The word *Sautrāntika* derives from *sūtrānta,* scripture, the tenets being based on the *sūtras,* in contrast to the *Sarvāstivāda,* which is based on the Abhidharma.
359 S. IV. 359: *Katamañ ca bhikkhave asaṅkhataṃ yo bhikkhave rāgakkhayo dosakkhayo mohakkhayo idaṃ vuccati bhikkhave asaṅkhataṃ.*
360 A. II. 34; It. 88: *yathā bhikkhave dhammā saṅkhatā vā asaṅkhata vā virāgo tesaṃ aggam*

akkhāyati yad idaṃ madanimmadano pipāsavinayo ālayasamugghāto vaṭṭūpacchedo taṇhakkhayo virāgo nirodho nibbānaṃ.

361 S. IV. 251 f.

362 S. V. 8: *Nibbānadhātuyā kho etaṃ bhikkhu adhivacanaṃ rāgavināyo dosavināyo mohavināyo āsavānaṃ khayo tena vuccatī ti. Yo kho bhikkhu rāgakkhayo dosakkhayo mohakkhayo idaṃ vuccati amataṃ ayam eva ariyo aṭṭaṅgiko maggo amatagāmimaggo.*

363 D. I. 83 f. and *passim* in the scriptures.

364 The Udāyi mentioned here is the "Great" Udāyi, as distinguished from the theras Lāludāyi and Kāludāyi who also figure in the Buddhist texts. See also D. III. 115 and S. V. 83.

365 S. IV. 279 ff.

366 S. II. 117: *bhavanirodho nibbānaṃ.*

367 S. V. 218: *Ajjhaparam brāhmaṇa pañhaṃ nāsakkhi pañhassa pariyantaṃ gahetuṃ nibbānogadaṃ hi brāhmaṇa brahmacariyaṃ vussati nibbānaparāyanaṃ nibbānapariyosānan ti.*

368 S. V. 2.

369 Dh. v. 243:

Tato malā malataraṃ avijjā paramaṃ malaṃ
etaṃ malaṃ pahatvāna nimmalā hotha bhikkhave.

370 *nāparaṃ itthattāyā ti.* See D. I. 83 f. and *passim* in the scriptures.

371 The term *yoga* also means a method of meditation or mental control which has been known in India from very early days. This technique is explained in the *Upaniṣads* and the *Bhagavadgītā.* The system of philosophy established by Patañjali (c. fifth century B.C.E.) in his *Yogasūtra* defines the term as the "cessation of mental activities" (*cittavṛttinirodha*). The term, however, is derived from *yuj,* to employ or join, and it means the practice of spiritual discipline or way to union with ultimate reality. The *Dhammapada* also says, "Indeed, from meditation wisdom arises" (*yogā ve jāyate bhūrī.* v. 282).

372 *kāma-yoga, bhava-yoga, diṭṭhi-yoga.* See D. III. 230; A. II. 11.

373 Dh. v. 254: *papañcābhiratā pajā nippapañcā Tathāgata.* See note 206.

374 *Ibid.* v. 255: *n'atthi Buddhānam iñjitaṃ.* See note 206.

375 *taṃ jīvaṃ sarīraṃ udāhu aññam jīvaṃ aññam sarīran ti.* D. I. 157, and frequently in the Buddhist texts.

376 D. I. 1 58: *yo so āvuso bhikkhu evaṃ jānāti evaṃ passati kallaṃ tass'etaṃ, vacanāya taṃ jīvaṃ taṃ sarīran ti vā aññam jīvaṃ aññam am sarīran ti vā.*

377 See Vin. I. 34; S. III. 71, IV. 19 f.; Sn. v. 591 and *passim; (ādīpita)* S. I. 31.

378 D. I. 76: *ayaṃ kho me kāyo rūpī cātum-mahā-bhūtiko mātā-pettika-sambhavo odana-kummās-upacayo aniccucchādana-parimaddana-bhedana-viddhaṃsana-dhammo, idañ ca pana me viññāṇaṃ etthasitaṃ ettha paṭibaddhan ti.*

379 D. I. 46.

380 It. 38 f.

381 D. I. 46: *kāyassa bhedā uddhaṃ jīvita-pariyādānā na dakkhinti devamanussā.*

382 *Vimuttimagga* and *Visuddhimagga, op. cit.,* p. 107.

383 Vism. 67–70.

384 *Rāgo ca doso ca moho ca vyādhi*
    jarā ca maraṇam pi ca sokam eva
    paridevadukkham pi ca domanassaṃ
    pāyasam ekādasa aggim āha.

385 *Vimuttimagga* and *Visuddhimagga, op. cit.,* p. 107.

386 D. II. 119 f.: *Katame ca te bhikkhave dhammā mayā abhiññāya desitā, ye vo sādhukaṃ uggahetvā āsevitabbā bhāvetabbā bahulīkātabbā yathayidaṃ brahmacariyaṃ addhaniyaṃ assa ciraṭṭhitikaṃ, tad assa bahujana-hitāya bahujana-sukhāya lokānukampāya atthāya hitāya sukhāya devamanussānaṃ? Seyyathīdaṃ cattāro sati-paṭṭhānā cattāro sammapaddhānā cattāro iddhipādā pañc' indriyāni pañca balāni satta bojjhaṅga ariyo aṭṭhaṅgiko maggo.*

387 *Ibid.* II. 134-36.

388 *Sabbasaṅkhārasamatho sabbūpadhi-paṭinissaggo taṇhakkhayo virāgo nirodho nibbānaṃ.* S. I. 136; A. II. 118.

389 *Katamañ ca bhikkhave dukkha-samudayaṃ ariya-saccaṃ? Yāyaṃ taṇhā ponobhavikā nandi-rāga-sahagatā tatra tatrābhinandinī, seyyathīdaṃ kāma-taṇhā bhava-taṇhā vib-hava-taṇhā.* Vin. I. 10; D. II. 308, III. 216, 275; M. I. 48, 299, III. 250 and *passim.*

390 It. 50; cf. Uv. III. vv. 7, 8.

391 Dh vv. 335, 336 and 337; Thag. 402; J. III. 387; Cf. Uv. III. vv. 9, 10, 11.

392 A. II. 10; Sn. v. 740; It. 15; Uv. III. v. 12.

393 Uv. III. v. 13:

    Tāṃ tu tṛṣṇām prahāya hi vītatṛṣṇo bhavābhave
    nāsuu punaḥ saṃsarate tṛṣṇā hy asya na vidyate.
    (No Pali equivalents.)

394 D. I. 156: *Puna ca paraṃ Mahāli bhikkhu āsavānaṃ khayā anāsavaṃ ceto-vimuttiṃ paññā-vimuttiṃ diṭṭhe va dhamme sayaṃ abhiññā sacchikatvā upasampajja viharati.*

395 See *Pali Text Society's Pali-English Dictionary,* pp. 272 and 390.

396 D. I. 235 ff.

397 *Ibid.* 250 f.: *So mettā-sahagatena cetasā ekaṃ disaṃ pharitvā viharati, tathā dutiyaṃ, tathā tatiyaṃ, tathā catutthaṃ. Iti uddham adho tiriyaṃ sabbadhi sabbattatāya sabbāvantaṃ lokaṃ mettā-sahagatena cetasā vipulena mahaggatena appāmāṇena avereṇa avyāpajjhena pharitvā viharati. Seyyathā pi Vāseṭṭha balavā saṅkha-dhamo appakasiren'eva catuddisā viññāpeyya, evaṃ bhāvitāya kho Vāseṭṭha mettāya ceto-vimut-tiyā yaṃ pamāṇa-kataṃ na taṃ tatrāvasissati na taṃ tatrāvatiṭṭhati. Ayam pi kho Vāseṭṭha Brahmāṇaṃ sahavyatāya maggo.*

398 D. II. 55–71.

399 Devas of the *rūpāvacara* who were reborn there because of their experience of third jhāna.

400 D. II. 70: *Yato kho Ānanda bhikkhu imāsañ ca sattannaṃ viññāṇaṭṭhitīnam imesañ ca dvinnaṃ āyatanānaṃ samudayañ ca atthāgamañ ca assādañ ca ādinavañ ca nissaraṇañ ca yathābhūtaṃ viditvā anupādā vimutto hoti, ayaṃ vuccati Ānanda bhikkhu paññā-vimutto.*

401 *Ibid.* II. 70 f.: *Rūpī rūpāni passati ayaṃ paṭhamo vimokkho, ajjhattaṃ arūpa-saññī bahiddhā rūpāni passati ayaṃ dutiyo vimokkho. Subhan't'eva adhimutto hoti. Ayaṃ*

tatiyo vimokkho. Sabbaso rūpasaññanaṃ samatikkamā paṭigha-saññānaṃ atthagamā nānatta-saññānaṃ amanisikārā ananto ākāso ti ākāsanañcāyatanaṃ upasampajja viharati ayaṃ catuttho vimokkho. Sabbaso nevasaññānāsaññāyatanaṃ samatikkamma saññā-vedayita-nirodhaṃ upasampajja viharati ayaṃ viharati ayaṃ satthamo vimokkho.

402 D. II. 71: *āsavānañ ca khayā anāsavaṃ ceto-vimuttiṃ paññā-vimuttiṃ diṭṭhe va dhamme sayaṃ abhiññā sacchikatvā upasampajja viharati, ayaṃ vuccati Ānanda bhikkhu ubha-tobhāga-vimutto, imāya ca Ānanda ubhato-bhāgāvimuttiyā aññā ubhato-bhāga-vimut-ti uttaritarā vā paṇītatatarā vā n'atthīti.*

403 Dh. v. 183.

404 A. IV. 281.

405 *Ibid.* I. 189 f.

406 D. I. 212.

407 D. II. 213; A. II. 256.

408 Vism. 373 ff.

409 S. I. 87.

410 D. II. 156: *Handa dāni bhikkhave āmantayāmi vo vayadhammā saṅkhāra appamādena sampādethā ti ayaṃ Tathāgatassa pacchimā vācā.*

411 D. I. 161 f.

412 D. I. 202.

413 *Ibid.* 1. 45.

414 D. II. 30, 33, 35.

415 Sn. vv. 620–47.

416 *Bho* is the vocative form of *bhavant* (cf. Skt. *bhoḥ*, the shortened voc. of *bhagoḥ*, of Vedic *bhagavant*): "sir, friend, my dear, or you." A familiar term of address in speaking to equals or inferiors. *Bhovādi:* "A person who addresses others as 'bho,'" so assuming familiarity. If this familiarity is not justified, the speaker is implying his superiority. From *bhovādi* was inferred a brahman by caste as contrasted with a "true" brahman.

417 *gandhabba:* a heavenly musician belonging to the *Cātummahārājika* realm; a being ready to take a new existence is also called *gandhabba.* In this context it is used in the former sense.

418 D. II. 37, 39.

419 *Ibid.* II. 100: *Kim pan' Ānanda bhikkhu-saṅgho mayi paccāsiṃsati? Desito Ānanda mayā dhammo anantaraṃ abāhiraṃ karitvā, na tatth' Ānanda Tathāgatassa dhammesu ācariya-muṭṭhi. Yassa nūna Ānanda evaṃ assa ahaṃ bhikkhu-saṅghaṃ pariharissāmīti vā mam'uddesiko bhikkhusaṅgho ti vā, so nūna Ānanda bhikkhu-saṅghaṃ ārabbha kiñ-cid eva udāhareyya..*

INDEX

A

Ābhassara (realm of the radiance) *devas*, 9, 36
Abhidhamma, 25, 48, 50, 51, 52
Absolute Reality, 5, 10, 15, 29
absolute truth (*yathābhūtam*), 9, 15, 24, 129-30
absorption (*appanā*), 62, 63, 70
ācariyas, 106
action. *See karma*
adhiṭṭhāna (determination), 47
āditta (burning), 133-34
affliction, 63, 70, 104, 121
Āgamas, 49, 50
aggregates (*khandhas*), 6, 26, 69
ahiṃsā (non-injury), 61
Ajātasattu, King, 40
ājīvikas (finders of subsistence), 13
ākāsānañcāyatana (dwelling on Infinity of Space), 9
ākiñcaññāyatana (dwelling on Nothingness), 9
alcohol. *See* intoxication
alertness, qualities for, 8, 143
amṛtam (deathlessness), 128, 132
Ānanda, 15, 17, 20, 21, 43, 86, 123, 131, 148
anattā doctrine, 10, 20-23, 45, 51, 132-33
anger
    and meditation, 61-62
    methods for overcoming, 62-69
Aṅguttara Nikāya, 50, 97
anicca, vii, 20-21, 23, 36, 45, 51, 73, 89
āpāṇakoṭika sīla (lifelong sila), 80
aparāpariyavedanīya (effect in some afterlife), 19
appamāda (vigilance)
    Buddha on, 109, 142, 143-44
    practice of, 25, 44, 71, 78, 118, 128
appanā (absorption), 62, 63, 70
Ārāda Kālāma, 145
arahantship, 41, 53, 86
arahat, 41, 52, 55-56, 86
Aristotle, xiv, 2-3, 12, 113
Ariya Saṅgha, 56, 82
arūpaloka (immaterial world), 8
arūpāvacara citta, 9, 141
arūpāvacara jhāna, 9
Aryan, 6, 7, 107
asaṃskṛta dharmas, 25, 128
āsavas (influxes)
    and Buddha's enlightenment, 15, 137

destruction of, 43, 55, 128
and Four Noble Truths, 87
and yogas, 132
asceticism, 13, 36, 37
    Buddha on, 13, 44-45, 90-91, 144
    and religious life, 131
    types of, 54
Asoka, Emperor, 15
Asoka Edicts, 97
Atharvaveda, and hell, 7
ātman, 10, 133
attachment (*upādāna*)
    Buddha on, 37, 45, 137
    as cause of future life, 19
    and Nibbāna, 132, 137
attainment, origin of, 143
aṭṭha sīla (eight precepts). *See* Precepts
Avesta, 6
avijjā (ignorance), 18, 105, 131, 137
awareness, and mindfulness, 42, 47

B

backbiting (*pisunāvācā*), 46
Banares, 44, 53
Banerjee, A.C, 25
barriers (*sīmāsambheda*), 63, 69, 70, 82
becoming (*bhava*), 19
benevolence, 7
bhakti (devotion), 31
Bhalluka, 52
bhava (becoming), 19
bhavacakka (wheel of life), 18
bhikkhunī (nun), 27, 49-50, 53-54
bhikkhu (monk)
    classes of, 50, 56-57
    and laity, 83-84
    Order of, 56
    place in Saṅgha, 22, 53, 82
    practice of, 32, 38, 42, 54, 65, 68, 87-88, 139
    requisites of, 54, 70
    rules for, 49-50
Bimbisāra, 40
birth (*jāti*), 19, 25
bodhisattva, 67
Bodhi tree (Ficus religiosa), 16, 34, 52, 145
Bodhivagga, 16

ABOUT
WISDOM PUBLICATIONS

WISDOM PUBLICATIONS, a not-for-profit publisher, is dedicated to making available authentic Buddhist works for the benefit of all. We publish translations of the sutras and tantras, commentaries and teachings of past and contemporary Buddhist masters, and original works by the world's leading Buddhist scholars. We publish our titles with the appreciation of Buddhism as a living philosophy and with the special commitment to preserve and transmit important works from all the major Buddhist traditions.

If you would like more information or a copy of our mail order catalog, please write or call us at:

WISDOM PUBLICATIONS
361 Newbury Street
Boston, Massachusetts, 02115 USA
Telephone: (617) 536-3358
Fax: (617) 536-1897

THE WISDOM TRUST

AS A NOT-FOR-PROFIT PUBLISHER, Wisdom Publications is dedicated to the publication of fine Dharma books for the benefit of all sentient beings and dependent upon the kindness and generosity of sponsors in order to do so. If you would like to make a donation to Wisdom you may send it to the above address. If you would like more information about book sponsorship, please contact our Boston office.

Thank you.

Wisdom Publications is a non-profit, charitable 501(c)3 organization and a part of the Foundation for the Preservation of the Mahayana Tradition (FPMT).

OTHER TITLES FROM
WISDOM PUBLICATIONS

THE MIDDLE LENGTH DISCOURSES OF THE BUDDHA
A New Translation of the Majjhima Nikaya
Translated by Bhikkhu Ñanamoli and Bhikkhu Bodhi
1995 Outstanding Academic Book Award—Choice Magazine
Tricycle Prize for Excellence in Buddhist Publishing for "Dharma Discourse"

The 152 discourses of this major collection combine a rich variety of contextual settings with deep and comprehensive teachings.
"...remarkable both in its scope and in its contemporary rendering of the Buddha's words." *—Tricycle: The Buddhist Review*
1424pp., 5 1/4 x 8 1/2, CLOTH, ISBN 0-86171-072-X, $75.00

THE LONG DISCOURSES OF THE BUDDHA
A Translation of the Digha Nikaya
Translated by Maurice Walshe

An invaluable collection of the teachings of Buddha which reveal his gentleness, compassion, and penetrating wisdom. These thirty-four discourses are among the oldest records of the Buddha's original teachings. (Previously titled *Thus Have I Heard*)
656pp., 5 1/4 x 8 1/2, CLOTH, ISBN 0-86171-103-3, $34.95

THE FIRST DISCOURSE OF THE BUDDHA
Venerable Dr. Rewata Dhamma

After attaining enlightenment, the Buddha delivered his first discourse to five disciples. Known as the Four Noble Truths, this teaching forms the foundation of all the Buddha's teachings. Includes a history of the Buddha's life and a modern translation of the Four Noble Truths.
128pp., 6 x 9, PAPER, ISBN 0-86171-104-1, $14.95

BEING NOBODY, GOING NOWHERE
Meditations on the Buddhist Path
Ayya Khema

"This book is a valuable guide to the path of meditative insight and loving compassion. It is direct, clear, and inspiring."—Sharon Salzberg, author of *Lovingkindness*
"Not just highly recommended but essential reading for hearts inclined to the path."
—DharmaCrafts
192 pp., 5 1/4 x 8 1/2, PAPER, ISBN 0-86171-052-5, $12.95

MINDFULNESS WITH BREATHING
A Manual for Serious Beginners
Ajahn Buddhadasa Bhikkhu

Here is a clear explanation of the meditation technique of anapanasati, or "mindfulness with in-breaths and out-breaths." If you have yet to sit down and "watch" your breath, this book will point out why you should and how to do it.

160 pp., 6 x 9, PAPER, ISBN 0-86171-111-4, $14.95

HEARTWOOD OF THE BODHI TREE
The Buddha's Teachings on Voidness
Buddhadasa Bhikkhu

A profound and beautiful book by the Thai master explaining the practice of non-clinging or sunnata, a thread that links every great school of Buddhism.

"...masterfully explains how to develop this profound practice in daily life."
—NAPRA Review
"...one of the most prolific and influential teachers in our modern era..."
—Turning Wheel
"...remarkable book..."—Inquiring Mind

152 pp., 6 x 9, PAPER, ISBN 0-86171-035-5, $14.95

MINDFULNESS IN PLAIN ENGLISH
Venerable Henepola Gunaratana

This step-by-step guide to insight meditation is truly practical. Gunaratana's deeply spiritual approach invites readers of all backgrounds to enjoy the fruits of meditative awareness.
"A masterpiece. I cannot recommend it highly enough."
—Jon Kabat-Zinn, author and director of Center for Mindfulness in Medicine and Health Care, UMASS
"Of great value to newcomers...especially people without access to a teacher."
—Larry Rosenberg, Director of Cambridge Insight Meditation Center

208 pp., 5 1/4 x 8 1/2, PAPER, ISBN 0-86171-064-9, $12.95

THE MIND AND THE WAY
Buddhist Reflections on Life
Ajahn Sumedho

Ajahn Sumedho offers advice on freeing the mind and opening the heart. "...[A] thorough summation of the principles of Buddhism.... Sumedho's personal stories are so humble and brilliantly illuminating that they lift this book high above most Buddhist guides...."
—*NAPRA Review*

20 pp. of photos, 228pp., 6 x 9, Paper, ISBN 0-86171-081-9, $16.95